# Principles of Communication

Anshuman Sharma

**Principles of Communication**

ISBN 978-93-5111-389-8



Published in 2014 in India by

**RANDOM PUBLICATIONS**

4376-A/4B, Gali Murari Lal, Ansari Road
New Delhi-110 002
Phone : +91-11-43580356, +91-11-23289044
e-mail: randomexports@gmail.com, sales@randompublications.com,
info@randompublications.com

Reprinted 2022

*Type Setting by* : Keystoneprintads, Delhi-110051
*Digitally Printed at* : Replika Press Pvt. Ltd.

# Preface

Communication is the activity of conveying information through the exchange of thoughts, messages, or information, as by speech, visuals, signals, writing, or behavior. It is the meaningful exchange of information between two or more living creatures. Pragmatics defines communication as any sign-mediated interaction that follows combinatorial, context-specific, and content-coherent rules. Communication is an inherently social interaction, and communicative competence is the ability to engage in inter-subjective interactions. Communication requires a sender, a message, and a recipient, although the receiver doesn't have to be present or aware of the sender's intent to communicate at the time of communication; thus communication can occur across vast distances in time and space. Communication requires that the communicating parties share an area of communicative commonality. The communication process is complete once the receiver understands the sender's message.

Communication is the vital aspect to change behaviour of the receiver. As a matter of fact no executive can be successful without communicating effectively with his superiors or subordinates. Message is in the form of words, symbols, signs, letters or actions. Communication is a tool of management to get the things done through people. The process of communication demands the necessity of a transmitter, message, symbols, channel, decoding, receiver, action and feedback. It is a continuous process or cycle of sending message and feedback. Communication is a primary tool for effecting behaviour change. We can isolate at least four independent dimensions of the communication process: content, noise, network characteristics and direction. The modern principles of communication systems such as the compact discs, television, the telephone and the computer as the motivation for you to study their basic principles. From analog to digital conversion, spectrum and bandwidth and packet and circuit switching, to electricity and electronics, modulation and multiplexing and computer processing, the author takes a thorough and phased approach in presenting major topics. The presented book consists of an exhaustive elaboration of varied sorts of communication management. The book is of tremendous potentiality of the readers.

The book Principles of Communication is based on an altogether new concept and a multi-dimensional definition of the word, rather, term communication, going much beyond its conventional definition 'to connect' and not limiting it to verbal, written, or print and electronic media, or radio, television, satellite, computer and cellular telephony means and tools of connectivity. Structured in modular format, the book covers audio technology, video systems, speech communication systems and written communication systems, applying key concepts in each area to real world communication systems. The reader a complete introduction to communication technologies and systems, offering you a solid understanding of the fundamentals, history and the future direction of this ever changing field. Geared towards non-technical business professionals and students, this unique resource integrates human physiology and factors, important inventors and business people and basic technological principles to explain the key concepts and developments of modern principles of communication. This book has incorporated in it the latest developments in this subject. The present edition is an attempt to provide the whole subject in a simple, lucid, and comprehensive manner. Research scholars, teachers and professionals can also find this book beneficial because each and every aspect is specifically presented and discussed in detail through ample examples.

I thank all members of my team who have helped in the preparation of the book. My special thanks go to "Random Publications" who have published the book.

*– Anshuman Sharma*

# Principles of Communication

# Contents

# 1

# Communication

Communication is a process of transferring information from one *entity* to another. Communication processes are sign-mediated interactions between at least two agents which share a *repertoire* of signs and *semiotic* rules.

Communication is commonly defined as "the imparting or interchange of thoughts, opinions, or information by speech, writing, or signs". Although there is such a thing as one-way commu-nication, communication can be perceived better as a two-way process in which there is an exchange and progression of thoughts, feelings or ideas (energy) towards a mutually accepted goal or direction (information).

Communication is a process whereby information is enclosed in a package and is channeled and imparted by a sender to a receiver via some medium. The receiver then decodes the message and gives the sender a feedback. All forms of communication require a sender, a message, and a receiver. Communication requires that all parties have an area of communicative commonality.

There are auditory means, such as speech, song, and tone of voice, and there are nonverbal means, such as body language, sign language, paralanguage, touch, eye contact, through media, i.e., picures, graphics and sound, and writing.

## INFORMATION COMMUNICATION REVOLUTIONS

Over time, technology has progressed and has created new forms of and ideas about communication. The newer advances include media and communications psychology. Media psychology is an emerging field of study. These technological advances revolutionized the processes of communication. Researchers have divided how communi-cation was transformed into three revolutionary stages:

In the 1st Information Communication Revolution, the first written communication began, with pictographs. These writings were made on stone, which were too heavy to transfer. During this era, written communication was not mobile, but nonetheless existed. In the 2nd Information Communication Revolution, writing began to appear on paper, papyrus, clay, wax, etc. Common alphabets were introduced, allowing the uniformity of language across large distances. Much later the Gutenberg printing-press was invented. Gutenberg created this printing-press after a long period of time in the 15th century. In the 3rd Information Communication Revolution, information can now be transferred via controlled waves and electronic signals.

Communication is thus a process by which meaning is assigned and conveyed in an attempt to create shared understanding. This process requires a vast repertoire of skills in intrapersonal and interpersonal processing, listening, observing, speaking, questioning, analyzing, and evaluating. It is through communication that collaboration and cooperation occur. There are also many common barriers to successful communication, two of which are message overload (when a person receives too many messages at the same time), and message complexity. Communication is a continuous process. The psychology of media communications is an emerging area of increasing attention and study.

## TYPES OF COMMUNICATION

Albert Mehrabian identified three major parts that convey meaning in human face to face communication: body language, voice tonality, and words. He conducted research to determine how people make meaning when a speaker says one thing but means another.

*If the speaker is sending a mixed message the listener will rely on the following cues to determine true meaning*:

- 55% of impact is determined by body language—postures, gestures, and eye contact.
- 38% by the tone of voice.
- 7% by the content or the words spoken.

Mehrabian says this only applies in situations where the speaker is talking about feelings or attitudes.

Although the exact percentage of influence may differ due to variables such as the perceptions or biases of the listener and the speaker, communication as a whole is meant to convey meaning and thus, in some cases, can be universal. A system of signals, such as voice sounds, intonations or pitch, gestures or written symbols can communicate thoughts or feelings. If a language employs communicating with signals, voice, sounds, gestures, or written symbols, can animal communications be considered to be a language? Animals do not have a written form of a language, but use a language to communicate with each another. In that sense, animal communication can be considered as a separate language.

Human spoken and written languages can be described as a system of symbols (sometimes known as lexemes) and the grammars (rules) by which the symbols are manipulated. The word "language" is also used to refer to common properties of languages. Language learning is normal in human childhood. Most human languages use patterns of sound or gesture for symbols which enable communication with others around them. There are thousands of human languages, and these seem to share certain properties, even though many shared properties have exceptions. There is no defined line between a language and a dialect, but the linguist Max Weinreich is credited as saying that "a language is a dialect with an army and a navy". Constructed languages such as Esperanto, programming languages, and various mathematical formalisms are not necessarily restricted to the properties shared by human languages.

Bernard Luskin, UCLA, 1970, advanced computer assisted instruction and began to connect media and psychology into what is now the field of media psychology. In 1998, the American Association of Psychology, Media Psychology Division 46 Task Force report on psychology and new technologies combined media and communication as pictures, graphics and sound increasingly dominate modern communication.

## Nonverbal Communication

Nonverbal communication is the process of communi-cating through sending and receiving wordless messages. Such messages can be communicated through gesture, body language or posture; facial expression and eye contact, object communication such as clothing, hairstyles or even architecture, or symbols and infographics, as well as through an aggregate of the above, such as behavioral communication. Nonverbal communication plays a key role in every person's day to day life, from employment to romantic engagements.

Speech may also contain nonverbal elements known as paralanguage, including voice quality, emotion and speaking style, as well as prosodic features such as rhythm, intonation and stress. Likewise, written texts have nonverbal elements such as handwriting style, spatial arrangement of words, or the use of emoticons. A portmanteau of the English words emotion (or emote) and icon, an emoticon is a symbol or combination of symbols used to convey emotional content in written or message form.

Other communication channels such as telegraphy fit into this category, whereby signals travel from person to person by an alternative means. These signals can in themselves be representative of words, objects or merely be state projections. Trials have shown that humans can communicate directly in this way without body language, voice tonality or words.

*Categories and Features G. W. Porter divides non-verbal communication into four broad categories*:

- *Physical*: This is the personal type of communication. It includes facial expressions, tone of voice, sense of touch, sense of smell, and body motions.

- *Aesthetic*: This is the type of communication that takes place through creative expressions: playing instru-mental music, dancing, painting and sculpturing.
- *Signs*: This is the mechanical type of communication, which includes the use of signal flags, the 21-gun salute, horns, and sirens.
- *Symbolic*: This is the type of communication that makes use of religious, status, or ego-building symbols.
- *Static Features*
- *Distance*: The distance one stands from another frequently conveys a non-verbal message. In some cultures it is a sign of attraction, while in others it may reflect status or the intensity of the exchange.
- *Orientation*: People may present themselves in various ways: face-to-face, side-to-side, or even back-to-back. For example, cooperating people are likely to sit side-by-side while competitors frequently face one another.
- *Posture*: Obviously one can be lying down, seated, or standing. These are not the elements of posture that convey messages. Are we slouched or erect ? Are our legs crossed or our arms folded ? Such postures convey a degree of formality and the degree of relaxation in the communication exchange.
- *Physical Contact*: Shaking hands, touching, holding, embracing, pushing, or patting on the back all convey messages. They reflect an element of intimacy or a feeling of (or lack of) attraction.

**Dynamic Features**

- *Facial Expressions*: A smile, frown, raised eyebrow, yawn, and sneer all convey information. Facial expressions continually change during interaction and are monitored constantly by the recipient. There is evidence that the meaning of these expressions may be similar across cultures.
- *Gestures*: One of the most frequently observed, but least understood, cues is a hand movement. Most people use hand movements regularly when talking. While some gestures (e.g., a clenched fist) have universal meanings, most of the others are individually learned and idiosyncratic.
- *Looking*: A major feature of social communication is eye contact. It can convey emotion, signal when to talk or finish, or aversion. The frequency of contact may suggest either interest or boredom.

**Visual Communication**

Visual communication as the name suggests is communication through visual aid. It is the conveyance of ideas and information in forms that can be read or looked upon. Primarily associated with two dimensional images, it includes: signs, typography, drawing, graphic design, illustration, colour and electronic resources. It solely relies on vision. It is form of communication with visual effect. It explores the idea that a visual message with text has a greater power to inform, educate or persuade a person. It is communication by presenting information through visual form.

The evaluation of a good visual design is based on measuring comprehension by the audience, not on aesthetic or artistic preference. There are no universally agreed-upon principles of beauty and ugliness. There exists a variety of ways to present information visually, like gestures, body languages, video and TV. Here, focus is on the presentation of text, pictures, diagrams, photos, et cetera, integrated on a computer display. The term visual presentation is used to refer to the actual presentation of information. Recent research in the field has focused on web design and graphically oriented usability. Graphic designers use methods of visual communication in their professional practice.

## Understanding the Field of Communication

The field of communication is typically broken into three distinct camps: human communication, mass communications, and communication disorders

Human Communication or Communication Studies is the study of how individuals communicate.

*Some examples of the distinct areas that human communication scholars study are*:

- Interpersonal Communication
- Organizational Communication
- Oral Communication
- Small Group Communication
- Intercultural Communication
- Nonviolent Communication
- Conflict
- Rhetoric
- Public Speaking
- Media and Communications Psychology

*Examples of Mass Communications include*:

- Mass communication
- Graphic communication
- Science communication
- Strategic Communication
- Superluminal communication
- Technical communication
- Public relations
- Broadcast Media
- Journalism
- Media and Communications Psychology

*Examples of Communication Disorders include*:

- Facilitated Communication
- Impairment of Language Modality
- Speech Disorders

## Oral Communication

Oral communication is a process whereby information is transferred from a sender to receiver usually by a verbal means but visual aid can support the process..

The receiver could be an individual person, a group of persons or even an audience. There are a few of oral communication types: discussion, speeches, presentations, etc. However, often when you communicate face to face the body language and your voice tonality has a bigger impact than the actual words that you are saying.

A widely cited and widely mis-interpreted figure, used to emphasize the importance of delivery, is that "communication is 55% body language, 38% tone of voice, 7% content of words", the so-called 55/38/7 rule. This is not however what the cited research shows – rather, when conveying *emotion,* if body language, tone of voice, and words *disagree,* then body language and tone of voice will be believed more than words. For example, a person saying "I'm delighted to meet you" while mumbling, hunched over, and looking away will be interpreted as insincere. Further discussion at Albert Mehrabian: Three elements of communication.

You can notice that the content or the word that you are using is not the determining part of a good communication. The "how you say it" has a major impact on the receiver. You have to capture the attention of the audience and connect with them. For example, two persons saying the same joke, one of them could make the audience die laughing related to his good body language and tone of voice. However, the second person that has the exact same words could make the audience stare at one another.

In an oral communication, it is possible to have visual aid helping you to provide more precise information. Often enough, we use a presentation programme in presentations related to our speech to facilitate or enhance the communi-cation process. Although, we cannot communicate by providing only visual content because we would not be talking about oral communication anymore.

## Communication Modeling

The first major model for communication came in 1949 by Claude Shannon and Warren Weaver for Bell Laboratories The original model was designed to mirror the functioning of radio and telephone technologies.

Their initial model consisted of three primary parts: sender, channel, and receiver. The sender was the part of a telephone a person spoke into, the channel was the telephone itself, and the receiver was the part of the phone where one could hear the other person. Shannon and Weaver also recognized that often there is static that interferes with one listening to a telephone conversation, which they deemed noise. In a simple model, often referred to as the transmission model or standard view of communication, information or content (e.g. a message in natural language) is sent in some form (as spoken language) from an emisor/ sender/ encoder to a destination/ receiver/ decoder.

This common conception of communication simply views communication as a means of sending and receiving information. The strengths of this model are simplicity, generality, and quantifiability.

*Social scientists Claude Shannon and Warren Weaver structured this model based on the following elements*:

- An information source, which produces a message.
- A transmitter, which encodes the message into signals
- A channel, to which signals are adapted for trans-mission
- A receiver, which 'decodes' (reconstructs) the message from the signal.
- A destination, where the message arrives.

*Shannon and Weaver argued that there were three levels of problems for communication within this theory*:

- *The technical problem*: How accurately can the message be transmitted?
- *The semantic problem*: How precisely is the meaning 'conveyed'?
- *The effectiveness problem*: How effectively does the received meaning affect behaviour?

*Daniel Chandler critiques the transmission model by stating It assumes communicators are isolated individuals*:

- No allowance for differing purposes.
- No allowance for differing interpretations.
- No allowance for unequal power relations.
- No allowance for situational contexts.

In 1960, David Berlo expanded on Shannon and Weaver's linear model of communication and created the SMCR Model of Communication. The Sender-Message-Channel-Receiver Model of communication separated the model into clear parts and has been expanded upon by other scholars.

Communication is usually described along a few major dimensions: Message (what type of things are communicated), source/ emisor/ sender/ encoder (by whom), form (in which form), channel (through which medium), destination/ receiver/ target/ decoder (to whom), and Receiver. Wilbur Schram also indicated that we should also examine the impact that a message has (both desired and undesired) on the target of the message.

Between parties, communication includes acts that confer knowledge and experiences, give advice and commands, and ask questions. These acts may take many forms, in one of the various manners of communication. The form depends on the abilities of the group communicating. Together, communication content and form make messages that are sent towards a destination. The target can be oneself, another person or being, another entity (such as a corporation or group of beings).

*Communication can be seen as processes of information transmission governed by three levels of semiotic rules*:

- Syntactic (formal properties of signs and symbols),
- Pragmatic (concerned with the relations between signs/expressions and their users) and
- Semantic (study of relationships between signs and symbols and what they represent).

Therefore, communication is social interaction where at least two interacting agents share a common set of signs and a common set of semiotic rules. This commonly held rules in some sense ignores autocommunication, including intrapersonal communication via diaries or self-talk, both secondary phenomena that followed the primary acquisition of communicative competences within social interactions.

In light of these weaknesses, Barnlund proposed a transactional model of communication. The basic premise of the transactional model of communication is that individuals are simultaneously engaging in the sending and receiving of messages. In a slightly more complex form a sender and a receiver are linked reciprocally. This second attitude of communication, referred to as the constitutive model or constructionist view, focuses on how an individual communicates as the determining factor of the way the message will be interpreted. Communication is viewed as a conduit; a passage in which information travels from one individual to another and this information becomes separate from the communication itself.

A particular instance of communication is called a speech act. The sender's personal filters and the receiver's personal filters may vary depending upon different regional traditions, cultures, or gender; which may alter the intended meaning of message contents. In the presence of "communication noise" on the transmission channel (air, in this case), reception and decoding of content may be faulty, and thus the speech act may not achieve the desired effect.

One problem with this encode-transmit-receive-decode model is that the processes of encoding and decoding imply that the sender and receiver each possess something that functions as a code book, and that these two code books are, at the very least, similar if not identical. Although something like code books is implied by the model, they are nowhere represented in the model, which creates many conceptual difficulties. Theories of coregulation describe communication as a creative and dynamic continuous process, rather than a discrete exchange of information. Canadian media scholar Harold Innis had the theory that people use different types of media to communicate and which one they choose to use will offer different possibilities for the shape and durability of society.

His famous example of this is using ancient Egypt and looking at the ways they built themselves out of media with very different properties stone and papyrus. Papyrus is what he called 'Space Binding'. it made possible the transmission of written orders across space, empires and enables the waging of distant military campaigns and colonial administration. The other is stone and 'Time Binding', through the construction of temples and the pyramids can sustain their authority gene-ration to generation, through this media they can change and shape communication in their society. The Krishi Vigyan Kendra Kannur under Kerala Agricultural University has pioneered a new branch of agri-cultural communication called Creative Extension.

## Communication Noise

In every communication models, noise is anything that interferes with the decoding of messages sent over the channel by an encoder.

*There are many examples of noise*:

- *Environmental Noise*: Noise that physically disrupts communication, such as standing next to loud speakers at a party, or a construction site next to a classroom making it hard to hear the professor.
- *Physiological-Impairment Noise*: physical maladies that prevent effective communication, such as actual deafness or blindness preventing messages from being received correctly.
- *Semantic Noise*: different interpretations of the meanings of certain words, like how the word "weed" can be interpreted as both an undesirable plant in your yard or marijuana, or how "LOL" is easily recognizable by most teens, but complete gibberish to older readers.
- *Syntactical Noise*: mistakes in grammar can disrupt communication, such as abrupt changes in verb tense during a sentence, or differing sentence structures between different cultures.
- *Organizational Noise*: poorly structured communi-cation can prevent the receiver from accurate interpretations, like unclear and badly stated directions can make the receiver even more lost, or how unfocused and disorganized lectures by professors are extremely hard for students to understand.
- *Cultural Noise*: stereotypical assumptions can cause misunderstandings, such as unintentionally offending Jews by wishing them a "Merry Christmas," or how Democrats and Republicans alike are bigoted about the other party's policies.
- *Psychological Noise*: certain attitudes can make communication difficult, like when great anger or sadness causes someone to lose focus on the present, or how more serious psychological diseases like autism severely hamper effective communication.

## Nonhuman Communication

Communication in many of its facets is not limited to humans, or even to primates. Every information exchange between living organisms — i.e. transmission of signals involving a living sender and receiver — can be considered a form of communication. Thus, there is the broad field of animal communication, which encompasses most of the issues in ethology. Also very primitive animals such as corals are competent to communicate. On a more basic level, there is cell signaling, cellular communication, and chemical communi-cation between primitive organisms like bacteria, and within the plant and fungal kingdoms. All of these communication processes are sign-mediated interactions with a great variety of distinct coordinations.

Animal communication is any behaviour on the part of one animal that has an effect on the current or future behaviour of another animal. Of course, human communication can be subsumed as a highly developed form of animal communi-cation. The study of animal communication, called *zoosemiotics'* (distinguishable from anthroposemiotics, the study of human communication) has played an important part in the development of ethology, sociobiology, and the study of animal cognition. This is quite evident as humans are able to communicate with animals, especially dolphins and other animals used in circuses. However, these animals have to learn a special means of communication. Animal communication, and indeed the understanding of the animal world in general, is a rapidly growing field, and even in the 21st century so far, many prior understandings related to diverse fields such as personal symbolic name use, animal emotions, animal culture and learning, and even sexual conduct, long thought to be well understood, have been revolutionized.

## Plants and Fungi

Among plants, communication is observed within the plant organism, i.e. within plant cells and between plant cells, between plants of the same or related species, and between plants and non-plant organisms, especially in the rootzone. Plant roots communicate in parallel with rhizobia bacteria, with fungi and with insects in the soil. This parallel sign-mediated interactions which are governed by syntactic, pragmatic and semantic rules are possible because of the decentralized "nervous system" of plants. The original meaning of the word "neuron" in Greek is "vegetable fibre" and as recent research shows, most of the intraorganismic plant communication processes are neuronal-like.

Plants also communicate via volatiles in the case of herbivory attack behaviour to warn neighboring plants. In parallel they produce other volatiles which attract parasites which attack these herbivores. In Stress situations plants can overwrite the genetic code they inherited from their parents and revert to that of their grand- or great-grandparents.

Fungi communicate to coordinate and organize their own growth and development such as the formation of mycelia and fruiting bodies. Additionally fungi communicate with same and related species as well as with nonfungal organisms in a great variety of symbiotic interactions, especially with bacteria, unicellular eukaryotes, plants and insects. The used semiochemicals are of biotic origin and they trigger the fungal organism to react in a specific manner, in difference while to even the same chemical molecules are not being a part of biotic messages doesn't trigger to react the fungal organism. It means, fungal organisms are competent to identify the difference of the same molecules being part of biotic messages or lack of these features. So far five different primary signalling molecules are known that serve to coordinate very different behavioral patterns such as filamentation, mating, growth, pathogenicity. Behavioral coordination and the production of such substances can only be achieved through interpretation processes: self or non-self, abiotic indicator, biotic message from similar, related, or non-related species, or even "noise", i.e., similar molecules without biotic content-

### Communication as Academic Discipline

Communication as an academic discipline, sometimes called "communicology," relates to all the ways we communicate, so it embraces a large body of study and knowledge. The communication discipline includes both verbal and nonverbal messages. A body of scholarship all about communication is presented and explained in textbooks, electronic publications, and academic journals. In the journals, researchers report the results of studies that are the basis for an ever-expanding understanding of how we all communicate.

Communication happens at many levels (even for one single action), in many different ways, and for most beings, as well as certain machines. Several, if not all, fields of study dedicate a portion of attention to communication, so when speaking about communication it is very important to be sure about what aspects of communication one is speaking about. Definitions of communication range widely, some recognizing that animals can communicate with each other as well as human beings, and some are more narrow, only including human beings within the different parameters of human symbolic interaction.

## TELECOMMUNICATION

Telecommunication is the transmission of messages over significant distances for the purpose of communication. In earlier times, telecommunications involved the use of visual smoke signals, semaphores, signal flags, the optical heliograph, or audio coded messages sent by drumbeats, messages sent with lung-blown horns, or messages sent by whistles, for example.

In the modern age of electricity and electronics, telecommunications has typically involved the use of electric means such as the telegraph, the telephone, and the teletype, developed in fibre optics, and/or the Internet. The first breakthrough into modern electrical telecommunications came with the development of the telegraph during the 1830s and 1840s. The use of these electrical means of communications exploded into use on all of the continents of the world during the 19th century, and these also connected the continents via cables on the floors of the ocean. These three systems of communications all required the use of conducting metal wires.

A revolution in telecommunications into wireless communications began in the first decade of the 20th Century, and in fact, Guglielmo Marconi, who was of Italian and British descent won the Nobel Prize in Physics in 1909 in recognition of his pioneering developments in wireless radio communications. Other early inventors and developers in the field of electrical and electronic telecommunications include Samuel F.B. Morse and Joseph Henry of the United States, Alexander Graham Bell of Canada, Lee de Forest of the U.S., who invented the amplifying vacuum tube called the triode, Edwin Armstrong of the U.S., and John Logie Baird of England.

Telecommunications play an important role in the world economy and the worldwide telecommunication industry's revenue was estimated to be $3.85 trillion in 2008. The service revenue of the global telecommunications industry was estimated to be $1.7 trillion in 2008, and is expected to touch $2.7 trillion by 2013

**Early Telecommunications**

In the Middle Ages, chains of beacons were commonly used on hilltops as a means of relaying a signal. Beacon chains suffered the drawback that they could only pass a single bit of information, so the meaning of the message such as "the enemy has been sighted" had to be agreed upon in advance. One notable instance of their use was during the Spanish Armada, when a beacon chain relayed a signal from Plymouth to London that signaled the arrival of the Spanish warships.

In 1792, Claude Chappe, a French engineer, built the first fixed visual telegraphy system (or semaphore line) between Lille and Paris. However semaphore systems suffered from the need for skilled operators and the expensive towers at intervals of ten to thirty kilometers (six to nineteen miles). As a result of competition from the electrical telegraph, the last commercial line was abandoned in 1880.

**The Telegraph and the Telephone**

The first commercial electrical telegraph was constructed by Sir Charles Wheatstone and Sir William Fothergill Cooke, and its use began on April 9, 1839. Both Wheatstone and Cooke viewed their device as "an improvement to the [already-existing, so-called] electromagnetic telegraph" not as a new device. The businessman Samuel F.B. Morse and the physicist Joseph Henry of the United States developed their own, simpler version of the electrical telegraph, independently. Morse successfully demonstrated this systen on September 2, 1837. Morse's most important technical contribution to this telegraph was the rather simple and highly-efficient Morse Code, which was an important advance over Wheatstone's telegraph system. The communications efficiency of the Morse Code anticipated that of the Huffman code in digital communications by over 100 years, but Morse had developed his code purely empirically, unlike Huffman, who gave a detailed theoretical explanation of how his method worked.

The first permanent transatlantic telegraph cable was successfully completed on 27 July 1866, allowing transatlantic electrical communication for the first time. An earlier transatlantic cable had operated for a few months in 1859, and among other things, it carried messages of greeting back and forth between President James Buchanan of the United States and Queen Victoria of the United Kingdom.

However, this transatlantic cable failed soon, and the project to lay a replacement line was delayed for five years by the War Between the States in the U.S. Also, note that these transatlantic cables would have been completely incapable of carrying telephone calls even if the telephone had been invented by then. The first translantic telephone cable which incorporated hundreds of electronic amplifiers was not ready to be used until 1956.

The conventional telephone now in use worldwide was first patented by Alexander Graham Bell in March 1876. That first patent by Bell was the *master patent* of the telephone, from which all other patents for electric telephone devices and features flowed. Credit for the invention of the electric telephone has been frequently disputed, and new controversies over the issue have arisen from time-to-time. As with other great inventions such as radio, television, light bulb, and the computer, there were several inventors who did pioneering experimental work on *voice transmission over a wire* and improved on each other's ideas. However, the really important innovater was Mr. Bell, who first made the telephone utility into a Big Business with his Bell Telephone Company in the United States, and Bell Canada.

The first commercial telephone services were set up in 1878 and 1879 on both sides of the Atlantic in the cities of New Haven, Connecticut, and London, England.

## Radio and Television

In 1832, James Lindsay gave a classroom demonstration of wireless telegraphy via conductor electricity I conductive water to his students. By 1854, he was able to demonstrate a transmission across the Firth of Tay from Dundee, Scotland, to Woodhaven, a distance of about two miles (3 km), again using water as the transmission medium. In December 1901, Guglielmo Marconi established wireless communication between St. John's, Newfoundland (Canada) and Poldhu, Cornwall (England), earning him the Nobel Prize in Physics for 1909, one which he shared with Karl Braun. However small-scale radio communication had already been demonstrated in 1893 by Nikola Tesla in a presentation before the National Electric Light Association.

On March 25, 1925, John Logie Baird of England was able to demonstrate the transmission of moving pictures at the department store Selfridge's in London, England. Baird's system relied upon the fast-rotating Nipkow disk, and thus it became known as the mechanical television. It formed the basis of experimental broadcasts done by the British Broadcasting Corporation beginning 30 September 1929. However, for most of the twentieth century television systems were designed around the cathode ray tube invented by Karl Braun. The first version of such a television to show promise was produced by Philo Farnsworth of the United States, and it was demonstrated to his family in Idaho on September 7, 1927.

### Computer Networks and the Internet

On 11 September 1940, George Stibitz was able to transmit problems using teletype to his Complex Number Calculator in New York and receive the computed results back at Dartmouth College in New Hampshire. This configuration of a centralized computer or mainframe with remote dumb terminals remained popular throughout the 1950s.

However, it was not until the 1960s that researchers started to investigate packet switching — a technology that would allow chunks of data to be sent to different computers without first passing through a centralized mainframe. A four-node network emerged on 5 December 1969; this network would become ARPANET, which by 1981 would consist of 213 nodes.

ARPANET's development centred around the Request for Comment process and on 7 April 1969, RFC 1 was published. This process is important because ARPANET would eventually merge with other networks to form the Internet and many of the protocols the Internet relies upon today were specified through the Request for Comment process. In September 1981, RFC 791 introduced the Internet Protocol v4 (IPv4) and RFC 793 introduced the Transmission Control Protocol (TCP) — thus creating the TCP/IP protocol that much of the Internet relies upon today.

However, not all important developments were made through the Request for Comment process. Two popular link protocols for local area networks (LANs) also appeared in the 1970s. A patent for the token ring protocol was filed by Olof Soderblom on 29 October 1974 and a paper on the Ethernet protocol was published by Robert Metcalfe and David Boggs in the July 1976 issue of *Communications of the ACM*.

## Key Concepts

A number of key concepts reoccur throughout the literature on modern telecommunication systems.

### *Basic Elements*

A basic telecommunication system consists of three primary units that are always present in some form:

- A transmitter that takes information and converts it to a signal.
- A transmission medium, also called the "physical channel" that carries the signal. An example of this is the "free space channel".
- A receiver that takes the signal from the channel and converts it back into usable information.

For example, in a radio broadcasting station the station's large power amplifier is the transmitter; and the broadcasting antenna is the interface between the power amplifier and the "free space channel". The free space channel is the transmission medium; and the receiver's antenna is the interface between the free space channel and the receiver. Next, the radio receiver is the destination of the radio signal, and this is where it is converted from electricity to sound for people to listen to.

Sometimes telecommunication systems are "duplex" (two-way) with a single box of electronics working as both a transmitter and a receiver, or a *transceiver*. For example, a cellular telephone is a transceiver. The transmission electronics and the receiver electronics in a transceiver are actually quite independent of each other. This can be readily explained by the fact that radio transmitters contain power amplifiers that operate with electrical powers measured in the watts or kilowatts, but radio receivers deal with radio powers that are measured in the microwatts or nanowatts. Hence, transceivers have to be carefully designed and built to isolate their high-power circuitry and their low-power circuitry from each other.

Telecommunication over telephone lines is called point-to-point communication because it is between one transmitter and one receiver. Telecommunication through radio broadcasts is called broadcast communication because it is between one powerful transmitter and numerous low-power but sensitive receivers.

## Analog and Digital Communications

Communications signals can be either by analog signals or digital signals. These are analog communication systems and digital communication systems. For an analog signal, the signal is varied continuously with respect to the information. In a digital signal, the information is encoded as a set of discrete values (for example, a set of ones and zeros).

During the propagation and reception, the information contained in analog signals will inevitably be degraded by undersirable physical noise.

(The output of a transmitter is noise-free for all practical purposes.) Commonly, the noise in a communication system can be expressed as adding or subtracting from the desirable signal in a completely random way. This form of noise is called *"additive noise"*, with the understanding that the noise can be negative or positive at different instants of time. Noise that is not additive noise is a much more difficult situation to describe or analyse, and these other kinds of noise will be omitted here.

On the other hand, unless the *additive noise* disturbance exceeds a certain threshold, the information contained in digital signals will remain intact. Their resistance to noise represents a key advantage of digital signals over analog signals.

## Communications Networks

A communications network is a collection of transmitters, receivers, and communications channels that send messages to one another. Some digital communications networks contain of one or more routers that work together to transmit information to the correct user. An analog communications network consists of one or more switches that establish a connection between two or more users. For both types of network, repeaters may be necessary to amplify or recreate the signal when it is being transmitted over long distances. This is to combat attenuation that can render the signal indistinguishable from the noise.

## Communication Channels

The term "channel" is an ambiguous one that has two different meanings, but they are easily sorted out by their contexts in practice. One meaning of a "channel" is simply the physical medium that exists between the transmitter and the receiver. Examples of this meaning of channel include the atmosphere for sound communications, glass optical fibers for some kinds of optical communications, coaxial cables for communications by way of voltages and electric currents in them, and free space for communications using visible light, infrared waves, ultraviolet light, and radio waves.

This channel is called, simply enough, the "free space channel". Note that the sending of radio waves from one place to another has absolutely nothing to do with the presence or absence of an atmosphere between the two. Radio waves travel through a perfect vacuum just as easily as they travel through air, fog, clouds, or any other kind of gas besides air. The term "on the air" for a radio or TV station transmitting is an archaic one dating back ninety years or more - to a time when 99.9% of people did not understand what was going on in a radio system.

The other meaning of the term "channel" in telecommunications is as follows. This kind of a communi-cations channel is some variety of subdivision of a transmission medium so that it can be used to send multiple streams of information simultaneously. For example, one radio station can broadcast radio waves into free space at frequencies in the neighborhood of 94.5 megahertz (MHz) while another radio station can also broadcast radio waves at frequencies in the neighborhood of 96.1 MHz. In the practical cases, each of these radio stations is allowed to transmit radio waves over a frequency bandwidth of about 180 kilohertz (KHz),centered at frequencies such as the above, which are called their "carrier frequencies". Each station in this example is separated from its adjacent stations by 200 KHz, and the difference between 200 KHz and 180 KHz equaling 20 KHz is an engineering allowance for the inperfections in the communication system - which is something that we always have to allow for.

In the example above, the "free space channel" has been divided into communications channels according to frequencies, and each channel is assigned to a separate frequency bandwidth to broadcast radio waves into. This system of dividing the medium into channels according to frequency is called, simply enough, "frequency-division multiplexing" (FDM).

Another way of dividing up a communications medium into channels is to allocate to each sender a recurring segment of time ("time slots" such as 20 milliseconds out of each second), and to allow each sender to send messages only within its own time slot. This method of dividing up the medium into communication channels is called, simply enough, "time-division multiplexing" (TDM), and is always used in optical fibre communication. On the other hand, there are radio communication systems that use TDM, but these systems *always* use FDM at the same time, because their allocated bandwidths are limited. Hence, these systems use a hybrid of TDM and FDM.

**Modulation**

The shaping of a signal to convey information is known as modulation. Modulation can be used to represent a digital message as an analog waveform. This is known as keying and several keying techniques exist (these include phase-shift keying, frequency-shift keying and amplitude-shift keying). Bluetooth, for example, uses phase-shift keying to exchange information between devices.

Modulation can also be used to transmit the information of analog signals at higher frequencies. This is helpful because low-frequency analog signals cannot be effectively transmitted over free space. Hence the information from a low-frequency analog signal must be superimposed on a higher-frequency signal (known as the carrier wave) before transmission. There are several different modulation schemes available to achieve this (two of the most basic being amplitude modulation and frequency modulation). An example of this process is a DJ's voice being superimposed on a 96 MHz carrier wave using frequency modulation (the voice would then be received on a radio as the channel "96 FM").

## Society and Telecommunication

Telecommunication has a significant social, cultural and economic impact on modern society. In 2006, estimates placed the telecommunication industry's revenue at $1.2 trillion (USD) or just under 3% of the gross world product (official exchange rate). The following sections discuss the impact of telecommunication on society.

## Economic Impact

### *Microeconomics*

On the microeconomic scale, companies have used telecommunication to help build global empires. This is self-evident in the case of online retailer Amazon.com but, according to academic Edward Lenert, even the conventional retailer Wal-Mart has benefited from better telecommunication infrastructure compared to its competitors. In cities throughout the world, home owners use their telephones to organize many home services ranging from pizza deliveries to electricians. Even relatively poor communities have been noted to use telecommunication to their advantage. In Bangladesh's Narshingdi district, isolated villagers use cell phones to speak directly to wholesalers and arrange a better price for their goods. In Cote d'Ivoire, coffee growers share mobile phones to follow hourly variations in coffee prices and sell at the best price.

### *Macroeconomics*

On the macroeconomic scale, Lars-Hendrik Röller and Leonard Waverman suggested a causal link between good telecommunication infrastructure and economic growth. Few dispute the existence of a correlation although some argue it is wrong to view the relationship as causal.

Because of the economic benefits of good telecommuni-cation infrastructure, there is increasing worry about the inequitable access to telecommunication services amongst various countries of the world—this is known as the digital divide. A 2003 survey by the International Telecommunication Union (ITU) revealed that roughly one-third of countries have fewer than one mobile subscription for every 20 people and one-third of countries have fewer than one land-line telephone subscription for every 20 people. In terms of Internet access, roughly half of all countries have fewer than one out of 20 people with Internet access. From this information, as well as educational data, the ITU was able to compile an index that measures the overall ability of citizens to access and use information and communication technologies. Using this measure, Sweden, Denmark and Iceland received the highest ranking while the African countries Nigeria, Burkina Faso and Mali received the lowest.

## Social impact

Telecommunication has played a significant role in social relationships. Nevertheless devices like the telephone were originally advertised with an emphasis on the practical dimensions of the device (such as the ability to conduct business or order home services) as opposed to the social dimensions. It was not until the late 1920s and 1930s that the social dimensions of the device became a prominent theme in telephone advertisements. New promotions started appealing to consumers' emotions, stressing the importance of social conversations and staying connected to family and friends.

Since then the role that telecommunications has played in social relations has become increasingly important. In recent years, the popularity of social networking sites has increased dramatically. These sites allow users to communicate with each other as well as post photographs, events and profiles for others to see. The profiles can list a person's age, interests, sexuality and relationship status. In this way, these sites can play important role in everything from organising social engagements to courtship.

Prior to social networking sites, technologies like SMS and the telephone also had a significant impact on social interactions. In 2000, market research group Ipsos MORI reported that 81% of 15 to 24 year-old SMS users in the United Kingdom had used the service to coordinate social arrangements and 42% to flirt.

## Other Impacts

In cultural terms, telecommunication has increased the public's ability to access to music and film. With television, people can watch films they have not seen before in their own home without having to travel to the video store or cinema. With radio and the Internet, people can listen to music they have not heard before without having to travel to the music store.

Telecommunication has also transformed the way people receive their news. A survey by the non-profit Pew Internet and American Life Project found that when just over 3,000 people living in the United States were asked where they got their news "yesterday", more people said television or radio than newspapers. The results are summarised in the following table (the percentages add up to more than 100% because people were able to specify more than one source).

| Local TV | National TV | Radi• | Local paper | Internet | National paper |
|---|---|---|---|---|---|
| 59% | 47% | 44% | 38% | 23% | 12% |

Telecommunication has had an equally significant impact on advertising. TNS Media Intelligence reported that in 2007, 58% of advertising expenditure in the United States was spent on mediums that depend upon telecommunication. The results are summarised in the following table.

| | Internet | Radio | Cable TV | Syndicated TV | Spot TV | Network TV | Newspaper | Magazine | Outdoor | Total |
|---|---|---|---|---|---|---|---|---|---|---|
| Percent | 7.6% | 7.2% | 12.1% | 2.8% | 11.3% | 17.1% | 18.9% | 20.4% | 2.7% | 100% |
| Dollars | $11.31 billion | $10.69 billion | $18.02 billion | $4.17 billion | $16.82 billion | $25.42 billion | $28.22 billion | $30.33 billion | $4.02 billion | $149 billion |

## Telecommunication and Government

Many countries have enacted legislation which conform to the *International Telecommunication Regulations* establish by the International Telecommunication Union (ITU), which is the "leading United Nations agency for information and communication technology issues." In 1947, at the Atlantic City Conference, the ITU decided to "afford international protection to all frequencies registered in a new international frequency list and used in conformity with the Radio Regulation." According to the ITU's *Radio Regulations* adopted in Atlantic City, all frequencies referenced in the *International Frequency Registration Board,* examined by the board and registered on the *International Frequency List* "shall have the right to international protection from harmful interference."

From a global perspective, there have been political debates and legislation regarding the management of telecommunication and broadcasting.

The history of broadcasting discusses some of debates in relation to balancing conventional communication such as printing and telecommunication such as radio broadcasting. The onset of World War II brought on the first explosion of international broadcasting propaganda.

Countries, their governments, insurgents, terrorists, and militiamen have all used telecommunication and broadcasting techniques to promote propaganda. Patriotic propaganda for political movements and colonization started the mid 1930s. In 1936, the BBC did broadcast propaganda to the Arab World to partly counter similar broadcasts from Italy, which also had colonial interests in North Africa.

Modern insurgents, such as those in the latest Iraq war, often use intimidating telephone calls, SMSs and the distribution of sophisticated videos of an attack on coalition troops within hours of the operation. "The Sunni insurgents even have their own television station, Al-Zawraa, which while banned by the Iraqi government, still broadcasts from Erbil, Iraqi Kurdistan, even as coalition pressure has forced it to switch satellite hosts several times."

## Modern Operation

### *Telephone*

In an analog telephone network, the caller is connected to the person he wants to talk to by switches at various telephone exchanges. The switches form an electrical connection between the two users and the setting of these switches is determined electronically when the caller dials the number. Once the connection is made, the caller's voice is transformed to an electrical signal using a small microphone in the caller's handset. This electrical signal is then sent through the network to the user at the other end where it is transformed back into sound by a small speaker in that person's handset. There is a separate electrical connection that works in reverse, allowing the users to converse.

The fixed-line telephones in most residential homes are analog — that is, the speaker's voice directly determines the signal's voltage. Although short-distance calls may be handled from end-to-end as analog signals, increasingly telephone service providers are transparently converting the signals to digital for transmission before converting them back to analog for reception. The advantage of this is that digitized voice data can travel side-by-side with data from the Internet and can be perfectly reproduced in long distance communication (as opposed to analog signals that are inevitably impacted by noise).

Mobile phones have had a significant impact on telephone networks. Mobile phone subscriptions now outnumber fixed-line subscriptions in many markets. Sales of mobile phones in 2005 totalled 816.6 million with that figure being almost equally shared amongst the markets of Asia/Pacific (204 m), Western Europe (164 m), CEMEA (Central Europe, the Middle East and Africa) (153.5 m), North America (148 m) and Latin America (102 m). In terms of new subscriptions over the five years from 1999, Africa has outpaced other markets with 58.2% growth. Increasingly these phones are being serviced by systems where the voice content is transmitted digitally such as GSM or W-CDMA with many markets choosing to depreciate analog systems such as AMPS.

There have also been dramatic changes in telephone communication behind the scenes. Starting with the operation of TAT-8 in 1988, the 1990s saw the widespread adoption of systems based on optic fibres. The benefit of communicating with optic fibers is that they offer a drastic increase in data capacity. TAT-8 itself was able to carry 10 times as many telephone calls as the last copper cable laid at that time and today's optic fibre cables are able to carry 25 times as many telephone calls as TAT-8. This increase in data capacity is due to several factors: First, optic fibres are physically much smaller than competing technologies. Second, they do not suffer from crosstalk which means several hundred of them can be easily bundled together in a single cable. Lastly, improvements in multiplexing have led to an exponential growth in the data capacity of a single fibre.

Assisting communication across many modern optic fibre networks is a protocol known as Asynchronous Transfer Mode (ATM). The ATM protocol allows for the side-by-side data transmission mentioned in the second paragraph. It is suitable for public telephone networks because it establishes a pathway for data through the network and associates a traffic contract with that pathway. The traffic contract is essentially an agreement between the client and the network about how the network is to handle the data; if the network cannot meet the conditions of the traffic contract it does not accept the connection. This is important because telephone calls can negotiate a contract so as to guarantee themselves a constant bit rate, something that will ensure a caller's voice is not delayed in parts or cut-off completely. There are competitors to ATM, such as Multiprotocol Label Switching (MPLS), that perform a similar task and are expected to supplant ATM in the future.

***Radio and Television***

In a broadcast system, the central high-powered broadcast tower transmits a high-frequency electromagnetic wave to numerous low-powered receivers. The high-frequency wave sent by the tower is modulated with a signal containing visual or audio information. The receiver is then tuned so as to pick up the high-frequency wave and a demodulator is used to retrieve the signal containing the visual or audio information. The broadcast signal can be either analog (signal is varied continuously with respect to the information) or digital (information is encoded as a set of discrete values).

The broadcast media industry is at a critical turning point in its development, with many countries moving from analog to digital broadcasts. This move is made possible by the production of cheaper, faster and more capable integrated circuits. The chief advantage of digital broadcasts is that they prevent a number of complaints with traditional analog broadcasts. For television, this includes the elimination of problems such as snowy pictures, ghosting and other distortion.

These occur because of the nature of analog transmission, which means that perturbations due to noise will be evident in the final output. Digital transmission overcomes this problem because digital signals are reduced to discrete values upon reception and hence small perturbations do not affect the final output. In a simplified example, if a binary message 1011 was transmitted with signal amplitudes [1.0 0.0 1.0 1.0] and received with signal amplitudes [0.9 0.2 1.1 0.9] it would still decode to the binary message 1011 – a perfect reproduction of what was sent. From this example, a problem with digital transmissions can also be seen in that if the noise is great enough it can significantly alter the decoded message. Using forward error correction a receiver can correct a handful of bit errors in the resulting message but too much noise will lead to incomprehensible output and hence a breakdown of the transmission.

In digital television broadcasting, there are three competing standards that are likely to be adopted worldwide. These are the ATSC, DVB and ISDB standards; the adoption of these standards thus far is presented in the captioned map. All three standards use MPEG-2 for video compression. ATSC uses Dolby Digital AC-3 for audio compression, ISDB uses Advanced Audio Coding (MPEG-2 Part 7) and DVB has no standard for audio compression but typically uses MPEG-1 Part 3 Layer 2. The choice of modulation also varies between the schemes. In digital audio broadcasting, standards are much more unified with practically all countries choosing to adopt the Digital Audio

Broadcasting standard (also known as the Eureka 147 standard). The exception being the United States which has chosen to adopt HD Radio. HD Radio, unlike Eureka 147, is based upon a transmission method known as in-band on-channel transmission that allows digital information to "piggyback" on normal AM or FM analog transmissions.

However, despite the pending switch to digital, analog television remains being transmitted in most countries. An exception is the United States that ended analog television transmission (by all but the very low-power TV stations) on the 12th of June 2009 after twice delaying the switch over deadline. For analog television, there are three standards in use for broadcasting colour TV . These are known as PAL (British designed), NTSC (North American designed), and SECAM (French designed). (It is important to understand that these are the ways from sending colour TV, and they do not have anything to do with the standards for black & white TV, which also vary from country to country. For analog radio, the switch to digital radio is made more difficult by the fact that analog receivers are sold at a small fraction of the price of digital receivers. The choice of modulation for analog radio is typically between amplitude modulation (AM) or frequency modulation (FM). To achieve stereo playback, an amplitude modulated subcarrier is used for stereo FM.

**The Internet**

The Internet is a worldwide network of computers and computer networks that can communicate with each other using the Internet Protocol. Any computer on the Internet has a unique IP address that can be used by other computers to route information to it. Hence, any computer on the Internet can send a message to any other computer using its IP address. These messages carry with them the originating computer's IP address allowing for two-way communication. The Internet is thus an exchange of messages between computers.

As of 2008 , an estimated 21.9% of the world population has access to the Internet with the highest access rates (measured as a percentage of the population) in North America (73.6%), Oceania/Australia (59.5%) and Europe (48.1%). In terms of broadband access, Iceland (26.7%), South Korea (25.4%) and the Netherlands (25.3%) led the world.

The Internet works in part because of protocols that govern how the computers and routers communicate with each other. The nature of computer network communication lends itself to a layered approach where individual protocols in the protocol stack run more-or-less independently of other protocols. This allows lower-level protocols to be customized for the network situation while not changing the way higher-level protocols operate. A practical example of why this is important is because it allows an Internet browser to run the same code regardless of whether the computer it is running on is connected to the Internet through an Ethernet or Wi-Fi connection.

Protocols are often talked about in terms of their place in the OSI reference model (pictured on the right), which emerged in 1983 as the first step in an unsuccessful attempt to build a universally adopted networking protocol suite.

For the Internet, the physical medium and data link protocol can vary several times as packets traverse the globe. This is because the Internet places no constraints on what physical medium or data link protocol is used. This leads to the adoption of media and protocols that best suit the local network situation. In practice, most intercontinental communication will use the Asynchronous Transfer Mode (ATM) protocol (or a modern equivalent) on top of optic fibre. This is because for most intercontinental communication the Internet shares the same infrastructure as the public switched telephone network. At the network layer, things become standardized with the Internet Protocol (IP) being adopted for logical addressing. For the World Wide Web, these "IP addresses" are derived from the human readable form using the Domain Name System (e.g. 72.14.207.99 is derived from www.google.com). At the moment, the most widely used version of the Internet Protocol is version four but a move to version six is imminent.

At the transport layer, most communication adopts either the Transmission Control Protocol (TCP) or the User Datagram Protocol (UDP). TCP is used when it is essential every message sent is received by the other computer where as UDP is used when it is merely desirable. With TCP, packets are retransmitted if they are lost and placed in order before they are presented to higher layers. With UDP, packets are not ordered or retransmitted if lost. Both TCP and UDP packets carry port numbers with them to specify what application or process the packet should be handled by. Because certain application-level protocols use certain ports, network administrators can manipulate traffic to suit particular requirements. Examples are to restrict Internet access by blocking the traffic destined for a particular port or to affect the performance of certain applications by assigning priority.

Above the transport layer, there are certain protocols that are sometimes used and loosely fit in the session and presentation layers, most notably the Secure Sockets Layer (SSL) and Transport Layer Security (TLS) protocols. These protocols ensure that the data transferred between two parties remains completely confidential and one or the other is in use when a padlock appears in the address bar of your web browser. Finally, at the application layer, are many of the protocols Internet users would be familiar with such as HTTP (web browsing), POP3 (e-mail), FTP (file transfer), IRC (Internet chat), BitTorrent (file sharing) and OSCAR (instant messaging).

**Local Area Networks**

Despite the growth of the Internet, the characteristics of local area networks (computer networks that do not run beyond a few kilometres) remain distinct. This is because networks on this scale do not require all the features associated with larger networks and are often more cost-effective and efficient without them. In the mid-1980s, several protocol suites emerged to fill the gap between the data link and applications layer of the OSI reference model. These were Appletalk, IPX and NetBIOS with the dominant protocol suite during the early 1990s being IPX due to its popularity with MS-DOS users. TCP/IP existed at this point but was typically only used by large government and research facilities. As the Internet grew in popularity and a larger percentage of traffic became Internet-related, local area networks gradually moved towards TCP/IP and today networks mostly dedicated to TCP/IP traffic are common. The move to TCP/IP was helped by technologies such as DHCP that allowed TCP/IP clients to discover their own network address — a functionality that came standard with the AppleTalk/IPX/ NetBIOS protocol suites.

It is at the data link layer though that most modern local area networks diverge from the Internet. Whereas Asynchronous Transfer Mode (ATM) or Multiprotocol Label Switching (MPLS) are typical data link protocols for larger networks, Ethernet and Token Ring are typical data link protocols for local area networks. These protocols differ from the former protocols in that they are simpler (e.g. they omit features such as Quality of Service guarantees) and offer collision prevention. Both of these differences allow for more economic set-ups.

Despite the modest popularity of Token Ring in the 80's and 90's, virtually all local area networks now use wired or wireless Ethernet. At the physical layer, most wired Ethernet implementations use copper twisted-pair cables (including the common 10BASE-T networks). However, some early implementations used coaxial cables and some recent implementations (especially high-speed ones) use optic fibres. Where optic fibre is used, the distinction must be made between multi-mode fibre and single-mode fibre. Multi-mode fibre can be thought of as thicker optical fibre that is cheaper to manufacture devices for but that suffers from less usable bandwidth and greater attenuation (i.e. poor long-distance performance).

# 2

# The Communication Process

Communication is a complex, ongoing process that brings us into contact with the people in our world. Often communication is viewed as a straightforward exchange of messages between a speaker and a listener, but this is a naïve view. As indicated in this chapter, communication is a symbolic process of sharing meanings. A key to interpreting communication is to find the meanings of messages, and those meanings are found in people, not in words. Your friend's meaning of trust or happiness may be quite different than yours.

Even a presumably simple, concrete word can cause misunderstandings. You may think of vacation as personal time spent away from the workplace with no thought of your job. Your boss may think vacation implies that employees will be away from the office but continuously available to discuss work-related problems via cell phone or e-mail. The closer both meanings are, the easier it is for you to communicate effectively.

Communication is a continuous process that begins with a first encounter between people and does not end until the last encounter in their lives. These encounters may involve functional messages that serve practical purposes, or, in cases of close ties, the encounters may also involve nurturing messages that convey a sense of caring and personal connection. Over time, members of a relationship develop increasingly predictable communication patterns and, if they become close, create a relational culture or similar worldview. In the following pages, Galvin andWilkinson address this complex issue, discussing the communication process as a constant symbolic interaction of sharing, exchanging, and coordinating meanings.

Through various examples, they apply this understanding of the communication process to explain the difference between specific types of communication, like interpersonal, impersonal, functional, and nurturing communication. Finally, they explore relational culture, a very specific and unique type of interpersonal communication, and discuss the commun-ication dynamics involved. The analysis in this chapter answers the question"How does communication work?" and establishes a basis of knowledge that prepares the reader for the chapters to follow. As you read this chapter, begin to formulate your answer to the question: What is communi-cation? How often have you heard someone say,"We just can't communicate," or"We are having communication problems"? These expressions appear regularly in everyday conversations as people struggle to solve a problem, start a relationship, manage a conflict, or find a new way of connecting in an established relationship. Such struggles occur in all areas of life, in classrooms and offices, at kitchen tables, and on athletic fields.

In our society people of different backgrounds come together to solve problems or make things happen, and in those situations they can find themselves frustrated because of"communication breakdowns." Although these dissatis-factions are not new, they are heightened by the fact that we live in an information age in which effective communication is expected and valued in all areas of life.

Over time we have had the opportunity to listen to many different people discuss their interpersonal frustrations as we lead communication workshops for family members, organizational employees, and community groups. In all these cases participants are invested in improving their handling of certain situations, in analyzing their relationships, and in developing new relational skills. As we discuss interpersonal communication in our workshops, we also describe the communication process and its elements as well as the specific characteristics of interpersonal communication that distinguish it from impersonal communi-cation.

We also address the concept of relational culture, or the development of a highly unique interpersonal relationship characterized by a unique system of meanings created and maintained by the partners. Our hope is to encourage participants to develop their knowledge and skills in relationship development and relationship maintenance in various contexts. We will introduce these issues in the following pages.

## THE COMMUNICATION PROCESS

Whenever we ask workshop participants how they would define communication, we hear responses such as"transmitting ideas,""talking and listening," or"sending messages using words and movements." Each person has some notion of what it means to communicate with another and knows how it feels when communication attempts are successful or unsuccessful, yet they have not thought deeply about the communication process itself. People seem to assume that communication works or it does not work, more as a matter of fate than as a process that can be changed or improved. Because communication itself is so complex, we could list multiple elaborate and highly technical definitions of it. For our purposes, however, a simple phrase is an appropriate starting point. As we view it, communication is the symbolic process of sharing meanings. Because this definition is almost deceptively simple, each of these key words needs to be developed.

## Symbolic

By saying that communication is symbolic, we mean that symbols are used to transmit messages. Symbols are representations of a person, event, place, or object. Words, or verbal expressions, are the most commonly understood symbols, but symbolic actions also include the whole range of nonverbal behaviors: facial expressions, vocal tone, eye contact, gestures, movement, body posture, appearance, context, and spatial distance. In addition, objects and ideas can be used as symbols. For example, friends often exchange gifts, food, or e-mails as symbols of connectedness. You have learned to use verbal and nonverbal symbols both as a message creator and as a message interpreter. As a speaker (or sender), you create messages by selecting the most appropriate symbols from a range of options in order to reach your intended receivers most effectively.

As a listener (or receiver), you attempt to interpret the symbols others convey to you. Although exchanging appropriate symbols appears rather simple and straight-forward, we are constantly amazed at the communication breakdowns that occur as symbols are misinterpreted.

Effective communicators are those who are able to select the most appropriate symbols or messages for specific other persons and who are able to interpret the intended message symbols of other speakers. As a child you learned to encode one type of message to ask your father for money and another to request a loan from your best friend. You learned to interpret your brother's gestures indicating if he is feeling sad, worried, or exhausted. You have learned who will be enraged if you roll your eyes at them, and who will decode your nonverbal cue as humorous. For effective communication to occur, the speaker and listener must share the same meanings for the symbolic messages they exchange.

## Process

Relational communication involves a process, a dynamic and continuous process. Each relationship develops its own communication history, a history that cannot be rewritten. Someone once said,"It's unfortunate you only get one chance to make a first impression." A relationship's communication pattern begins at the first moment of contact- at a party, in a classroom, in a meeting. The relationship may start in any number of ways: a question, a glance, an introduction, or a smile. Once contact is made, the relationship begins to develop its history, which is constructed and reflected by its communication patterns.

A relationship's ongoing development may be interrupted by physical or psychological distance; relational partners may move in and out of each others' lives over many years, but the history of the relationship continues from that first meeting. Sometimes people say they wish to wipe out a time period of their relationship or forget a painful argument that occurred.

Individuals may choose to emphasize or deemphasize certain communication events throughout their relationship history, but they can never go back to"how things used to be," or delete a piece of that history.

Although some models of the communication process portray it as a circular process, our preferred model for understanding this process comes from the thinking of Frank Dance,whoproposed a helical representation. Imagine the form of a helix, in which the continuousness of the process is represented by the infinity sign. This model depicts the ever-widening scope of the relationships as participants continuously reencounter each other, a process that continues indefinitely.

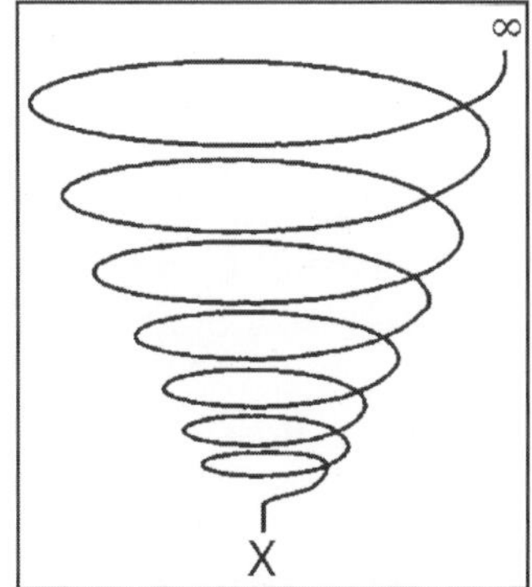


Whereas a circular model suggests that communication returns to the same place, the helical model implies the ever-changing, progressive, and evolving nature of relational interactions. The helix representation provides support for the concept that"you can't put a relationship into reverse and erase a difficult period of time."We have stopped counting the times workshop participants say,"If only things could go back to the way they were two years ago," or,"I want to wipe out the last six months of our marriage." In reality each encounter has inalterably added to their relationship, and this history cannot be denied.

People in relationships cannot wipe out a huge hurtful fight, long periods of verbal aggression or silence, or, in romantic situations, the affair.Yet most friends, partners or colleagues can learn to manage their history in effective ways: through emphasizing positives, talking through the conflicts, and behaving in ways that affirm their ties. A conflictual father and son cannot pretend they never hurt one another with words or fists; friends cannot erase sarcastic comments.

All they can do is work through the issues that currently keep them from dealing with each other in constructive or caring ways, and attempt to change their present communication patterns as they continue in their relational process. People can always choose to change, to do things differently. Such choices represent one of the most exciting parts of the relational development process.

## Sharing

Even though the words speaker and listener are commonly used in communication terminology, communi-cation is not a process of trading messages. It does not resemble a poor tennis match in which one Player A hits the ball and then just stands there until the Player B hits the return. Symbolic messages do not travel from Person One to Person Two and back to Person One again in some turn-taking ritual. Rather, at its most basic level, communication requires mutual and continuous involvement, sometimes referred to as the transactional nature of communication.

This mutual influence process is similar to a skilled tennis match in which both players are always in motion based on what they anticipate the other will do. Similarly, in communication encounters both parties remain actively involved in the process.

For example, even though Michael may appear more talkative, Vanessa conveys nonverbally that she is bored or pleased or annoyed, thus influencing Michael's choice of future message symbols. Both are actively and continuously involved in every moment of the interactions; thus, the mutual influence process that characterizes interpersonal interaction. Diagrammed, the transactional nature of communication looks like Figure.

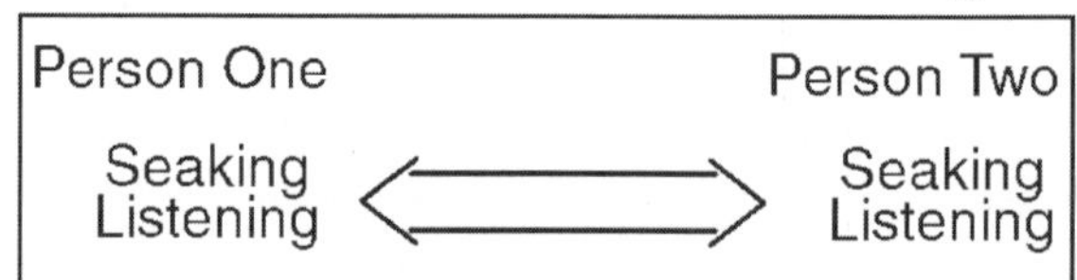


As relationships develop over time, the transactional process becomes more complex. Your perception of another person and that individual's perception of you combine to form a context for your interactions. If you see Person X as warm and supportive, you will relate to him or her in an open manner. Person X is then likely to see you as open and friendly and relate to you with increasing warmth or support. Thus, your perceptions of each other affect each interaction as well as the overall perception of the relationship. The situation can also be reversed, creating a negative context. If you see another person as judgmental or sarcastic, this may lead you to interact in a defensive or combative manner.

You may be caught up in a type of negative spiral. Each communication exchange occurs within the context of a mutually constructed relationship. If the definition of a relationship remains relatively unchanged, for example boss and employee, romantic partners, and parent and child, the nature of the communication process becomes fixed. Each new encounter reinforces the good or the bad. A boss who constantly relates to staff members as incompetent may stifle their attempts to be innovative.

A parent who treats children as responsible persons fosters their ability to handle new situations. This process is captured in the statement"Over time we create an image of another person and relate to the image we create." Individuals construct a reality of themselves and of others through their interactions, and relate to those realities they constructed. The attempt to understand and adapt to another represents a communication challenge.

## Meanings

Although verbal and nonverbal symbols permit us to transmit thoughts and feelings, the symbols must be mutually understood for the meanings to be truly shared. Common meanings make it possible for us to communicate. Since there is no absolute standard for all symbols, we are constantly trying to connect with people, even our family members, who do not share exactly the same meanings for the symbols that we use.

Therefore it is important to remember the expression "Words don't mean; people do." Each person's background, including physiological state, family and cultural background, and unique experiences, influences how he or she perceives the world and attaches meanings to symbols. The experience of being nearsighted, athletic, extraverted, dyslexic, artistic, or shy affects how you perceive the world and relate to others. Your family of origin (the family or families in which you were raised) served as your first communication classroom, teaching you how to interpret messages and how to use communication to manage key relational issues such as intimacy and conflict. In addition, your cultural background, socioeconomic level, and educational experiences influence your perceptions. Based on your culture, you may interpret big hugs, multiple-course meals, and shouting voices as symbols of caring.

If you grew up in a lower-middle-class neighborhood, you will have different meanings for money and security than someone who grew up in an affluent community. Finally, your own unique circumstances influence how you assign meanings. A painful custody battle affects how you discuss divorce. Early school experiences influence how you participate in college classes. Living abroad affects how willing you are to interact with people of different cultures. Fortunately, most people report many similar experiences, but no two people develop the same set of meanings.

Each is a unique entity with particular meanings for certain symbols. Ninety dollars may represent a large purchase to one person, but her partner assumes that only purchases above $500 are large. A nickname may seem funny to you and insulting to your friend. Screaming may be viewed as an acceptable or terrible way to resolve conflicts. Breakdowns in communication often occur because of missed meanings. Only with knowledge and empathy can you walk in someone else's shoes, experience the world from a different perspective, and create messages that reflect that point of view.

Frequently, focus is placed on the words rather than on the entire range of verbal and nonverbal symbols that are constantly being used to create and interpret the meanings of messages. Therefore, at any point in time each person involved in communication is contributing to the process-and experiencing the transactional nature of the communication process. Effective communication requires the psychological presence of both parties-attention and connectedness are indicators that both parties are focused on the encounter. We find the following simple exercise very useful for demonstrating how individuals may differ in translating the meaning of everyday terms. Imagine yourself saying these phrases to a particular person. Think about exactly what you would hope that other person would do if you said these words to him or her. I need more respect from you. I feel there is a lack of trust in our relationship. Each of the italicized words receives many different responses.

*Depending on the person responding, more respect may be indicated by*:

- Listening to me,
- Asking for my opinion,
- Following my advice.

*Trust may be indicated by*:

- Keeping what I say confidential,
- Telling me your real feelings,
- Telling me when a painful event happens.

These are only examples of the many meanings that people have for the two common terms respect and trust. Shared meanings are critical because they help to create the context for a relationship in which participants learn to predict how the other will react to particular verbal and nonverbal messages.

**Interpersonal Communication**

Not all communication should be considered inter-personal communication. Frequently, you are engaged in impersonal interactions. When you ask for directions, pay for a purchase, or call for a doctor's appointment, you are not automatically involved in interpersonal communication. If you ask a teacher for clarification, discuss a project with a boss, or plan a family reunion with a distant cousin, you may be involved in necessary, functional interactions but you do not share a strong, significant relationship.

Interpersonal communication occurs when two or more people engage in voluntary, ongoing, interdependent interactions that involve meaningful interpretation of their verbal and nonverbal behaviors. In short, this implies a perception of the relationship as positive, reflecting a choice to continue to relate to each other over time in order to deepen the relationship and make it increasingly unique.

There may be exceptions to this description, such as when you interact involuntarily with particular teachers or managers for a long period of time, learn how to communicate effectively with them, and eventually develop a voluntary interpersonal relationship. In the case of involuntary but required relationships, it is likely that the person with the less power is adapting to the person with greater power, setting up a one-up/one-down interaction pattern. Such relationships tend to remain impersonal, although, on occasion, these persons develop a friendship. Relationships move from impersonal to increasingly personal as closeness develops. Therefore, you need to think about relationships on a continuum from impersonal to interpersonal, understanding that a particular relationship may move forward and backward at different times.

**Patterns**

In ongoing relationships, communication becomes patterned and predictable. As you relate with another person, you begin to create increasingly predictable interaction patterns. The more intense and personal the relationship becomes, the more unique the relational patterns. Relational patterns involve verbal and nonverbal communication acts that are:

- Recurring
- Relationship defining.

Over time, while people in a relationship develop their own ways of interacting, they evoke certain responses from each other and play off them.

For example, you may know that you and Tony will joke around when you see each other, whereas you and Alberto will talk about poker.

You may share your romantic problems with Sarah but never with Gail, who you know equally well. Observing an ongoing significant relationship, you may see a remarkably complex pattern, similar to a dance, emerge.

*For example*:

- X makes a statement; Y answers with a complaint.
- X responds with a kidding remark; Y counters with sarcasm.
- X retorts angrily; Y suggests talking is useless.

One or the other stomps away. In his book Couplehood, Paul Reiser describes numerous examples of everyday patterns between partners. Like all businesses, couples engage in endless meetings to discuss areas of management concern and division of labour.

"You know, we really should call the post office and tell them to hold our mail while we're away."

"We? You mean me, don't you?"

"No, I mean we. I didn't say'you.' I said'we.' You or me."

"Oh, really? Are you going to ever call the post office?"

A moment to think."No.""

Then you mean'me,' don't you?"

"Yeah."

As in many other areas of life, relationships become predictable; these patterns tend to create or constitute the relationship.

**Functional and Nurturing Communication**

In many relationships, the bulk of everyday communi-cation tends to be functional rather than nurturing. Functional communication involves managing day-to-day necessities and exchanging impersonal information such as getting plans coordinated, meals fixed, schedules arranged, and group projects finished-all the details that keep life running smoothly. We estimate that 90 per cent of the communication that goes on between friends or colleagues, parents and children, and even spouses or partners tends to be functional communi-cation. If the only communication between closely connected persons is functional, that relationship is severely limited. If the necessary and desirable functional interactions are not accompanied by communication that is more personal, distance will characterize their ties, limiting their relationship. Nurturing communication occurs when participants send messages that are caretaking of the relationship-messages that indicate that the other person and the relationship are valued.

Such nurturing communicationmayinclude a hug, a special birthday celebration, a thinking-of-you phone call or IM, a deep conversation about feelings, or a direct personal statement such as"I'm glad we're friends." Nurturing communication involves emotional closeness and carries the"I care about you" messages. People who nurture each other confirm the other's existence-" You are there; I recognize you; I care about you."

Through our work with partners and families, we have developed an informal guideline that states the following: If there is 10 per cent nurturing communication going on in any relationship, that relationship is healthy. When 10 per cent of the behaviors in a relationship are nurturing, we believe the people involved will feel cared for and valued. In our experience, when individuals in relationships come for counseling, functional messages account for about 95 per cent of their communication and the remaining 5 per cent is negative, often openly hostile.

Nurturing messages disappeared from their relational life. Nurturing takes different forms in different relationships, but no matter what the form of expression, everyone needs to experience it.

Coworkers, friends, and family members can all be involved in levels of nurturing communication. Individuals who have been nurtured are likely to be good nurturers; those who have not been nurtured can learn to nurture others, but often this takes conscious effort and hard work. Nurturing communication serves as the lifeblood of any relationship. Without it, the relationship remains static and functional; with it, the relationship renews itself through continual growth.

**Relational Culture**

Persons in strong, highly developed interpersonal relationships eventually create their own relational culture. Relational culture describes a jointly constructed worldview, a personally developed set of understandings that affect the attitudes, actions, and identities of the relational partners. Over time many partners or best friends adapt to each other until they experience an evolving, unique set of meanings that are reflected in their relational culture.

These private meanings, conveyed verbally and nonverbally, separate the partnership from other relationships; nicknames, joint storytelling, inside jokes, and code words contribute to the creation of a"world built for two." We find Julia Wood's description captures the essence of a relational culture:"processes, structures and practices that create, express and sustain personal relationships and the identities of partners".

Communication patterns serve as the basis for relational cultures as they are constructed, maintained, or changed through communication. A strong relational culture is the hallmark of an intense, intimate interpersonal relationship. In a world of many stresses and changes, we need our relationships to sustain us and nourish us as human beings. Communication is central to the process of constructing meaningful and fulfilling relational support. The ability to build and nurture such relationships is a critical life skill, one to be learned and valued.

# 3

# Consideration of Communication

Audience is the most important consideration in any communication. People are different and have different needs. They will need to write one way if their audience is EMS personnel, another way if your audience is scientific researchers, and a completely different way if your audience is the general public.

## OFTEN FORGOTTEN

Audience is the most important consideration in any communication, but it is the one we most often forget. We assume people are just as interested in our subject as we are, so we pack our reports full of detail and nuance.

We assume people won't take us seriously unless we include pages and pages of data and tables to prove our point. We forget what the audience cares about and focus on the wrong messages.

Or, even worse, we don't even understand how to best communicate with our audience, so they don't even receive the messages we're sending them. I guarantee you've all done this. We all have.

### How to you Write for Audience

- Go through the questions in Step 2 and thoughtfully come up with answers.
- Try to ask additional questions specific to your subject matter.
- Put yourself in the shoes of your audience. What would they want to know?
- Talk to your audience. Find out specifically what they'd like to know.
- Test your material out on some members of your audience and get their feedback. This can be one of the most beneficial tools of all.

### Make It Visually Appealing

All readers, regardless of your audience, are more likely to read something that is visually appealing than something that is not. No, you don't have to be a graphic designer to make your document visually appealing. You just need to know a few simple tricks.

**Use White Space**

Don't crowd your document with too much text and other stuff. Most people would rather read a four-page document with effective "breathing" space than a jam-packed, text-heavy two-page document. So keep your margins big, and incorporate other areas of space throughout your document.

**Break Up Text**

There's nothing worse than seeing tons of monotonous text. Try to break text into different sections. Pull some areas of text into a side-bar – away from the main body of text. Use 3-4-inch-wide columns instead of the full width of your paper. Pull out a good quote and make it big. If you have a list of several items:

**Use Headings**

A great way to break up long areas of text is to Create Big headings to *break up the different sections* and paragraphs. This will make your document look more interesting, and it will also help people jump around to the sections they are most interested in.

**Use Font Sizes, Bold And Italics**

In addition to headings, you can also differentiate different areas of text through font sizes, bold, and italics. These techniques help to draw emphasis to certain areas and provide variety and interest to your document as a whole.

**Use Different Fonts**

Fonts can also be used to help differentiate text in your document. Just don't use too many fonts; generally two or three is all you'll need. A simple rule is to try to use blocky sans serif fonts for headings, such as Arial or Trebuchet, and serif fonts for the areas of lots of text, such as Times New Roman or Garamond (the web is the only exception to this rule - serif fonts are difficult to read on a web page).

**Use Colour**

Colour is one of the greatest ways to add visual appeal to any document. Again, don't use too many colors or it will look unprofessional. Often just adding one or two colors (besides black) can dramatically spice up your document. If you aren't able to print in colour, you can do a lot with different variations of black-and-white shading.

**Use Pictures:**

Pictures can replace a thousand words. It's really true. Pictures can replace a thousand words. It's really true. You can try to describe the senseless pain of a sick child, or you can show a picture of the child and the job is done for you. Make sure you use pictures as much as you can. Often you can turn data and even words into pictures, which will make concepts simpler for your audience to understand. Just make sure your pictures help communicate your message and don't distract your readers from it.

These are just some of the simple, established techniques for turning a boring old document into a visually stimulating one – one that your readers might actually want to read. Which is kind of the idea, right?

How do you know if your document is visually appealing enough? Test it. People are often very happy to share the opinions about visual appeal. You may in fact get more opinions than you want! But certainly, many people will be able to suggest simple techniques you can incorporate to give your document a visual face-lift.

**Make It Readable**

You could make your document visually stimulating, but if the language is too difficult, no one will want to read it.

*Here are a few techniques for readability*:

- *Keep language short and sweet*: If you can say something in fewer words, do it. It takes practice and good editing to write this way. Do the best you can to make your writing clear and concise.
- *Keep sentences and paragraphs short*: Sentences should be no more than 20 words, and paragraphs should be no more than four short sentences.
- *Make the language appropriate for the audience*: If you are writing for the general public, you must write at no more than a 6th grade level. Even for many advanced and educated audiences, your language should generally be more than a 9th grade level. This means you should try to replace certain words with simpler words. For instance, instead of saying "facilitate," say "help." Instead of saying "physician," say "doctor."
- *Avoid jargon or technical language*: Even if you are communicating with people who "should" understand certain language, such as medical terminology, don't assume the language will be clear to everyone. Maybe there will be outsiders who read the document, or maybe the individual is new or has simply forgotten that "hemorrhage" means "bleeding." The general rule is: if you can say it in a simpler way, do it.

Even if you are the greatest writer and editor in the world, you will make mistakes and leave room for improvement. Always get someone to edit your work.

**Make It Credible**

A great document could be totally dismissed if it doesn't appear credible, trustworthy, and professional.

*Here are a few tips:*

- *Always include your organization name*: Your organization name, or the agency that is paying for the time in creating the document, should appear somewhere on the document where it is easy to find. If you have a logo, include that too.
- *Always include contact information*: If people have questions, who should they contact? Leaving off this information looks sloppy and unprofessional. If you have a website, this is also a great tool for people who want more information.
- *Include references, where appropriate*: If you are communicating to the general public, you often will not want to include references. They will take your word for it. For many other audiences, such as in academics or even professional peers, if you make some far out claim, they will at least want to see a reference to support that claim. Just because you are trying to shorten and simplify a document does not mean you let it become less credible.
- *Don't overstate your conclusions*: There is a difference between making your results important and making them dramatic. Be careful. Don't be tempted to exaggerate your results and findings. People will notice your "drama" and question the validity of your arguments.
- *Be honest and accurate at all times*: You have an important responsibility to remain honest and credible to your results at all times. Readers trust you that the information you present is valid. You owe it to them and to yourself to make sure this is true.

## COMMUNICATING STATISTICS

Statistics are the heart and soul of your data communication. After all, the numbers are the primary thing you often need to communicate to your audience. However, that does not mean the numbers should overwhelm the reader. When communicating your data to others, there are a few important tips to remember:

### Statistical Tips

- *Don't overload your reader with statistics*: Give them enough to get the point across. You can always give them additional data if they ask for it.
- *Choose meaningful data*: When narrowing down your data choices, try to choose the ones that show the magnitude of the problem, data that provide context or meaning, and data that are new or noteworthy.
- *Avoid statistical terminology*: Statistical terminology should be avoided when there are simpler ways to explain results. Most people have

low math literacy, even highly educated persons. Unless you're communicating to scientists, the term "statistically significant" is rarely meaningful. Instead, say "more likely" or "less likely."

- *Avoid statistical data terms*: Avoid saying p-value, confidence limit, correlation, regression, and chi square. Instead, try to say things like number, count, per cent, rate, and average. These are data terms almost anyone can understand.
- *As much as possible, try to turn numbers into words*: For example, instead of presenting an odds ratio as 2.0, say that smoking doubles the risk of having a heart attack. Even with relatively simple data, like percents, it can be useful to turn the data into words. Instead of saying "25% of children do not wear seatbelts," say "one out of every four children does not wear a seatbelt." This is a more clear and helpful way of saying the same thing.

**Communicating with Charts and Graphs**

A wonderfully illustrative method of displaying complex data. Another important technique for dealing with data is to make good use of charts and graphs. Charts are a wonderfully illustrative method of displaying data that would otherwise be to complex for many audiences. Here are some tips for charting:

*Charting Tips*:

- *Use charts to get the reader's attention*: Use charts particularly for data points that you want the reader to take notice of. Charts stand out well in a document, so you can use that to your advantage.
- *Non-scientific-audiences*: For non-scientific audiences, use easy-to-understand charts, such as pie charts, bar charts, line graphs, and tables. Avoid using complex charts, such as stacked bar charts, scatterplots, etc.
- *Use explanations and bullet points*: Wherever possible, try to include explanations or bullet points beneath the chart. This will help to ensure that your audience interprets the chart correctly and that the message is not lost on them. You can also include additional information or data in these bullets that cannot be seen in the chart.
- *Use stand-alone charting*: Charts should be able to stand on their own, with or without the text. Therefore, always include titles, legends, and other labels.
- *Chart garbage*: Get rid of unnecessary chart "garbage" that clutters up your document and takes away from the data's message. This includes many of the default settings in charting programs like Microsoft® Excel. Get rid of the horizontal gridlines, the ugly grey background the chart borders, the excessive tick marks, etc. Even 3-D can be a distraction from the actual message of the data.

- *Don't have too many data points on one chart*: For example, pie charts should have no more than six slices, line graphs should have no more than four lines, and bar charts are most effective if they contain only a few bars, etc.
- *Using tables*: Tables should be used when no other good charting options are available. Tables are excellent for displaying lots of data; but because they require more decoding, they are the least preferred charting method.

Regardless of what data, statistics, or charts you include in your document, just make sure you double-check your numbers to ensure they are accurate. There's nothing more embarrassing than presenting a report full of data and having someone point out a calculation error. Your whole report could be discredited from a simple mistake. Also, you may want to have a statistician check over your numbers to make sure you are presenting data in a mathematically correct way.

## Provide a Take-Home Message

You can present an excellent analysis of an important topic, but unless you help the reader know what to do with the information, it will be forgotten before you know it. The final step in a good communication project is to provide a memorable take-home message.

### *Here are the Steps for Providing an Effective Take-home Message*

- *State the conclusion*: Briefly summarize your key findings and state your conclusion. This should be just one or two points that people can easily digest and remember. Make sure that your conclusion is fully supported by your data and is not an exaggeration.
- *Provide possible recommendations based on your findings*: What should be done given the findings? Does the subject need further study? Does your agency need to implement a new programme or policy? Make sure that your recommendations follow naturally from the findings of your document; this is not the time to wax eloquent on your ideas for the improvement of other systems outside your research area. Also, make sure that you remain as unbiased as possible in your recommendations; your audience may be put off if you argue for your "one favourite solution" without proper consideration of the alternatives. Remember, you are there to inform, suggest, and work with others to decide the next step.
- *Suggest an action, if appropriate*: Having an action is a powerful way to end any communication; it helps solidify your message in the reader's mind and encourages them to implement your message in their own sphere. Action is the holy grail of communi-cation – it is

every advertiser's dream. In many cases, it may not be appropriate for you to suggest one action too strongly (for some of the reasons under #2). However, there are many times when you will want to.

Including an action is one of the best ways to make your communication message memorable and effective to your audience. For instance, you can suggest the reader go to the website to learn more, remember a certain rule when performing a medical procedure, support your programme, talk to friends and family about your message, do one simple thing to keep their home safer, etc. You want to find the "obvious" actions you can suggest that will not be a question of debate or strategy among your leaders or peers.

**There we Have it**

You have gone through all the steps of communicating your data effectively. Please let us know if you have any questions or if you would like personalized technical assistance on a communication project you are working on. Just remember to always communicate clearly and often with those around you. Hopefully, you've learned a few tips to make your communications go more smoothly the next time!

# 4

# Effective Communications

The ability to communicate effectively is essential. Communicating is more than speaking; it involves your entire presence. How you present yourself has a great deal of impact on your students' interest and desire to learn. As a Navy instructor, you must be able to communicate your knowledge, skills, and experiences to the students in order to facilitate the learning process. How you communicate often has more impact than the content of your message. The skills and techniques explained in this chapter will assist you in strengthening your ability to communicate effectively.

**Effective Communication Principles**

The purpose of effective communications in a training environment is to ensure students accurately understand the material presented by the instructor.

*There are basically two principles you need to understand that have to do with communicating effectively*:

- The identification and removal of barriers
- The communication process itself.

**Barriers to Effective Communication**

The existence of certain barriers increases the potential for poor communication. By being aware of these barriers, you can reduce them and enhance the clear understanding of your students.

**Lack of Common Core Experience**

One barrier is the lack of common core experience. You are unlikely to find any group in which students have the same common core experience. For example, if you say that a kiwi tastes like a kumquat, students who have tasted one would have the experience to make the proper relationship.

However, for the students who have tasted neither, the comparison would have no meaning. To prevent that problem, determine student experience level before you prepare your lesson. Then check for understanding as you use examples and analogies with your explanations.

**Overuse Of Abstractions**

Abstractions are concepts, ideas, or words that are not directly related to the subject being discussed. To avoid confusion you should speak in concrete terms—be specific. Be aware of the background and experience level of your students and use appropriate terms and examples.

Remember, you will normally have more experience in the subject matter than any of your students, so you have the responsibility of ensuring understanding.

This requires that you not only present the information, but also that you check to ensure the students understand exactly what you intended.

**Fear**

Fear may be one of the greatest barriers to effective communication. The fear of showing ignorance, fear of disapproval, fear of losing status, and fear of judgment are common barriers. Many times, students will have anxieties or fears about their abilities. Students may hesitate to take part in your discussions because they have a lack of confidence and are afraid they will appear ignorant. That, in turn, brings about a fear of judgment and a fear of losing status in front of their peers.

Try to understand your students' fears. Provide a threat-free learning environment by being encouraging and nonjudgmental of the students. Remember how long it took you to learn your subject matter. Take the time to recognize the individual differences in your students so that you will know how to motivate them. Since you have control of the class, you must direct the class energy in a positive direction.

Do not allow fellow students to make fun of or exhibit disapproval of a struggling student. Avoid embarrassing any of your students or offending human values. Follow the basic principle of motivation by giving them positive feedback.

**Environmental Factors**

Environmental factors such as noise and temperature may interfere with the communication process. Obviously, noise is a barrier to hearing what is being said. If students are overly hot or cold it may be difficult from them to listen attentively. However, more subtle factors may also affect the communication process.

The colour of the walls, uncomfortable seats, the location of pictures or illustrations, and the arrangement of students in relation to the instructor may all become barriers to effective communication.

You should constantly strive to identify and eliminate barriers to effective communication. Some will be obvious while others maybe very difficult to detect. Your awareness of barriers, along with a knowledge of the communication process, will assist you in communicating effectively.

## THE COMMUNICATION PROCESS

The communication process consists of a message being sent and received. The message may be verbal or non-verbal. The same basic principles apply whether humans, animals, other forms of life, or combinations of these are involved. Your challenge, as an instructor, is to not merely communicate with your students—but to communicate effectively.

Effective communication involves a message being sent and received. Added to this however, is the element of feedback to ensure that the message sent was received exactly as intended. This concept may be illustrated using the three-step communications model.

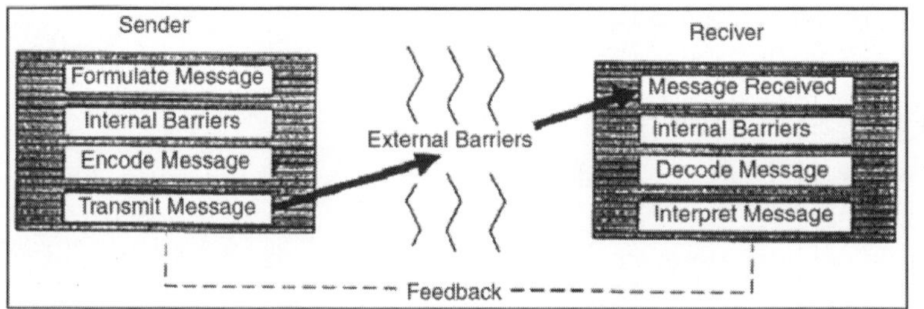


**Fig**. Three-step Communication Process.

### Sending The Message

There are four elements involved in sending a message. First, as the instructor (sender), you formulate the message you intend to communicate. Next, you consider possible barriers that may affect the message. This includes your experience, the terms you will use, and even your feeling toward the subject or the students. External barriers such as noise must also be considered. Third, you encode the message; that is, you put the message into the words you want to use. Last, you clearly communicate (send) the message.

### Receiving The Message

There are also four elements involved in receiving a message. The students (receivers) will first hear and/or see the message you sent. Second, the message is affected by external barriers, if any, and the students' own internal barriers. Possible internal barriers may include the students experience level, their understanding of the terms used, their attitude toward the material, or the way they feel about you. Third, your students decode the message through the use of mental images. For instance, when you say the word circus, the receiver does not "see" the letters that form the word. Instead, a mental image of some sort appears. How many different mental images might arise among your students for this one word alone? A clown, a big top, lions, acrobats, and so forth. Fourth, the students interpret the message. Clearly, at this point in the process there is no way for you to determine that all of the students received the message you intended. To determine this, you must get feedback.

### Feedback

Feedback, which may take several forms, provides essential information about your success in communicating the message. To get feedback, have the students respond to oral questions and encourage them to ask questions. The students' non-verbal behaviors also provide important clues as to their understanding of the material. Facial expressions and body movements often indicate when students are unsure about the meaning of your message. You should be careful in accepting a "yes" response when you ask "Do you understand?" Obtain meaningful feedback by asking questions that require the students to provide answers which indicate that they in fact do understand exactly what you intended.

## EFFECTIVE COMMUNICATION SKILLS AND TECHNIQUES

There are many skills and techniques you must master to bean effective communicator and instructor. Many of these skills you already possess, all that is required is that you use them to their best advantage. Others, you need to learn and practice.

## LISTENING

Listening is one of our most important communication skills. It is an active process of hearing and understanding that demands concentration and attention. Both you and your students have responsibilities in the communication process. You must ensure that the learning environment is free of distractions that might interfere with the students' ability to listen. Be alert to the non-verbal behaviors of your students.

Facial expressions reveal much of what is happening in the mind of a student. A quizzical look indicates some misunderstanding has occurred or a question needs to be addressed.

A student leaning slightly forward and maintaining good eye contact with you is probably interested and sincere about learning. An affirmative head nod indicates approval, agreement, or understanding. Conversely, eye contact out the window or someplace other than the front of the room may indicate boredom or lack of interest.

Fidgeting in the chair or a slouched posture may also bean indication of something other than effective listening. Raised hands and relevant questions are sure signs that you are communicating effectively. Learn to determine if students are listening by the type of feedback they provide.

Effective listening depends on motivation, and you are the prime motivator in your classroom. Students should arrive for instruction ready to learn. They should participate and ask questions as they arise. Students must understand that they have responsibility for their own learning. This requires active listening on their part.

## EFFECTIVE INSTRUCTOR DELIVERY TECHNIQUES

Delivery style has a major impact on student motivation and determines to a great extent how well students listen. Studies have shown that spoken words alone account for only seven per cent of the impact of the message. The following Factors are important considerations in your delivery of instruction.

### Articulation

Articulation is simply understandable speech. You can achieve good articulation in two ways. First, enunciate; speak clearly. Second, pronunciate; accent syllables and reproduce consonant and vowel sounds in conformity with the accepted standard—the dictionary.

To be a good speaker, make crisp, distinct enunciation your goal. Avoid slurring and mumbling. Avoid slang such as jist, git, gonna, whut, watcha, or hafta. In rehearsal, exaggerate your enunciation beyond what is required in normal speech. Apply the principle of sharpened enunciation not only in your classes but in ordinary conversation. Make it a habit. If you have a regional accent, such as a Southern drawl or a New England twang, don't try to eliminate it—make the most of it! It's part of your personality. A slight accent is pleasant and adds interest and personality to your speech. However, be sure that people from other parts of the country can understand you.

### Grammar

Grammar concerns the correct usage of the spoken or written word. It is like a code. When you use the code correctly, the message comes through clearly and quickly. But when you make encoding errors, the one who receives the message has to labour to extract the precise meaning. Sometimes your message never comes through exactly right. However, as an instructor, never commit glaring grammatical errors like "him and me is going," "I seen," "he give," or "it run."

### Rate Of Speech

As a speaker, you should neither talk at a slow, plodding rate that puts your listeners to sleep nor rattle off words so rapidly that they run together. As a rule, speak fast enough to be interesting yet slow enough to be understood. Just as a good baseball pitcher keeps the batter alert by changing the speed of the ball, take advantage of a vocal change of pace to hold the interest of your audience. Your rate of speech should be governed by the complexity of the thought, idea, or emotion you are communicating.

Use a fast rate for joy, excitement, or vigorous action. Use a slow rate for a deliberate or methodical presentation. Add emphasis by either slowing or speeding your rate. The normal rate of delivery is 125 to 150 words per minute.

## To Improve Common Rate Difficulties, Observe the Following Suggestions

Slow, ponderous rate. Force yourself to think faster so that you can speak faster. Using a tape recorder, read aloud and interpret the meaning of the words by the rate at which you speak them.

Then play back the recording. If your rate is still too slow, record the same reading selection again but force yourself to use a faster rate of speech to cut down the total playback time.

### *Fast, Machine-gun Delivery*

Curb your impatience to blurt out ideas. Take time to make them clear. Force yourself to slow down. Recognize the listeners' need to absorb ideas; give them time to do so by saying words clearly and by pausing longer between ideas. Read aloud, observing the marks of punctuation. Express the meaning of the words carefully at the rate that fits your interpretation. Taking care to enunciate more precisely will generally slow your rate.

### *Halting, Choppy Rate*

Concentrate on speaking complete ideas or sentences. Take a deep breath before you begin a sentence; breathe between, not in the middle of, ideas or phrases. Sometimes a choppy rate results from tenseness, nervousness, or lack of familiarity with the subject matter.

### *Pauses*

In writing, punctuation marks separate thoughts and ideas and give the desired meaning and emphasis to words. In speaking, pauses serve the same functions to a large degree. You may use pauses to gain humorous, dramatic, or thought-provoking effects. Use them as a vocal means of punctuating for effect. Proper use of pauses gives listeners a chance to absorb ideas and gives the speaker a chance to breathe and concentrate on the next point. Pauses also give emphasis, meaning, and interpretation to ideas.

*The following suggestions will help you overcome common pausing difficulties*:

- *Not enough pauses*: Begin by reading aloud something that you like. Force yourself to pause between ideas and at periods, commas, and other punctuation marks. Try to adopt the attitude of the artist who makes a few brush strokes and then steps back to evaluate the results.
- *Too many pauses*: A lack of knowledge of the subject, failure to organize material thoroughly, or inadequate rehearsals usually result in too many pauses in the speaker's delivery. Study your material and organize it on paper. Then rehearse until your thoughts and words flow smoothly. Thorough familiarity with the subject matter increases verbal fluency.

- *Overuse of verbal connectors*: Pauses, properly placed in the flow of speech, are often more effective than words. Filling pauses with meaningless, guttural sounds gives listeners the impression that you are not confident of what you are saying, and that you are not prepared to speak to them. Too many "uhs" and "ahs" may be detrimental to an otherwise effective lesson presentation. To improve on this difficulty, use the same techniques suggested for eliminating too many pauses and leave out the "uhs" and "ahs."

**Inflection**

Inflection is a change in the normal pitch or tone of the speaker's voice. Just as musical notes become melody when arranged in different relative positions on the musical scale, your voice becomes more interesting and words more meaningful when you use changes in pitch. Using inflection can increase the emphasis on certain words. The following example illustrates how inflection on different words changes the meaning of a question.

*Say the question to yourself, raising your pitch (but not your volume) on the underlined words, as indicated*:

- What am I doing?
- What am I doing?
- What am I doing?
- What am I doing?

Inflection is the key to expression of mood. It can be emotional, persuasive, or convincing. Using inflection can move an audience to tears or laughter and create a lasting impression. Without inflection, the audience may fall asleep. Like pauses, inflection is a way of punctuating speech; it can put the question mark at the end of a question, make a statement of fact more positive, or help to put an exclamation mark at the end of a strong statement. Inflection is the principal difference between just saying words and speaking ideas with meaning:

*Try the following suggestions to improve inflection*:

- *Read aloud and communicate your emotions*: Inflection conveys feeling and meaning. However, feeling also produces good inflection. As an instructor, you must show your feeling about what you say. To practice using inflection, read aloud and communicate your emotions. Using a tape recorder is a good way to improve inflection because you must communicate emotion entirely through your voice; gestures or visible facial expressions provide no help.
- *Downward and upward inflection*: Generally, downward inflection at the end of a sentence expresses conviction. However, downward inflection within the sentence itself gives a sense of finality to the thought and creates a mental break in the listeners' thoughts. Use slight upward inflection within the sentence to indicate that the

thought is not yet complete; that serves to bind ideas together and to give unity to the thought. Use upward inflection at the end of a sentence only when you ask a question or imply uncertainty.

## Force

Forceful speech combies the volume or carrying power of the voice with the demonstrated vitality, strength, and conviction of the speaker; it includes the proper placement of stress or emphasis on key words and phrases. Like rate, pauses, and inflection, force is a way of conveying conviction, of giving meaning, or of adding emphasis. Yet, unlike rate, pauses, and inflection, it cannot be set apart distinctly. Force involves rate, pauses, and inflection plus carrying power, fullness of tone (or body), and proper regulation of loudness. Listeners will not respond to a speaker who shouts and is insensitive to their feelings. Neither will they be convinced by the cool, detached manner of a speaker who is consistently calm, quiet, or patronizing. To communicate, you must awaken reactions and feelings in your listeners. Knowledge of the subject and of the sequence in which you plan to present ideas will help you to calmly lead the thoughts of your audience. You can then drive home a point with power and let silence underline the significance of your words.

Through your gestures, voice, movement, eye contact, and choice of words, you can convey force to your listeners. But your listeners will neither hear you nor see you unless you project words and actions with a vitality and strength of conviction. Force is not loudness, shouting, wild gesturing, or vulgar language. Force is knowing what you want to say and then saying it with implicit firmness and undeniable confidence.

*The following common difficulties with force have accompanying suggestions for improvement*:

- *Lack of volume*: To increase volume, select someone in the back of the room and concentrate on making him or her hear you. Rehearse in an empty classroom and speak to an imaginary person in the back of the room. Since these exercises will make you aware of the distance involved, they will motivate you to increase your volume. When you speak with increased volume, you will be able to feel your diaphragm working.
- *Dropping volume at end of words or sentences*: Dropping volume usually results when a speaker incorrectly associates a drop in volume with downward inflection. Develop the habit of paying attention to the sound of your own voice so that you can judge whether you are being heard. Practice lowering the pitch of your voice without dropping the volume. Record your voice so that you can hear how you sound to others. Read aloud, and concentrate on projecting every word in a thought or idea to an imaginary listener seated in the back of the room.

- *Failure to give emphasis to main points or key words*: To emphasize main points and key words, you must first know your subject well. Then you can communicate main and subordinate ideas by stressing key words and phrases using volume, pitch, rate, and pauses. That will result in convincing and authoritative presentations.

## SPEECH IMPROVEMENT

This chapter has addressed specific ways to correct common difficulties; however, two methods will improve all aspects of your speaking voice. First, listen closely to polished speakers on television, such as popular newscasters. Their techniques of speech make them good models for study. Don't try to imitate them exactly, but study how they use their voices to give meaning to their words and emphasis to their ideas. Second, listen to yourself daily as you instruct and casually converse with your contemporaries.

## EYE CONTACT

The most powerful element of instructor presence in front of a class is direct eye contact with your audience. By looking directly in the eyes of each of your students, you personalize the lesson being presented and stimulate the desire for them to listen more intently. Each student should have your direct eye contact several times during an instructional period. Make and maintain this eye contact for 3 to 5 seconds. This time interval is appropriate for personal contact without being overbearing or creating some level of discomfort for individual students.

Scan the entire class without developing a mechanical pattern. Avoid the common pitfall of talking to the chalkboard or visual aid panel or to any other training aid you may be using. Maintaining effective eye contact enhances your credibility. Another important reason for looking directly at your students is to observe their nonverbal reactions to your instruction.

## BODY MOVEMENT

Body movement is an important part of successful communication; it reinforces, emphasizes, and clarifies verbally expressed ideas. Because body movement is so easily adaptable for communicating, skilled pantomimic actors can tell complicated stones involving many characters through physical movement alone. However, your actions while instructing must reinforce rather than contradict your words. Make sure the image you present and your body movements strengthen your communication. Movement is the motion of the whole body as you travel about the classroom. Movement attracts the attention of the listener because the eye instinctively follows moving objects and focuses on them.

Movement can help you convey thoughts to your audience. The basic rule in movement is moderation. Do not remain glued to one spot, but do not keep on the move all the time. As your skill and experience increase, your movement will become less obvious and more meaningful. Learn to modify the degree of movement to make it natural and meaningful.

Plan your movement so that you are at the proper place at the proper time. For example, when using an overhead projector with a transparency, plan movement so that you are at the machine when it should be turned on; when you need to open the curtains, plan movement so that you are at the curtain control point at the time the curtain should be opened.

## GESTURES

A gesture is a natural movement of any part of the body that conveys a thought or emotion or reinforces oral expression. Your arms, hands, and facial expressions are your principal tools of gesture. Your gestures will depend to a large extent on whether your personality is vigorous and dynamic or calm and easygoing. Regardless of your personality, gestures will add to the effectiveness of your speech if you relax your shoulders, arms, and hands and concentrate on communicating to the audience the meaning and importance of your ideas. When the gesture is natural, it is effective. If the gesture is artificial, posed, or strained, it detracts rather than reinforces.

Practice gestures as a natural part of your speaking manner; they should arise spontaneously from enthusiasm and conviction. Descriptive gestures portray an object or illustrate an action. Describe the size, shape, or movement of an object by imitation. Show a vigorous punch by striking with your fist; show height by holding your hand at the desired level; show speed by a quick sweep of your arm. Pantomime a complicated or humorous movement as you describe it. Use your hands to sign a message, such as a "V" formed with two fingers as a symbol of victory.

### Facial Expression is a Type of Gesture

To change opinions or to inspire or interest people, your face must show what you are feeling and thinking. Facial expressions show many feelings, such as joy, dejection, anger, and poise. The most common fault in facial expression is the deadpan face that shows a total lack of expression. Another common difficulty is the use of a constantly intense expression, usually manifested by a frown. Overcome this problem by relaxing all over; then use your intensity only on key ideas. Finally, remember that you are neither a wooden statue nor a clown. You are a human being. The more natural you appear and act, the more you will influence your listeners. The classroom is no place for a poker face.

## ATTITUDE

Your speech reveals how you feel about what you say. It has an emotional impact on others. Thus, emotion indicates how you feel about all that surrounds you—it shows your attitude. Attitude affects the words you use. The four specific indicators of a good speaking attitude are sincerity, confidence, enthusiasm, and humour. Sincerity, from the speaker's point of view, is the apparent earnest desire to convince the audience of the truth and value of an idea. The two sources of sincerity are a personal, intense belief in your subject and a belief in the value of your subject to your listeners. The first of these sources is ideal because intense personal belief is natural sincerity that shows in your every word or gesture. The second source is more rational than emotional. If you know your teaching material is valuable, you will present it in an honest and forthright manner.

You will not rely on gimmicks or questionable reasoning to make your presentation look good. By showing that you believe in what you say, you convince your students of the importance of the subject. Sincerity shows in a number of ways: directness of manner, facial expressions, clarity of explanation, proper combination of humility and authority, and the effective use of the voice and body to reinforce and emphasize ideas.

Remember that students must see, hear, and feel that you believe in what you say. Confidence is a personal attitude or feeling of assurance. It is belief in your ability to perform a task well. To be confident and control stage fright requires two prerequisites: knowledge of the subject and belief in your ability to speak. You obtain knowledge of a subject through research and study. Belief in your ability comes from rehearsal and experience. These requirements are entirely up to you to accomplish in your own way.

## ENTHUSIASM

Enthusiasm is the outward manifestation of sincerity and confidence. From the speaker's standpoint, enthusiasm is a strong personal excitement or feeling about a cause or a subject. Enthusiasm is not shouting; it is not phony, overdramatic speech; it is not waving of the arms and leaping about on the platform. Rather, it is the way you show your belief in your subject! How you show enthusiasm is governed by your personality. If you are a vigorous and dynamic person, you may show enthusiasm by brisk, energetic movement; sweeping gestures; a rapid rate of speech; widely-varying inflection; and plenty of vocal force.

If you have a more subdued nature, you will move and gesture with less energy and speak in more measured tones. You will use force only on the key words and ideas; make more use of the pause for effect; and maintain a calm, pleasant, but confident and authoritative manner. Most instructors show enthusiasm by combining characteristics from both of these styles.

## HUMOUR

You may be a sincere, confident, and enthusiastic instructor, yet still lack the humour needed for effective instruction. If you lack a sense of humour, you will seem unreal, inhuman, or very conceived. Humour shows that you are, after all, just another human being and that you have a warm, lively interest in all that goes on around you. Having a sense of humour does not necessarily imply an ability to tell funny jokes, although tasteful, relevant jokes certainly have a place in good instruction.

A more effective type of humour is spontaneous humour. Take advantage of unexpected humorous classroom situations that sometimes arise—make a brief comment, pause, or simply smile. Humour directed at yourself is very effective. Most people laugh when someone important is receptive to being the object of good humour. In addition to decency, the only rule to follow in using humour is good judgment. Take care not to direct humour at a specific person. Students may resent having a classmate singled out. Be sure your humour is good natured and lightly done. Clean humour is as American as the hot dog and will often assist student learning.

**Feed Back**

Observation of your students provides important feedback that will help you in evaluating the effectiveness of your communications skills. Puzzled brows, frowns, and whispered questions between students indicate that you have not communicated effectively. The students have unconsciously shown signs of a lack of understanding. The observation of these signs and their on-the-spot analysis is called feedback. That again underlines the importance of maintaining good eye contact with your students. Students can also send signs of positive feedback.

*You may often knowledge*: When you see a student's observe students at the very moment they gain new face light up, you are seeing understanding take place. This positive feedback is one of the most personally rewarding experiences of an instructor.

Feedback is important because it indicates how you must adjust your instruction to communicate effectively. If the students have obviously not learned, then you must modify your instructional approach. Feedback makes the learning process an intercommunication between the students and the instructor. *As such*: it is critical to the success of the instructional mission.

**Oral Questions**

For two-way communication to take place between you and the students, you must use good, thought-provoking questions throughout the lesson. The use of oral questions allows you to determine from time to time if you are maintaining essential communication. When properly planned, implemented, and evaluated, oral questioning improves effectiveness and, more importantly, student learning. The greatest resource for enhancing your classroom instruction is the students themselves. Training is most effective and learning more permanent when the students take an active part in the process. Students need to interact with the subject matter and the instructor during the lessons rather than just at test or performance time. The responsibility of active class participation lies with you, the instructor. Avoid over using the questioning technique of asking "are there any questions?" That does not stimulate much thought or generate productive class participation. As an instructor, always remember that one purpose of questioning is to help students get involved in learning the material at hand. Some instructors have mastered the technique of teaching a lesson almost entirely through the use of oral questions. Questions add variety to a lesson and require active student involvement.

However, questions are only as effective as the manner in which they are used. You can defeat the whole purpose of the questioning technique by using it improperly, so make sure you learn how to use questions properly. If you don't have a natural knack for oral questioning, you can develop some degree of skill by setting yourself a goal for improvement and then practicing constantly.

Try to decrease the amount of one-way communication in the classroom by asking questions as much as you make statements. You will find that you have a natural compulsion to "tell," which is understandable. After all, that is probably what your instructors did. Studies show that in a typical classroom, someone is talking two-thirds of the time; and of that time, the instructor does two-thirds of the talking.

Through good questioning techniques, you can increase and improve the amount of student responses beyond the one-word contribution. A key point to remember is that the intent of a question is to elicit a response. Effective use of questions will result in more student learning than any other single technique. Becoming skillful in the art of questioning will increase your effectiveness as an instructor.

## PURPOSES OF ORAL QUESTIONING

The primary purpose of oral questioning is to stimulate the students to think. Navy requirements call for people who can operate complex equipment and carry out those troubleshooting and maintenance procedures needed to keep the equipment operating at peak performance. To perform those duties effectively, sailors must be trained to analyse, compare, and interpret facts, data, and methods, all of which require a high caliber of thinking. Oral questioning also provides you with a practical means for establishing the level of instruction. Students may vary greatly in the quantity and quality of background knowledge they have acquired through previous training and experience.

You must determine the level of achievement of the students before proceeding with the presentation of new subject matter. Although you may use a pretest or a questionnaire for this purpose, the quickest and simplest means is a series of oral questions. Oral questioning has three other important purposes: First, it arouses interest in the subject matter. Second, it focuses attention upon a particular area of the subject matter. Third, it drills students on subject matter they must recall precisely, such as correct terminology, functions of parts, and safety precautions.

*Use questions to achieve the following benefits*:

- Discover each student's interests, abilities, and depth of knowledge.
- Arouse student interest in the subject matter of the lesson.
- Stimulate discussion, and keep it closely tied to the subject matter.
- Review and summarize important points.
- Test students' knowledge of what the lesson has covered, and check the effectiveness of the instruction.

## CHARACTERISTICS OF A GOOD ORAL QUESTION

Questions that are poorly worded, vague in meaning, or ambiguous will frustrate both you and the students. Students who do not comprehend the true meaning of poorly phrased questions will hesitate longer than usual and then give uncertain answers. You may feel dissatisfied with the answers and reprimand the students for their lack of attention and understanding. The students, knowing that they have answered unsatisfactorily through no fault of their own, may lose enthusiasm and withdraw from active participation. You can avoid frustrations of this kind by planning your questions well in advance as well as carefully choosing and arranging words and phrases. The construction of good oral questions requires three considerations; level of instruction, use of interrogative, and clarity of meaning.

### Level of Instruction

In asking questions, use simple words, correct grammar, and complete sentences. Use words the students know and understand. As the course progresses, introduce new terms and more technical phraseology. Ask questions at times that suit your presentation of course material. Plan questions that require students to think before answering. Don't use questions that give away the answer or that students can answer with a simple yes or no.

### Use of Interrogative

Use the interrogatory word or phrase at the beginning of your question so that students know immediately when you are asking a question. Let's consider two examples where this is not done:

- The two sizes of firehose most frequently used in the Navy are what?
- You can determine whether or not explosive vapors are in a compartment by what means?

Questions worded in this way handicaps the students in at least two ways. First, the students are expecting a declarative statement, not a question. Second, they cannot identify the meaning of the question until the final words are spoken. Note the improvement in these same questions when the interrogatory word or phrase is placed at the beginning:

- What are the two sizes of firehose used most frequently in the Navy?
- By what means can you determine whether or not explosive or toxic vapors are in a compartment?

### Clarity of Meaning

Avoid the use of catch or trick questions as a teaching device, especially for beginners. Make sure the wording of the question conveys to the students the true or intended meaning. The students must understand what you want, regardless of whether they know the correct answer. "Where are storm warnings flown aboard ship?" is a good question; but "Where are storm warnings flown?" fails to indicate what point is being tested. Make your questions brief, and limit them to one thought. To include too many factors in a single question confuses the students.

Ask well-stated, clearly understood questions in a normal conversational tone as part of the lesson. After each lesson, reevaluate your questions in light of how the student responses contributed to better learning.

## TYPES OF ORAL QUESTIONS

Learn to use oral questions throughout the lesson. Use them in the introduction to create interest and focus attention on the subject matter and during the lesson presentation to ensure student understanding. Then use them at the end of the presentation for review and drill purposes. Feel free to ask factual, thought-provoking and interest-arousing questions as often as you choose. Other types of questions may serve one or more useful purposes if used sparingly, but may prove ineffective if you use them too often.

### Factual Question

The factual question asks for specific information; for example, "When was the first U.S. nuclear powered submarine built?" Although the primary purpose of the factual question is to help students memorize facts, it may, under certain conditions, have important secondary purposes. For example, you could use a factual question to arouse interest, to focus attention upon certain parts of the subject matter, and to assist in determining the level of instruction.

### Thought-Provoking Question

A thought-provoking question normally begins with such interrogatory expressions as "What is the advantage of," "What is the difference between," "Why is this method considered superior to," " How would you solve the problem if," and so forth. The value of this type of question is that a single question, properly used will stimulate the students to think. Prepare good, thought-provoking questions on key lesson points in advance.

**Interest-Arousing Question**

An interest-arousing question may sound, superficially, like a factual question. "How many Navy ships were involved in collisions at sea during the past year?" Since the question calls for an exact number, students will doubtless attempt to recall the collisions about which they have read or heard.

When asking an interest-arousing question, however, you are not interested in exact numbers, exact names of ships, or exact situations. Your main purpose in asking the question is to focus the students' attention and get them thinking about the subject you are about to present.

Multiple-Answer Question A multiple-answer question is one that has more than one correct answer. It can be used to increase student participation or cause students to think about the other students' answers. A multiple-answer question generates a high interest level and improves listening skills. A factual, thought-provoking, or multiple-answer question may also be one that is interest-arousing. That depends upon your intention in asking the question, not upon its form or content.

However, if you overestimate the knowledge of your students, a question intended to be factual may turn out to be thought-provoking. If you underestimate the students' knowledge, a question intended to be thought-provoking may turn out to be factual. As previously mentioned, certain kinds of questions are effective if used occasionally but are detrimental if used frequently. Typical of these types of questions are the yes or no question, the leading question, and the canvassing question.

**Yes/No Question**

The yes or no question, of course, calls for a simple answer—yes or no. This type of question has value in arousing interest, focusing attention, encouraging student participation, and serving as a lead-in to other kinds of questions, such as "Why do you believe that to be true?" An excessive use of yes or no questions tends to encourage students to guess.

**Leading Question**

A leading question is one that suggests its own answer; for example, "You wouldn't smoke in the paint locker, would you?" or "The 40mm gun is larger than the 20mm gun, isn't it?" If used properly, leading questions have value in focusing attention, in arousing interest, and in emphasizing a point. You can also use leading questions to help the student think the matter through to the right answer. If you notice students groping for the right answer, ask a question that directs their attention to information they know but have overlooked in answering the question. That has value when used skillfully because it builds a student's confidence. Occasionally. use the leading question to help awkward students, saving them the embarrassment of failure in front of the class. If used too frequently, leading questions discourage any real thinking and become boring to the students.

### Canvassing Question

Use a canvassing question to determine those who are familiar with a specific area of subject matter. If you are teaching damage control for instance, you may ask "How many of you have been involved in an actual shipboard fire?" A show of hands provides information about student experiences that you may find useful as your lesson progresses. It gives you a great opportunity to bring some real life examples into your lesson and to provide some individual recognition for student contributions. Canvassing questions can also help to determine class level.

## TECHNIQUES OF ORAL QUESTIONING

The AAUW Report: How School Shortchange Girls was addressed earlier. Gender bias has also played a significant role in questioning techniques within the school system. As mentioned earlier, boys demand more attention and get it. When boys call out answers, teachers usually listen while the same behaviour exhibited by girls is corrected. Even when boys do not volunteer, teachers are more likely to call on them than girls. Girls receive less teacher praise, fewer remedial comments on their work, and less specific comments about their performance. The implication for you as an instructor is to be aware these behaviors will continue in class unless you correct them. Set the same standards for responding to questions and enforce them uniformly. Provide remediation to both males and females in coaching them through incorrect responses.

Do not spend an inordinate amount of time taking questions from males alone. Know that females may be hesitant to respond to questions, but by providing a safe environment for all your students, you will gain culturally-sensitive class and curriculum include more favorable attitudes toward other groups, a reduction in stereotyping, and increased academic achievement.

### Five Step Questioning Technique

A recommended technique of oral questioning consists of five steps: asking the question; pausing; calling upon a student; evaluating the student's answer; and finally, emphasizing the correct answer. Put time and thought into making each step count in the teaching process. The first step in good questioning techniques is to state the question. Since the intent of questioning is to provoke thought, ask the question before calling on a person to answer. That encourages each member of the class to formulate an answer.

Many instructors make the mistake of calling on a student before stating the question. That allows the rest of the students to relax and not formulate an answer. When you state the question first and then pause for a few seconds, everyone will begin actively thinking of an answer.

This thinking process enables students who you do not select to answer the question time to think so that they may add to the response. Identifying there spondent before asking the question may startle and fluster some students so much that they may not be able to respond, even if they know the answer. State the question clearly, giving one central thought, by placing the interrogative word at the beginning of the statement to alert students that a question is coming. Do not repeat the question or change the wording of the question unless necessary. After asking a question, pause to allow the students time to think through their answers.

Vary the duration of the pause depending on the difficulty of the question and the level of the students. Most instructors fail to pause long enough after asking their questions.

Calling on a student too quickly is as detrimental as calling on the student before asking the question. After pausing for a reasonable time, call on a student by name to answer the question. That satisfies a basic student need for recognition.

If students feel you recognize their individual efforts, they will put forth greater effort. When selecting a person to respond, consider both the difficulty of the question and the individual abilities of students. Consistently assigning a difficulty question to a slower learner will remotivate that student. Spread the questions around without establishing a predictable pattern. A predictable pattern includes calling on students either in alphabetical or seating order or calling upon a select few whose names you know. Scattering questions also prevents mental loafing.

Faster learners will dominate the class if you do not control student participation. Achieve a balance between calling on volunteer respondents and nonvolunteers. Allow only one student to answer at a time, but encourage all students to participate and volunteer answers. Although you may not call upon every student, let students know you expect them to take an active part.

The next step is to comment on the given answer or acknowledge the response. That demands a careful and quick mental evaluation of the answer for accuracy and completeness. Provide feedback to the responder and class on the quality of the answer. When a student gives an incorrect answer, be critical only of the answer and not the student. Be sure to provide positive reinforcement for correct answers.

The strength of the reinforcement depends on the difficulty of the question asked and the relative difficulty level for the student selected. Do not overdo the reinforcement. A simple "correct" or "thank you" may suffice. The fifth and last step in the process, which is optional, is to emphasize or repeat the answer given.

Avoid the tendency to repeat each answer as that has the effect of diminishing the student's response. Remember that the student's answer has an importance for the class as well as for you. Insist that answers be clearly spoken; heard by all; phrased intelligibly; and if possible, stated in the terminology of the lesson.

## Other Questioning Techniques

*The following techniques may be used in addition to or in conjunction with the five step questioning technique*:

- Focus on the non-volunteer students; avoid eye contact with the active participants when asking a question. This will encourage the quieter students to reply. Assign a question to a student who does not have a hand raised; then provide appropriate recognition for that student's contribution. This technique will increase class involvement, attention, and participation because all students will know you may call on them regardless of whether they volunteer.
- Sometimes you may need to prompt a student who has given a weak, incorrect, or an "I don't know" response to your question. Help the student to arrive at a correct answer by asking questions that contain direct hints or clues to the correct answer. The key to effective prompting is to begin on a simple enough level that the student can relate to the material. The questions in the prompting sequence depend on the student's previous response. To begin the sequence, refer to material the student already knows. If the initial student response was partially correct, provide reinforcement by telling the student what was right.

  Then ask prompting questions until the student can give the entire correct response. If the student's first answer is "I don't know," rephrase the question or provide an example to eliminate any confusion, ambiguity, or vagueness in the original question. Acknowledge the final correct student response in the same manner as if the student had given the correct response the first time. Do not allow the prompting technique to result in student badgering.
- Seek further clarification when a student gives a response that is poorly organized, lacking in detail, or incomplete. Do not provide the student with any hints (prompts), clues, or additional information, but ask the student to do so. Request clarification when you believe the student has guessed at an answer by asking the student to justify the answer. Example: "What else can you add?"
- Use the reverse technique (answering a question with a question) to get students to think, make associations, and discover the answer to their own questions. Example: The student asks, "Why did the Chief give that order?" The instructor might respond, "If you were in the same situation, what order would you have given?"
- Use a redirected question to increase class involvement and provide recognition for students' answering questions. A redirected question occurs when you assign a question asked by one student to another member of the class for answering. Note: Never use this technique

unless you know the answer and believe the student to whom you redirect the question also knows the answer.

- Use the technique of refocusing when you want the student to relate a correct answer to another topic. This technique helps students to consider the implications of their response within a broader framework by noting relationships with other topics studied.

As an instructor, you give an impression to your class from your appearance, speech, habits, questions, and overall manner every time you present a lesson. This impression has a strong impact on the learning process. You must be an enthusiastic, positive motivator in your classroom. You control the energy and dynamics of the learning process. Remembering and applying effective communication and oral questioning techniques will improve your presentations and assist your students in learning the material.

# 5

# Models of the Communication Process

We teach the same models of communication today that we taught forty years ago. This can and should be regarded as a mark of the enduring value of these models in highlighting key elements of that process for students who are taking the process apart for the first time. It remains, however, that the field of communication has evolved considerably since the 1960's, and it may be appropriate to update our models to account for that evolution.

This paper presents the classic communication models that are taught in introducing students to interpersonal communication and mass communication, including Shannon's information theory model (the active model), a cybernetic model that includes feedback (the interactive model, an intermediary model (sometimes referred to as a gatekeeper model of the two-step flow), and the transactive model.

It then introduces a new ecological model of communication that, it is hoped, more closely maps to the the range of materials we teach and research in the field of communication today. This model attempts to capture the fundamental interaction of language, medium, and message that enables communication, the socially constructed aspects of each element, and the relationship of creators and consumers of messages both to these elements and each other.

While the field of communication has changed considerably over the last thirty years, the models used in the introductory chapters of communication textbooks are the same models that were used forty years ago. This is, in some sense, a testament to their enduring value. Shannon's model of the communication process provides, in its breakdown of the flow of a message from source to destination, an excellent breakdown of the elements of the communication process that can be very helpful to students who are thinking about how they communicate with others.

It remains, however, that these texts generally treat these models as little more than a baseline. They rapidly segue into other subjects that seem more directly relevant to our everyday experience of communi-cation. In interpersonal communication texts these subjects typically include the social construction of the self, perception of self and other, language, nonverbal communi-cation, listening, conflict management, intercultural communication, relational communication, and various communication contexts, including work and family.

In mass communication texts these subjects typically include media literacy, media and culture, new media, media industries, media audiences, advertising, public relations, media effects, regulation, and media ethics. There was a time when our communication models provided a useful graphical outline of a semesters material. This is no longer the case. This paper presents the classic models that we use in teaching communication, including Shannon's information theory model (the active model), a cybernetic model that includes feedback (the interactive model, an intermediary model (sometimes referred to as a gatekeeper model of the two-step flow), and the transactive model.

Few textbooks cover all of these models together. Mass Communication texts typically segue from Shannon's model to a two-step flow or gatekeeper model. Interpersonal texts typically present Shannon's model as the "active" model of the communication process and then elaborate it with interactive (cybernetic) and transactive models. Here we will argue the value of update these models to better account for the way we teach these diverse subject matters, and present a unifying model of the communication process that will be described as an ecological model of the communication process. This model seeks to better represent the structure and key constituents of the communication process as we teach it today.

## Shannon's Model of the Communication Process

Shannon's model of the communication process is, in important ways, the beginning of the modern field. It provided, for the first time, a general model of the communication process that could be treated as the common ground of such diverse disciplines as journalism, rhetoric, linguistics, and speech and hearing sciences. Part of its success is due to its structuralist reduction of communication to a set of basic constituents that not only explain how communication happens, but why communication sometimes fails. Good timing played a role as well. The world was barely thirty years into the age of mass radio, had arguably fought a world war in its wake, and an even more powerful, television, was about to assert itself.

It was time to create the field of communication as a unified discipline, and Shannon's model was as good an excuse as any. The model's enduring value is readily evident in introductory textbooks. It remains one of the first things most students learn about communication when they take an introductory communication class. Indeed, it is one of only a handful of theoretical statements about the communication process that can be found in introductory textbooks in both mass communication and interpersonal communication.

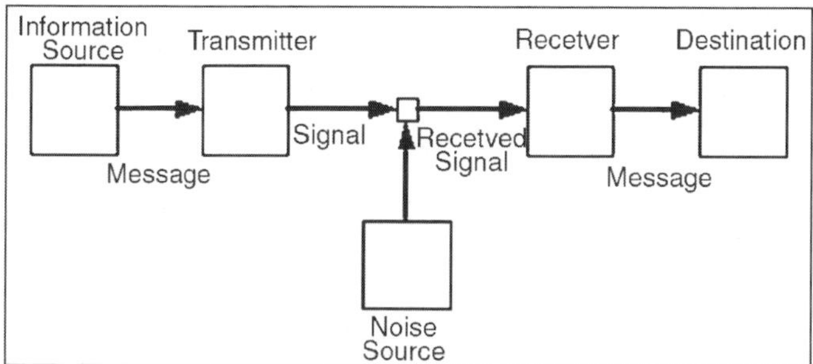


**Fig**. Shannon's (1948) Model of the Communication Process.

*Shannon's model, as shown in Figure, breaks the process of communication down into eight discrete components*:

- *An information source*: Presumably a person who creates a message.
- *The message,* which is both sent by the information source and received by the destination.
- *A transmitter*: For Shannon's immediate purpose a telephone instrument that captures an audio signal, converts it into an electronic signal, and amplifies it for transmission through the telephone network. Transmission is readily generalized within Shannon's information theory to encompass a wide range of transmitters. The simplest transmission system, that associated with face-to-face communication, has at least two layers of transmission. The first, the mouth (sound) and body (gesture), create and modulate a signal. The second layer, which might also be described as a channel, is built of the air (sound) and light (gesture) that enable the transmission of those signals from one person to another. A television broadcast would obviously include many more layers, with the addition of cameras and microphones, editing and filtering systems, a national signal distribution network (often satellite), and a local radio wave broadcast antenna.
- *The signal, which flows through a channel*: There may be multiple parallel signals, as is the case in face-to-face interaction where sound and gesture involve different signal systems that depend on different channels and modes of transmission. There may be multiple serial signals, with sound and/or gesture turned into electronic signals, radio waves, or words and pictures in a book.
- A carrier or channel, which is represented by the small unlabeled box in the middle of the model. The most commonly used channels include air, light, electricity, radio waves, paper, and postal systems. Note that there may be multiple channels associated with the multiple layers of transmission.

- Noise, in the form of secondary signals that obscure or confuse the signal carried. Given Shannon's focus on telephone transmission, carriers, and reception, it should not be surprising that noise is restricted to noise that obscures or obliterates some portion of the signal within the channel. This is a fairly restrictive notion of noise, by current standards, and a somewhat misleading one. Today we have at least some media which are so noise free that compressed signals are constructed with an absolutely minimal amount information and little likelihood of signal loss. In the process, Shannon's solution to noise, redundancy, has been largely replaced by a minimally redundant solution: error detection and correction. Today we use noise more as a metaphor for problems associated with effective listening.
- A receiver. In Shannon's conception, the receiving telephone instrument. In face to face communication a set of ears (sound) and eyes (gesture). In television, several layers of receiver, including an antenna and a television set.
- A destination. Presumably a person who consumes and processes the message.

Like all models, this is a minimalist abstraction of the reality it attempts to reproduce. The reality of most communication systems is more complex. Most information sources (and destinations) act as both sources and destinations. Transmitters, receivers, channels, signals, and even messages are often layered both serially and in parallel such that there are multiple signals transmitted and received, even when they are converged into a common signal stream and a common channel. Many other elaborations can be readily described.. It remains, however, that Shannon's model is a useful abstraction that identifies the most important components of communi-cation and their general relationship to one another. That value is evident in its similarity to real world pictures of the designs of new communication systems, including Bell's original sketches of the telephone, as seen in Figure.

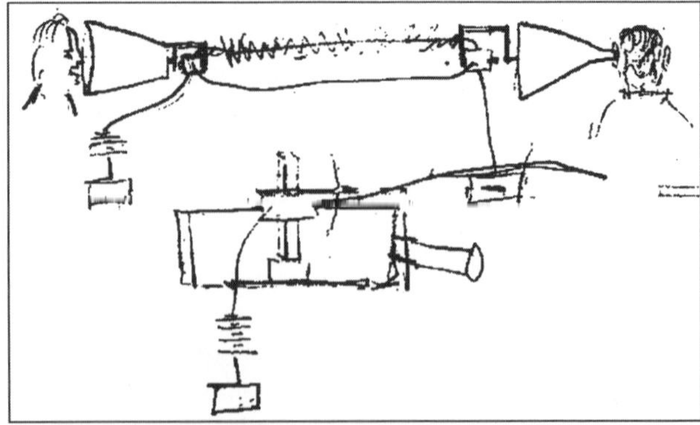

**Fig**. Bell's Drawing of the Workings of a Telephone, from his Original Sketches

Bell's sketch visibly contains an information source and destination, transmitters and receivers, a channel, a signal, and an implied message (the information source is talking). What is new, in Shannon's model (aside from the concept of noise, which is only partially reproduced by Bell's batteries), is a formal vocabulary that is now generally used in describing such designs, a vocabulary that sets up both Shannon's mathematical theory of information and a large amount of subsequent communication theory. This correspondence between Bell's sketch and Shannon's model is rarely remarked.

Shannon's model isn't really a model of communication, however. It is, instead, a model of the flow of information through a medium, and an incomplete and biased model that is far more applicable to the system it maps, a telephone or telegraph, than it is to most other media. It suggests, for instance, a"push" model in which sources of information can inflict it on destinations. In the real world of media, destinations are more typically self-selecting"consumers" of information who have the ability to select the messages they are most interested in, turn off messages that don't interest them, focus on one message in preference to other in message rich environments, and can choose to simply not pay attention. Shannon's model depicts transmission from a transmitter to a receiver as the primary activity of a medium. In the real world of media, messages are frequently stored for elongated periods of time and/or modified in some way before they are accessed by the"destination". The model suggests that communication within a medium is frequently direct and unidirectional, but in the real world of media, communication is almost never unidirectional and is often indirect.

## Derivative Models of the Communication Process

One of these shortcomings is addressed in Figure 2's intermediary model of communication (sometimes referred to as the gatekeeper model or two-step flow). This model, which is frequently depicted in introductory texts in mass communication, focuses on the important role that inter-mediaries often play in the communication process. Mass communication texts frequently specifically associate editors, who decide what stories will fit in a newspaper or news broadcast, with this intermediary or gatekeeper role.

There are, however, many intermediary roles associated with communication. Many of these intermediaries have the ability to decide what messages others see, the context in which they are seen, and when they see them. They often have the ability, moreover, to change messages or to prevent them from reaching an audience (destination). In extreme variations we refer to such gatekeepers as censors. Under the more normal conditions of mass media, in which publications choose some content in preference to other potential content based on an editorial policy, we refer to them as editors (most mass media), moderators (Internet discussion groups), reviewers (peer-reviewed publications), or aggregators (clipping services), among other titles. Delivery workers (a postal delivery worker, for instance) also act as intermediaries, and have the ability to act as gatekeepers, but are generally restricted from doing so as a matter of ethics and/or law.

**Fig**. An Intermediary Model.

Variations of Figure 3's gatekeeper model are also used in teaching organizational communication, where gatekeepers, in the form of bridges and liaisons, have some ability to shape the organization through their selective sharing of information. These variations are generally more complex in depiction and often take the form of social network diagrams that depict the interaction relationships of dozens of people. They network diagrams often presume, or at least allow, bi-directional arrows such that they are more consistent with the notion that communication is most often bidirectional.

The bidirectionality of communication is commonly addressed in interpersonal communication text with two elaborations of Shannon's model (which is often labeled as the action model of communication): the interactive model and the transactive model. The interactive model, a variant of which is shown in Figure, elaborates Shannon's model with the cybernetic concept of feedback, often without changing any other element of Shannon's model.

The key concept associated with this elaboration is that destinations provide feedback on the messages they receive such that the information sources can adapt their messages, in real time. This is an important elaboration, and as generally depicted, a radically oversimplified one. Feedback is a message (or a set of messages). The source of feedback is an information source. The consumer of feedback is a destination. Feedback is transmitted, received, and potentially disruptable via noise sources. None of this is visible in the typical depiction of the interactive model. This doesn't diminish the importance of feedback or the usefulness of elaborating Shannon's model to include it. People really do adapt their messages based on the feedback they receive. It is useful, however, to notice that the interactive model depicts feedback at a much higher level of abstraction than it does messages.

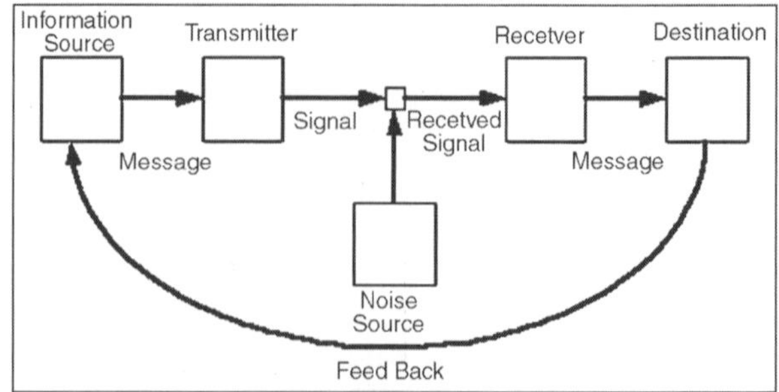


**Fig**. An Interactive Model.

This difference in the level of abstraction is addressed in the transactional model of communication, a variant of which is shown in Figure. This model acknowledges neither creators nor consumers of messages, preferring to label the people associated with the model as communicators who both create and consume messages.

The model presumes additional symmetries as well, with each participant creating messages that are received by the other communicator. This is, in many ways, an excellent model of the face-to-face interactive process which extends readily to any interactive medium that provides users with symmetrical interfaces for creation and consumption of messages, including notes, letters, C.B. Radio, electronic mail, and the radio.

It is, however, a distinctly interpersonal model that implies an equality between communicators that often doesn't exist, even in interpersonal contexts. The caller in most telephone conversations has the initial upper hand in setting the direction and tone of a a telephone callr than the receiver of the call.

In face-to-face head-complement interactions, the boss (head) has considerably more freedom (in terms of message choice, media choice, ability to frame meaning, ability to set the rules of interaction) and power to allocate message bandwidth than does the employee (complement). The model certainly does not apply in mass media contexts.

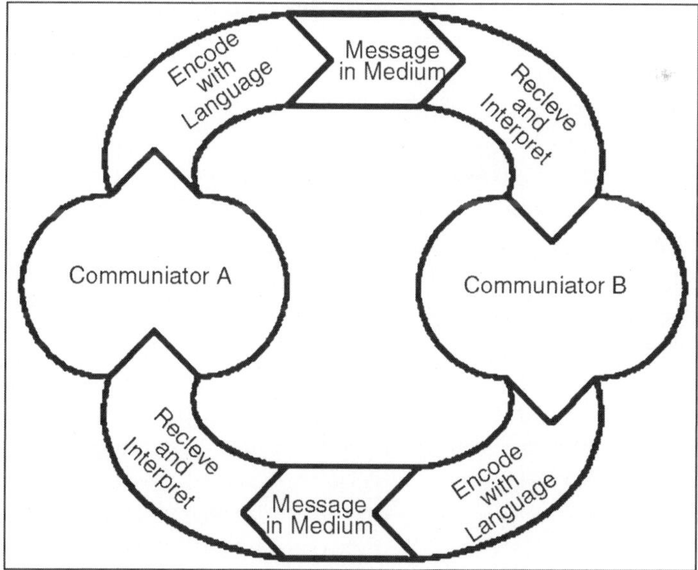


**Fig**. A Transactional Model.

The"masspersonal" media of the Internet through this implied symmetry into even greater relief. Most Internet media grant everyone symmetrical creation and consumption interfaces. Anyone with Internet access can create a web site and participate as an equal partner in e-mail, instant messaging, chat rooms, computer conferences, collaborative composition sites, blogs, interactive games, MUDs, MOOs, and other media. It remains, however, that users have very different preferences in their message consumption and creation. Some people are very comfortable creating messages for others online. Others prefer to"lurk"; to freely browse the messages of others without adding anything of their own. Adding comments to a computer conference is rarely more difficult than sending an e-mail, but most Internet discussion groups have many more lurkers (consumers of messages that never post) than they have contributors (people who both create and consume messages). Oddly, the lurkers sometimes feel more integrated with the community than the contributors do.

**A New Model of the Communication Process**

Existing models of the communication process don't provide a reasonable basis for understanding such effects. Indeed, there are many things that we routinely teach undergraduates in introductory communication courses that are missing from, or outright inconsistent with, these models.

*Consider that*:

- we now routinely teach students that"receivers" of messages really"consume" messages. People usually have a rich menu of potential messages to choose from and they select the messages they want to hear in much the same way that diners select entrees from a restaurant menu. We teach students that most"noise" is generated within the listener, that we engage messages through"selective attention", that one of the most important things we can do to improve our communication is to learn how to listen, that mass media audiences have choices, and that we need to be"literate" in our media choices, even in (and perhaps especially in) our choice of television messages. Yet all of these models suggest an"injection model" in which message reception is automatic.
- we spend a large portion of our introductory courses teaching students about language, including written, verbal, and non-verbal languages, yet language is all but ignored in these models (the use of the term in Figure is not the usual practice in depictions of the transactive model).
- we spend large portions of our introductory courses teaching students about the importance of perception, attribution, and relationships to our interpretation of messages; of the importance of communication to the perceptions that others have of us, the perceptions we have of ourselves, and the creation and maintenence of the relationships we have with others. These models say nothing about the role of perception and relationshp to the way we interpret messages or our willingness to consume messages from different people.
- we spend large portions of our introductory courses teaching students about the socially constructed aspects of languages,

messages, and media use. Intercultural communication presumes both social construction and the presumption that people schooled in one set of conventions will almost certainly violate the expectations of people schooled in a different set of expectations. Discussions of the effects of media on culture presume that communi-cation within the same medium may be very different in different cultures, but that the effects of the medium on various cultures will be more uniform. Existing general models provide little in the way of a platform from which these effects can be discussed.

- When we use these models in teaching courses in both interpersonal and mass communication; in teaching students about very different kinds of media. With the exception of the Shannon model, we tend to use these models selectively in describing those media, and without any strong indication of where the medium begins or ends; without any indication of how media interrelate with languages, messages, or the people who create and consume messages. without addressing the ways in which they are. while these media describe, in a generalized way, media,

The ecological model of communication, shown in Figure, attempts to provide a platform on which these issues can be explored. It asserts that communication occurs in the intersection of four fundamental constructs: communication between people (creators and consumers) is mediated by messages which are created using language within media; consumed from media and interpreted using language.This model is, in many ways, a more detailed elaboration of Lasswell's classic outline of the study of communication: "Who... says what... in which channel... to whom... with what effect". In the ecological model, the"who" are the creators of messages, the"says what" are the messages, the"in which channel" is elaborated into languages (which are the content of channels) and media (which channels are a component of), the"to whom" are the consumers of messages, and the effects are found in various relationships between the primitives, including relationships, perspectives, attributions, interpretations, and the continuing evolution of languages and media.

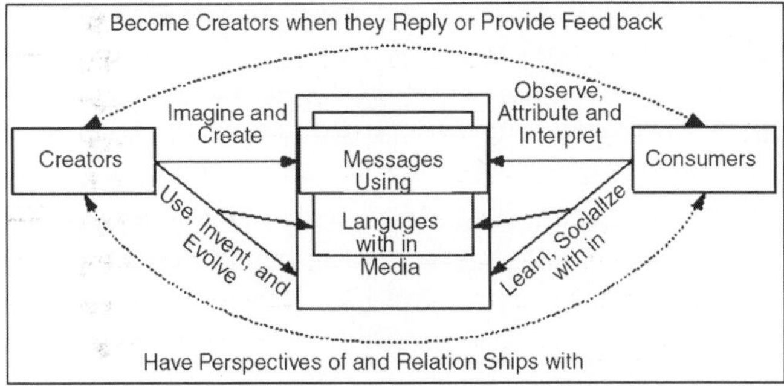


**Fig.** A Ecological Model of the Communication Process

*A number of relationships are described in this model*:

- Messages are created and consumed using language
- Language occurs within the context of media
- Messages are constructed and consumed within the context of media
- The roles of consumer and creator are reflexive. People become creators when they reply or supply feedback to other people. Creators become consumers when they make use of feedback to adapt their messages to message consumers. People learn how to create messages through the act of consuming other peoples messages.
- The roles of consumer and creator are introspective. Creators of messages create messages within the context of their perspectives of and relationships with anticipated consumers of messages. Creators optimize their messages to their target audiences. Consumers of messages interpret those messages within the context of their perspectives of, and relationships with, creators of messages. Consumers make attributions of meaning based on their opinion of the message creator. People form these perspectives and relationships as a function of their communication.
- The messages creators of messages construct are necessarily imperfect representations of the meaning they imagine. Messages are created within the expressive limitations of the medium selected and the meaning representation space provided by the language used. The message created is almost always a partial and imperfect representation of what the creator would like to say.
- A consumers interpretation of a messages necessarily attributes meaning imperfectly. Consumers intepret messages within the limits of the languages used and the media those languages are used in. A consumers interpretation of a message may be very different than what the creator of a message imagined.
- People learn language by through the experience of encountering language being used within media. The languages they learn will almost always be the languages when communicating with people who already know and use those languages. That communication always occurs within a medium that enables those languages.
- People learn media by using media. The media they learn will necessarilly be the media used by the people they communicate with.
- People invent and evolve languages. While some behaviour expressions (a baby's cry) occur naturally and some aspects of language structure may mirror the ways in which the brain structures ideas, language does not occur naturally. People invent new language when there is no language that they can be socialized into. People evolve language when they need to communicate ideas that existing language is not sufficient to.

- People invent and evolve media While some of the modalities and channels associated with communi-cation are naturally occurring, the media we use to communicate are not.

A medium of communication is, in short, the product of a set of complex interactions between its primary consituents: messages, people (acting as creators of messages, consumers of messages, and in other roles), languages, and media. Three of these consituents are themselves complex systems and the subject of entire fields of study, including psychology, sociology, anthropology (all three of which study people), linguistics (language), media ecology (media), and communication (messages, language, and media). Even messages can be regarded as complex entities, but its complexities can be described entirely within the scope of languages, media, and the people who use them.

This ecological model of communication is, in its most fundamental reading, a compact theory of messages and the systems that enable them. Messages are the central feature of the model and the most fundamental product of the interaction of people, language, and media. But there are other products of the model that build up from that base of messages, including (in a rough ordering to increased complexity) observation, learning, interpretation, socialization, attribution, perspectives, and relationships.

**Discussion: Positioning the Study of Media in the Field of Communication**

It is in this layering of interdependent social construction that this model picks up its name. Our communication is not produced within any single system, but in the intersection of several interrelated systems, each of which is self-standing necessarily described by dedicated theories, but each of which is both the product of the others and, in its own limited way, an instance of the other.

The medium is, as McLuhan famously observed, a message that is inherent to every message that is created in or consumed from a medium. The medium is, to the extent that we can select among media, also a language such that the message of the medium is not only inherent to a message, but often an element of its composition.

In what may be the most extreme view enabled by the processing of messages within media, the medium may also be a person and consumes messages, recreates them, and makes the modified messages available for further consumption. A medium is really none of these things. It is fundamentally a system that enables the construction of messages using a set of languages such that they can be consumed. But a medium is also both all of these things and the product of their interaction. People learn, create, and evolve media as a vehicle for enabling the creation and consumption of messages.

The same might be said of each of the constituents of this model. People can be, and often are, the medium (insofar as they act as messengers), the language (insofar as different people can be selected as messengers), or the message (one's choice of messenger can be profoundly meaningful). Fundamentally a person is none of these things, but they can be used as any of these things and are the product of their experience of all of these things. Our experience of messages, languages, media, and through them, other people, is fundamental in shaping who we become and how we think of ourselves and others. We invent ourselves, and others work diligently to shape that invention, through our consumption of messages, the languages we master, and the media we use.

Language can be, and often are, the message (that is inherent to every message constructed with it), the medium (but only trivially), the person (both at the level of the"language instinct" that is inherent to people (following Pinker, xxxxx) and a socialized semiotic overlay on personal experience), and even"the language" (insofar as we have a choice of what language we use in constructing a given message). Funda-mentally a language is none of these things, but it can be used as any of these things and is the product of our use of media to construct messages. We use language, within media, to construct messages, such as definitions and dictionaries) that construct language. We invent and evolve language as a product of our communication.

As for messages, they reiterate all of these constituents. Every message is a partial and incomplete precis of the language that it is constructed with, the medium it is created in and consumed from, and the person who created it. Every message we consume allows us to learn a little more about the language that we interpret with, the medium we create and consume messages in, and the person who created the message. Every message we create is an opportunity to change and extend the language we use, evolve the media we use, and influence the perspective that consumers of our messages have of us.

Yet fundamentally, a message is simply a message, an attempt to communicate something we imagine such that another person can correctly intepret the message and thus imagine the same thing. This welter of intersecting McLuhanesque/Burkean metaphors and interdependencies provides a second source of the models name. This model seeks, more than anything, to position language and media as the intermediate building blocks on which communication is built. The position of language as a building block of messages and and communication is well understood. Over a century of study in semantics, semiotics, and linguistics have produced systematic theories of message and language production which are well understood and generally accepted.

The study of language is routinely incorporated into virtually all programs in the field of communication, including journalism, rhetoric and speech, film, theater, broadcast media, language arts, speech and hearing sciences telecommunications, and other variants, including departments of"language and social interaction".

The positioning of the study of media within the field of communication is considerably more tenuous. Many depart-ments, including most of those named in this paragraph, focus almost entirely on only one or two media, effectively assuming the medium such that the focus of study can be constrained to the art of message production and interpretation, with a heavy focus on the languages of the medium and little real introspection about what it means to use that medium in preference to another or the generalized ways in which all media are invented, learned, evolved, socialized, selected or used meaningfully.

Such is, however, the primary subject matter of the newly emerging discipline of media ecology, and this model can be seen as an attempt to position media ecology relative to language and messages as a building block of our communication. This model was created specifically to support theories of media and position them relative to the process of communication. It is hoped that the reader finds value in that positioning.

**Theoretical and Pedogogical Value**

Models are a fundamental building block of theory. They are also a fundamental tool of instruction. Shannon's information theory model, Weiner's Cybernetic model, and Katz' two step flow each allowed allowed scholars decompose the process of communication into discrete structural elements. Each provides the basis for considerable bodies of communication theory and research. Each model also provides teachers with a powerful pedagogical tool for teaching students to understand that communication is a complex process in which many things can, and frequently do, go wrong; for teaching students the ways in which they can perfect different skills at different points in the communication process to become more effective communicators. But while Shannon's model has proved effective across the primary divides in the field of communication, the other models Katz' and Weiner's models have not. Indeed, they in many ways exemplify that divide and the differences in what is taught in courses oriented to interpersonal communication and mass communication.

Weiner's cybernetic model accentuates the interactive structure of communication. Katz' model accentuates its production structure. Students of interpersonal communi-cation are taught, through the use of the interactive/cybernetic and transactive models that attending to the feedback of their audience is an important part of being an effective communicator. Students of mass communication are taught, through the intermediary/gatekeeper/two-step flow model, that controlled production processes are an important part of being an effective communicator.

The difference is a small one and there is no denying that both attention to feedback and attention to detail are critical skills of effective communicators, but mass media programs focus heavily on the minutiae of production, interpersonal programs focus heavily on the munitiae of attention to feedback. Despite the fact that both teach both message production the languages used in message production, and the details of the small range of media that each typically covers, they discuss different media, to some extent different languages, and different approaches to message production. These differences, far more than more obvious differences like audience size or technology, are the divides that seperate the study of interpersonal communication from mass communication.

The ecological model of communication presented here cannot, by itself, remediate such differences, but it does reconsitute and extend these models in ways that make it useful, both pedogogically and theoretically, across the normal disciplinary boundaries of the field of communication. The author has made good use of the model in teaching a variety of courses within several communication disciplines, including on interpersonal communication, mass media criticism, organizational communication, communication ethics, communication in relationships and communities, and new communication technologies.

In introductory Interpersonal Communication classes the model has shown considerable value in outlining and tying together such diverse topics as the social construction of the self, verbal and non-verbal languages, listening, relationship formation and development, miscommunication, perception, attribution, and the ways in which communication changes in different interpersonal media. In an Organizational Communication class the model has proved value in tying comtemporary Organizational models, including network analysis models, satisficing, and Weick's model to key organizational skills like effective presentation, listening, and matching the medium to the goal and the stakeholder. In a communication ethics class it has proved valuable in elaborating the range of participants in media who have ethical responsibilities and the scope of their responsibilities.

In a mass media criticism class it has proved useful in showing how different critical methods relate to the process of communication and to each other. In each course the model has proved valuable, not only in giving students tools with which they can decompose communication, but which they can organize the course materials into a cohesive whole.

While the model was originally composed for pedagogical purposes, the primary value for the author has been theoretical. The field of communication encompasses a wide range of very different and often unintegrated theories and methods. Context-based gaps in the field like the one between mass media and interpersonal communication have been equated to those of"two sovereign nations," with"different purposes, different boundaries","different methods", and"different theoretical orientations", causing at least some to doubt that the field can ever be united by a common theory of communication. The author repeatedly finds these gaps and boundaries problematic

It may be be that complex model of the communication process that bridges the theoretical orientations of interpersonal, organizational, and mass media perspectives can help to bridge this gap and provide something more than the kind of metamodel that Craig calls for. Defining media directly into the process of communication may help to provide the kind of substrate that would satisfy Cappella's suggestion we can"remake the field by altering the organizational format", replacing contexts with processes that operate within the scope of media. This perspective does exactly that. The result does not integrate all of communication theory, but it may provide a useful starting point on which a more integrated communication theory can be built. The construction of such theory is the author's primary objective in forwarding this model for your comment and, hopefully, your response.

# 6

# Value of Communication

Communication is, by definition, a two-way process - an interaction. Presentation tends to be one way only, so is there anything at all that we can take from research underlying communication and how people learn, that is of any relevance to the topic of this book?

Assuming that the intention of your presentation is to inform your audience, so that something is learned from you, what do we know in general about how people learn?

*People learn best when*:

- They are motivated
- They recognise their need to learn
- The learning is relevant, in context and matches their needs
- The aims of the learning are clear
- They are actively involved
- A variety of learning methods is used
- It is enjoyable.

Presenting at meetings is not of course just about giving information ('I told them, therefore they know it') but about imparting it in such a way that people understand and take something away from it. Can we draw a parallel with the information-giving process between doctors and patients? There is in fact much evidence from research into medical communication showing that the following behaviours result in the effective transmission of information from doctor to patient:

- Decide on the key information that the patient needs to understand.
- Signpost to the patient what you are going to discuss.
- Find out what the patient knows or understands already.
- Make it manageable - divide it into chunks.
- Use clear, unambiguous language.
- Pace the information so that the patient does not feel overwhelmed.



- Check what the patient has understood.
- Invite questions.

Adopting these behaviours means that, as a doctor, you are doing your best to ensure that your patient both hears and understands what has been said. What can we take from these two sets of principles that is directly relevant to giving presentations at meetings?

## Preparation

### *Know your Audience*

Decide what it is about your topic that you want your audience to understand. The presenter is usually in the situation of knowing a lot more about the subject than many of the people in the audience. Find out about your audience. What is their level of knowledge likely to be? How many are likely to be there? The smaller the number, the greater the potential for interaction. Is the language in which you are giving your presentation your audience's first language? Regardless of first language, will your audience have a feel for the technical/medical/scientific terminology with which you are so familiar? Above all, avoid the temptation to try to impart more information than your audience can possibly assimilate. Message - keep it simple.

### *Don't let Yourself Get too Anxious*

Anxiety on the part of either the giver or receiver can act as a barrier to effective communication. Most experienced presenters will tell you that they are always anxious before starting their talk and this does not necessarily get better over time. It is normal and can be advantageous - a certain amount of adrenaline actually makes for a more exciting presentation. Lack of anxiety often results in the presentation appearing a bit flat. On the other hand, too much anxiety is a problem not only for the speaker but also for the audience. An audience can feel embarrassed and show more concern for the state of mind of the speaker than for what is being communicated. Sometimes deepbreathing exercises can help. Most people find that once they get started, anxiety drops to manageable levels. As with an examination, the worst time is just before you turn over the paper.

### *Rehearse Your Presentation*

An important key to anxiety reduction is to know that you are properly prepared. Not only should you be sure about what you are going to say but how long it will take to say it. This means practising your presentation, preferably in front of colleagues whom you trust and who will give you constructive feedback. It is highly unprofessional to over-run and encroach on other speakers' time. A good chairperson will not permit this anyway, with the inevitable result that your talk will be incomplete or rushed at the end. Rehearsal is important.

### *Prepare Prompt Cards*

What do you take in with you in the form of notes to your presentation? If all you do is read directly from a prepared script, there will be no effective communication with your audience. You might as well have distributed a photocopy of your talk and asked the audience to sit and read it. Reading also removes any opportunity for eye contact, for judging how the presentation is being received, or for spontaneity. Have you ever laughed at a joke that has been read out to you? A far better solution is to use prompt cards. Prompt cards carry only the key points of your talk. They serve partly as an aide memoire and partly as a means of reducing the anxiety of drying up.

### *Check Out the Venue and Equipment*

Arrive at the venue early enough to check out the room size and layout, the location of light switches and the equipment you are intending to use. If you have opted for a PowerPoint presentation, check that the system is compatible with your computer/CD. Always bring back-up overhead transparencies - just in case disaster strikes. Check that your slides/overheads are visible from the back of the hall. Be sure you know how to operate the equipment - OHP controls, laser pointers, lectern layout, video recorders, etc. The audience will be irritated if you are apparently experimenting with your equipment at the start of your presentation.

## CONTENT

### Say what you're Going to Say; say it; then say What you've Said

All presentations should have a beginning, a middle, and an end. First, you describe the purpose of the talk and the key areas you will be considering. Second, you deliver the main content of the talk.

*This should cover*:

- Why the work was done
- How it was done
- What was found
- What it means.

Finally, you should summarise what you have said in a clear and concise way. Don't worry about repeating yourself. Repetition aids understanding and learning.

### How to Present at Meetings

### *Put your Talk in Context*

It is often erroneously assumed that an audience understands the context of a presentation. An example will illustrate this.

*Try to memorise as many of the following statements as you can*:

- A newspaper is better than a magazine.
- A seashore is a better place than the street.
- At first, it is better to run than to walk.
- You may have to try several times.
- It takes some skill but it's easy to learn.
- Even young children can enjoy it.
- Once successful, complications are minimal.
- Birds seldom get too close.
- Rain, however, soaks very fast.
- Too many people doing the same thing can also cause problems.
- One needs lots of room.
- If there are no complications, it can be very peaceful.
- A rock will serve as an anchor.
- If things break loose from it, however, you will not get a second chance.

It's hard, isn't it? Now reread the statements in the knowledge that the title (i.e. the context) of the exercise is'making and flying a kite'.This time, you will find it easier to recall the statements. Although this example may seem a little unusual, there is much documented evidence in educational research showing that learners are often not able to relate new knowledge to whatever they already know about a certain subject. Having a context through which new information can be related to existing knowledge results in better memory recall. It is also important to put your presentation into a more general context - how it relates to others speaking in the same session, the meeting or conference theme.

## Delivery

### *Pretend You are on Stage*

Giving a talk is not unlike being on stage. First impressions matter, so do not shuffle, fidget, mumble, or talk to the projector screen. You do not want the audience to be distracted from what you are saying by how you behave. Remember that your non-verbal communication is as important as the words that you use. Grab the attention of your audience right from the start; you can appeal to their curiosity, tell an anecdote, use a powerful and pertinent quote. Smile and look confident. Speak slowly and clearly and vary your tone of voice. Look around your audience as you talk. Catch their eyes and engage them by being enthusiastic, even passionate, about your subject.

### *Decide on Your Mode of Delivery*

The medium of presentation needs some careful thought. The obvious contenders are flipcharts, overheads, and PowerPoint presentations. Which is best for you? With which are you most comfortable? Which is the most impressive? Which best illustrates the material you wish to present? These are questions only you can answer. You must weigh up the pros and cons and make a decision.

### *Make Your Visual Aids Clear and Simple*

Just as doctors can reinforce the information they give to patients with written materials or simple diagrams or drawings, your visual aids should illuminate or illustrate your words. If you are showing a slide for instance, it is enormously helpful to state what in general it is about as you show it. If your audience needs to read something on your slide or overhead, stay silent for a few seconds. You will be very familiar with your material but do not assume that your audience shares your understanding; for example say what the'x' and'y' axes represent on a graph; explain the key to your histograms. We would probably all like a pound for every slide or overhead that we have been shown in a scientific presentation that is impossible to see or interpret, for which the presenter apologises to the audience. So why show it? Why not make a new slide which summarises the point that the original was attempting to make?

### *Consider Varying the Delivery Mode*

Attention span is limited, especially if your audience is sitting through a series of presentations. In a presentation lasting more than 15-20 minutes, it is worth thinking about switching modes of delivery - for instance, to use a video clip to illuminate a particular point which you wish to drive home. Think about the visual impact of being shown an operating technique, for instance, versus a verbal description of it. Or a real patient describing a condition they suffer from, versus your description of what such a patient might say.

### *Don't Go Over the Top*

We have all been to presentations that were dazzling - dual projection, fancy animated PowerPoint slides, video clips, etc. But have we remembered a thing about the content of these glitzy presentations? Probably not. What is crucial is not to allow the medium to overwhelm the message. It may seem an obvious point, but the greater the number of modes of delivery, the greater the risk of technical failure.

## How to Present at Meetings

### *Don't be Frightened of Questions*

What is unpredictable, and invokes much anxiety, is the prospect of being asked difficult or awkward questions at the end. There will always be questioners who are trying to score points, gain attention, or display knowledge rather than genuinely trying to find out more about your work or ideas. The audience is usually aware of this and will be on your side. If you know that there are areas in your presentation that may confound or compromise some of the evidence that you are presenting, address these in the body of your talk to preempt obvious points of attack from questioners. Remember that good research provokes as many questions as it answers and occasionally a member of the audience will ask the question that you had not thought of that will trigger your next research proposal.

Doctors should not pretend that they know the answer to a patient's question when they do not. Similarly, admit to your audience if you cannot answer one of its questions, agree to find out the answer and remember to follow it up. You can sometimes engage your audience more actively if you throw the question back.

***Look Out for Non-verbal Communication***

How you check what the audience has understood from your talk is clearly difficult though not impossible. The questions that you are asked at the end of the talk may give you some insight into the level of comprehension. But what does it mean if no questions are asked at all? What is conveyed to you nonverbally from the audience during your presentation may be just as revealing. Do people look interested or puzzled?

How many have gone to sleep? How many are fidgeting or have actually left the room? If you spot any such behaviour, either bring your talk to a conclusion or do something to wake up the audience, such as asking a question or telling an amusing anecdote. There is real satisfaction to be had from giving a presentation that is well thought out, properly rehearsed, and confidently and enthusiastically delivered.

Indeed, anything less indicates lack of respect for your audience and will leave you feeling embarrassed and disinclined ever to repeat the experience. Abraham Lincoln said, memorably:'If I had 6 hours to chop down a tree, I should spend the first 4 hours sharpening the axe'.

The message is clear. Your presentation will be great if your preparation has been thorough. Take heart from the experience of most presenters which is that although they may feel very nervous beforehand, once started they actually enjoy the experience. There are few highs to be compared with knowing that your careful preparation paid off and you got it absolutely right.

## INTERPERSONAL COMMUNICATION

Interpersonal communication is the foundation of human interaction. Its importance for innovation and change can hardly be overemphasized. Communication is a two-way process of giving and receiving information through any number of channels. Whether one is speaking informally to a colleague, addressing a conference or meeting, writing a newsletter article or formal report, the following basic principles apply:

- Know your audience.
- Know your purpose.
- Know your topic.
- Anticipate objections.
- Present a rounded picture.
- Achieve credibility with your audience.
- Follow through on what you say.
- Communicate a little at a time.
- Present information in several ways.
- Develop a practical, useful way to get feedback.
- Use multiple communication techniques.

Communication is complex. When listening to or reading someone else's message, we often filter what's being said through a screen of our own opinions. One of the major barriers to communication is our own ideas and opinions. This is an old communications game, telegraph, that's played in a circle. A message is whispered around from person to person. What the exercise usually proves is how profoundly the message changes as it passes through the distortion of each person's inner"filter."

**Environmental Factors**

*Communication can be influenced by environmental factors that have nothing to do with the content of the message. Some of these factors are*:

- The nature of the room, how warm it is, smoke, comfort of the chair, etc
- Outside distractions, what is going on in the area.
- The reputation/credibility of the speaker/writer.
- The appearance, style or authority of the speaker.
- Listener's education, knowledge of the topic, etc.
- The language, page layout, design of the message.

People remember:

- 10% of what they read
- 20% of what they hear
- 30% of what they see
- 40% of what they hear and see

**Communication with Decision Makers**

Innovation and change often depends upon persuading potential users of the benefits of an innovation. To deal persuasively with decision makers, it is necessary to know and understand their interests and opinions.

*The following questions are helpful in organizing technology transfer efforts*:

- Who are the key people to persuade?
- Who will make the decisions about innovation and change?
- What are these decision makers' past experiences with innovation and change?

- What are the decision makers' current attitudes toward innovation and change? Are they neutral, friendly, hostile or apathetic?
- What is the most appropriate way to approach the decision maker?
- What are the work styles of the decision makers? Are they highly formal people who want everything in writing and all appointments scheduled in advance? Or are they more flexible, responding favorably to personal telephone calls and informal meetings?
- What networks or groups is the decision maker a part of?
- What programs or services will the new innovation improve?
- What programs or services will the new innovation cause problems with?
- How will the innovation or change benefit the decision maker?

## Principles of Effective Persuasion

Whether making a formal presentation at a meeting or writing a report or fact sheet, the following principles hold.

- Do not oversell or overstate your case. Make effective use of understatement.
- Outline the topic you are trying to cover into two parts. The first part should give broad background information, while the second part provides a detailed summary.
- Persuasion depends on clarity and simplicity. Avoid the use of jargon and buzz words.
- Be prepared to back up claims or facts immediately.
- Incorporate major anticipated objections into your programme or presentation.
- Address all relevant aspects of a topic, especially those that may affect the functioning of an organization.
- Use graphics and audiovisuals appropriately.
- Consider ways to get meaningful input from people. Find out what they think about the innovation or change.

## Selling New Ideas

### *Creating Isn't Selling*

Often the creators of an innovation feel that convincing others of the idea's value is somehow superfluous to their activities. To them, conceiving the idea is enough. This combines with their inner conviction that their idea will"sell itself." Change agents provide a link between creators of new techniques and users.

## Ideas Need Selling

Someone must recognize when an idea is good. It is important that when an idea is good it is sold to those who can act on it--those who have the power to evaluate and adopt it. Understanding users is an important activity for any change agent. People must be convinced that a particular idea or innovation has enough merit to warrant adoption.

**Selling Ideas Takes Effort**

Selling innovations requires preparation, initiative, patience, and resourcefulness. It may take more effort than originating the idea. In an age of technical complexity and information overload, new ideas seldom stand out. Information on new ideas must be targeted to the appropriate users and relate to their needs and motivations.

**Once is Not Enough**

A new idea has to be suggested many times before it will"catch on." Initial failures at promoting a new idea are to be expected, so don't get discouraged if you don't get the results you want the first time. Some ideas take years to catch on. However, first exposures are crucial to future prospects. Do it right the first time

**Feedback (Listening)**

Getting and giving feedback is one of the most crucial parts of good communication. Like any other activity, there are specific skills that can enhance feedback.

*Listening is a key part of getting feedback*:

- *Listen to the Complete Message*: Be patient. This is especially important when listening to a topic that provokes strong opinions or radically different points-of-view. In these situations, it's important not to prejudge the incoming message. Learn not to get too excited about a communication until you are certain of the message.
- *Work at Listening Skills*: Listening is hard work. Good listeners demonstrate interest and alertness. They indicate through their eye contact, posture and facial expression that the occasion and the speaker's efforts are a matter of concern to them. Most good listeners provide speakers with clear and unambiguous feedback.
- *Judge the Content, Not the Form of the Message*: Such things as the speaker's mode of dress, quality of voice, delivery mannerisms and physical chara-cteristics are often used as excuses for not listening. Direct your attention to the message--what is being said--and away from the distracting elements.
- *Weigh Emotionally Charged Language*: Emotionally charged language often stands in the way of effective listening. Filter out"red flag" words (like"liberal" and"conservative," for instance) and the emotions they call up. Specific suggestions for dealing with emotionally charged words include

- Take time to identify those words that affect you emotionally.
- Attempt to analyse why the words affect you the way they do.
- Work at trying to reduce the impact of these words on you.

**Eliminate Distractions**

Physical distractions and complications seriously impair listening. These distractions may take many forms: loud noises, stuffy rooms, overcrowded conditions, uncomfortable temperature, bad lighting, etc. Good listeners speak up if the room is too warm, too noisy, or too dark.

There are also internal distractions: worries about deadlines or problems of any type may make listening difficult.If you're distracted, make an effort to clear your head. If you can't manage it, arrange to communicate at some other time.

**Think Efficiently and Critically**

On the average, we speak at a rate of 100 to 200 words per minute. However, we think at a much faster rate, anywhere from 400 to 600 words per minute. What do we do with this excess thinking time while listening to someone speak? One technique is to apply this spare time to analyzing what is being said.

*They critically review the material by asking the following kinds of questions*:

- What is being said to support the speaker's point of view? (Evidence)
- What assumptions are being made by the speaker and the listener? (Assumptions)
- How does this information affect me? (Effect)
- Can this material be organized more efficiently? (Structure)
- Are there examples that would better illustrate what is being said?
- What are the main points of the message?

**Sending Messages**

*Messages should be clear and accurate, and sent in a way that encourages retention, not rejection*:

- Use Verbal Feedback Even If Nonverbal Is Positive And Frequent. Everyone needs reassurance that they are reading nonverbal communication correctly, whether a smile means"You're doing great,""You're doing better than most beginners," or"You'll catch on eventually."
- Focus Feedback On Behaviour Rather Than On Personality. It's better to comment on specific behaviour than to characterize a pattern of behaviour. For example, instead of calling a colleague inefficient, specify your complaint:"You don't return phone calls; this causes problems both in and outside your office."
- Focus Feedback On Description Rather Than Judgment. Description tells what happened. Judgment evaluates what happened. For

example, in evaluating a report don't say,"This is a lousy report!!" Instead, try:"The report doesn't focus on the information that I think needs emphasis," or"This report seems to have a lot of grammatical and spelling mistakes."

- Make Feedback Specific Rather Than General. If feedback is specific, the receiver knows what activity to continue or change. When feedback is general, the receiver doesn't know what to do differently. For example, in an office situation, instead of saying"These folders are not arranged correctly," it's better feedback to say,"These should be arranged chronologically instead of alphabetically."
- In Giving Feedback, Consider the Needs and Abilities of the Receiver. Give the amount of information the receiver can use and focus feedback on activities the receiver has control over. It's fruitless to criticize the level of activity, if the decision to grant the necessary monies for materials, personnel or technology is made at a different level.
- Check to See if the Receiver Heard What You Meant to Say. If the information is important enough to send, make sure the person understands it. One way of doing this is to say,"I'm wondering if I said that clearly enough. What did you understand me to say?" or"This is what I hear you saying. Is that right?"

**Selecting the Best Communication Method**

In communicating with decision makers, use the most appropriate communications method. One way to do this is to ask yourself the following questions.

- What is the purpose of your message? Do you plan to tell them something new? Inform? Do you plan to change their view? Persuade?
- What facts must be presented to achieve your desired effect?
- What action, if any, do you expect decision makers to take?
- What general ideas, opinions and conclusions must be stressed?
- Are you thoroughly familiar with all the important information on the innovation?
- What resources and constraints affect adoption of the innovation? How much time is available? How much money is available
- Which method, or combination of methods, will work most effectively for this situation? Personal contact--requires scheduling, time and interpersonal skills.

Telephone contact--requires good verbal skills and an awareness of voice tones as nonverbal communication.

# ORAL COMMUNICATION

## SPEAKING TO COMMUNICATE

Spoken communication occurs in many different settings during the course of successful innovation and change.

*These may be divided into three main types*:

- The formal and informal networks in which peers exchange information, such as professional asso-ciations, work units, work teams, etc.
- The activities of change agents, opinion leaders, etc.
- The contacts established at team meetings, con-ferences, training courses, etc.

Whether to use oral communication is a decision we all make frequently in the course of a workday. The change agent must be able to identify those situations in which oral communication is the most appropriate one to use. Don Kirkpatrick suggests the -following guidelines for making such decisions.

### Use Oral Communication

- The receiver is not particularly interested in receiving the message. Oral communication provides more opportunity for getting and keeping interest and attention.
- *It is important to get feedback*: It's easier to get feedback by observing facial expressions (and other nonverbal behaviour) and asking questions.
- *Emotions are high*: Oral communication provides more opportunity for both the sender and the receiver to let off steam, cool down, and create a suitable climate for understanding.
- *The receiver is too busy or preoccupied to read*: Oral communication provides more opportunity to get attention.
- *The sender wants to persuade or convince*: Oral communication provides more flexibility, oppor-tunity for emphasis, chance to listen, and opportunity to remove resistance and change attitudes.
- *When discussion is needed*: A complicated subject frequently requires discussion to be sure of understanding.
- *When criticism of the receiver is involved*: Oral communi-cation provides more opportunity to accomplish this without arousing resentment. Also, oral communi-cation is less threatening because it isn't formalized in writing.
- When the receiver prefers one-to-one contact.

### Presentation Styles

There are different styles of making a presentation and different people will use the approach that suits them.

- *Good Old Boy*: This is usually an experienced person who is the peer of most of the audience. Generally, there is a lot of good information but it may be poorly organized or poorly delivered.
- *The Entertainer*: This person relies on jokes and stories to get their point across. Good visual aids could be an important feature of the presentation. Sometimes there is too much emphasis on satisfying the audience that little information is actually transferred.
- *The Academic*: This person tends to be very precise and deliberate in presenting information. There is considerable content and it usually is well organized. Unfortunately. it can also be boring and irrelevant and not relate well to the audience.
- *The Reader*: This person decides to read his material word for word. The material is often not especially prepared for an oral presentation and can be overly technical, boring and hard to understand. All topics are covered and what is said is precise and accurate.
- *The Snail*: This person is nervous about the presentation and goes into a shell. Like a snail, this person also moves slowly and the presentation seems to last forever.

  What is best? You have to have a style you are comfortable with. Ideally, you have the rapport of the good old boy, the organization and content of the academic, the ability to get and maintain interest of the entertainer, and the precision of the reader. If you do this you will avoid the slow pace of the snail and effectively present information to your listeners. *The Gadgeteer*: This person uses every gimmick and technique in his or her presentation and visual aids. It can be overdone with the message getting lost among the bells and whistles.

## Components of an Effective Oral Report

*Introduction Capture the attention of the group right from the start*:

- Give the necessary explanation of the background from which the problem derived.
- Clearly state and explain the problem.
- Clearly state your objectives.
- Indicate the method(s) used to solve the problem.
- Suggest the order in which you will provide information.

*Organization*:

- Provide sufficient introductory information.
- Use transitions from one main part to the next and between points of the speech.
- Use summary statements and restatements.
- Make the main ideas of the report clearly distinguishable from one another.

*Content*:

- Have adequate supporting data to substantiate what you say.
- Avoid using extraneous material.
- Present supporting data clearly--in terms of the ideas or concepts you are trying to communicate.
- Were the methods of the investigation clearly presented?
- Visual Aid Supports
- Use clear drawings, charts, diagrams or other aids to make explanations vivid and understandable.
- Make visual aids fit naturally into the presentation.
- Be completely familiar with each visual used.
- Don't clutter your report with too many visual aids.

*Conclude your report with finality in terms of one or more of the following*:

- The conclusions reached
- The problem solved
- The results obtained
- The value of such findings to the county
- Recommendations offered

*Question Period*:

- Give evidence of intelligent listening in interpreting the questions.
- Organize answers in terms of a summary statement, explanation, and supporting example.
- Show flexibility in adapting or improvising visual aids in answering questions.

*Delivery*:

- Be natural,"communicative" in your delivery.
- Use frequent eye contact to maintain rapport with the audience.
- Vary your delivery with appropriate movements and gestures.
- Speak distinctly.
- Display confidence and authority.
- Express enthusiasm for your ideas.

## VISUAL COMMUNICATION

There's an old saying that"a picture is worth a thousand words." Life would indeed be difficult without paintings, photographs, diagrams, charts, drawings, and graphic symbols. These are some of the reasons why SHOWING is such an important form of communication.

- Most people understand things better when they have seen how they work.
- Involved, complex ideas can be presented clearly and quickly using visual aids.
- People retain information longer when it is presented to them visually.

- Visuals can be used to communicate to a wide range of people with differing backgrounds.
- Visuals are useful when trying to condense information into a short time period.

  Visual aids--used imaginatively and appropriately--will help your audience remember more. Consider the following:
- People think in terms of images, not words, so visuals help them retain and recall technical information.
- Visuals attract and hold the attention of observers.
- Visuals simplify technical information.
- Visuals may be useful in presenting technical infor-mation to a nontechnical audience.

**Questions to Ask about Visual Aids**

- Is my objective clear?
- What are my key points? Do they deserve the emphasis that a visual aid gives?
- What visual aid or aids have I planned to use?
- Will the visual aid clarify my spoken words? Will it support my spoken words rather than replace them?
- Is each visual aid simple, orderly and consistent? Is it free from incompatible and complicating ideas, symbols, art techniques and typefaces? Can my audience quickly and easily grasp what they see or must it be read to them? Avoid making it a reading session.
- Is it symbolic or pictorial? Which treatment is best for my subject? Which treatment is best from the standpoint of my audience?
- Is my visual direct and to the point? Is the art functional or ornate? Is it really one visual aid or several?

  If my subject is complex, will it be presented in easily comprehensible units? (Drop-ons or overlays) Was my artwork designed just for this presentation?
- Is my visual aid realistic? Does it give all the pertinent facts? Have the facts been distorted?
- Is my visual aid as effective as it can be made? Have I used all the available techniques to make it so?
- Did I put enough effort into the planning of the visual aid? Have I sought criticism from others?
- Will it achieve my objectives? Will my audience understand, appreciate and believe it? If my presen-tation calls for some action by the audience, will it stimulate them to do so willingly?
- Have I overlooked anything in the use of the visual aid? Have I tested the visual aid? Have I planned one or more rehearsals; if not, why? Will my visual aid material be visible to the entire audience?

**Visual Aid Checklist**

*Slides*:

- Does the projector work properly? Bulb, lenses, change mechanism, fan.
- Does each slide present a simple, clear message?
- Are the slides arranged and numbered consistently and consecutively?
- Are the slides clean and mounted properly?
- Will the audience be able to see slide details in the location I plan to use?
- Does the slide tray have a title slide at the beginning and a blind slide at the end to avoid blinding the audience with light?

*Power Point or Transparencies*:

- Is the lettering large enough to be seen by the audience?
- Is the projector placed so that the audience has an unobstructed view?
- Is the projector and slide colour scheme adequate for the lighting of the room being used?
- Does the projected image fit the screen?
- Are my slides in proper order?
- Does each present a clear message?
- Is the projector compatible with the computer being used?

*Video Tape*:

- Do you have the correct machine for the tape you plan to show (Beta or VHS)?
- Is the equipment in proper working order?
- Is the tape set to start at the proper place and does it"track" properly?
- Will the WHOLE audience be able to see the presentation?
- Is the sound level on the monitor(s) set at the proper level?

*The Location*:

- Does the room match the size of the audience?
- Is the location accessible to the physically disabled?
- Can the lighting be controlled for showing slides and transparencies? If so, is a reading light available?
- Is the location equipped with a projector cart or table?
- Are electrical outlets conveniently located--do I need extension cords?
- Is the room equipped with an adequate screen?
- If using video equipment, can monitors be set up at appropriate locations?
- Does the room have a speakers table or podium?
- Will the location be available prior to your meeting so you can set up and test your equipment?

- Is the room equipped with a newsprint easel or chalkboard?
- Does the room have chairs and tables or desks? Can they be rearranged if needed?
- Is the main entrance separated from the speaker area so that late arrivals will not disrupt your presentation?

Always check out the room and equipment in advance to see that it works properly! Never assume that it will work without trying it first. As a general rule, the more complicated the technolgy for an oral presentation, the more likely it will fail

*Checklist for Tables and Charts*:

- Be ruthless with numbers: use the fewest possible that will still convey the point of the visual. Do not exceed twenty numbers or a single slide.
- Combine numbers into larger sums wherever possible; eliminate any number that does not contribute significantly to your message.
- Consider using a chart (pie, bar, etc.) for presenting some information, especially if you want to draw comparisons between two or more items.
- When preparing charts use colors or patterns with a lot of contrast.
- Split information into two or three smaller tables rather than using one huge table. Use no more than three or four columns per table.
- Have a short, yet descriptive, title that states the point of the visual. Put it at the top. Include a date at the bottom.
- Label columns clearly and at the top. Show the units (dollars or tons, for example). On the left, label the statistics being compared.
- Avoid footnotes and symbols that may not be generally understood by your audience.
- Use light horizontal lines if they improve readability.
- Be consistent. Do not mix pounds and tons, years and months, gross and net.
- Avoid decimal points whenever possible. Use round numbers for tables and graphs.
- Highlight the most important numbers with boxes, underlining, or colour.
- If arithmetic operations are not obvious, state them: (less), or"Less Depreciation Expense."
- Eliminate zeros by expressing numbers in thousands or millions, if possible.
- Show negative numbers in parentheses, not with minus signs.

## WRITTEN COMMUNICATION

Written materials often bear the greatest burden for the communication of new ideas and procedures. Effective writing is the product of long hours of preparation, revision and organization. One book that follows its own rules is Strunk and White's Elements of Style, a short book which argues persuasively for clarity, accuracy, and brevity in the use of English. Its entire philosophy is contained in one paragraph:

- Vigorous writing is concise. A sentence should contain no unnecessary words, a paragraph no unnecessary sentences, for the same reasons that a drawing should have no unnecessary lines and a machine no unnecessary parts. This requires not that the writer make all his sentences short, or that he avoid all detail and treat his subjects only in outline, but that EVERY WORD TELL.

Clear, vigorous writing is a product of clear, vigorous thinking. Clarity is born of discipline and imagination. Kirkpatrick gives the following guidelines for using written communication:

*Use Written Communication When*:

- The sender wants a record for future references.
- The receiver will be referring to it later.
- The message is complex and requires study by the receiver.
- The message includes a step by step procedure.
- Oral communication is not possible because people are not in the same place at
- The same time.
- There are many receivers. Caution: the receivers must be interested in the subject and will put forth the time and effort to read and understand.
- It is cheaper. Caution: the same as above.
- A copy of the message should go to another person.
- The receiver prefers written.

*Advantages of Written Materials*:

- Highly technical topics can be presented using words and diagrams.
- Written material provides a permanent record that can be referred to from time to time or passed on to others.
- Written material can be duplicated in large quantities or distributed on the Internet relatively inexpensively.
- It is fairly easy to distribute written material to many people, but this practice is getting increasingly expensive and its effectiveness questionable.
- Written material is preferred when it is desirable to get the same information to a group of people.
- Written records and reports are sometimes useful in legal matters.
- Written material may be useful for documenting the success or progress of some project or activity.

*Disadvantages of Written Material*:

- People seldom take the time and effort to read technical materials.

- The preparation of written documents is time-consuming.
- Once prepared in large quantities, printed documents are difficult to change.
- Written material provides little feedback for the sender.
- Technical documents are often too long and complex for the majority of readers.
- A portion of the population may not be able to read written material.

Too much reliance on written material as a communi-cation method may obscure the true needs of potential users.

# 7

# Human Communication

Nonverbal communication is communication without words. You communicate nonverbally when you gesture, smile or frown, widen your eyes, move your chair closer to someone, wear jewelry, touch someone, or raise your vocal volume-and when someone receives these signals. Even if you remained silent and someone attributed meaning to your silence, communication would have taken place.

If, on the other hand, you gestured or smiled and no one perceived these movements, then communication would not have taken place. This doesn't mean that both sender and receiver have to give the same meanings to the signals (the gestures, the smile). It merely means that for communication to be said to have occurred, someone must send and someone must receive the message signals. Nonverbal messages may communicate specific meanings, just as verbal messages do; they may also metacommunicate, or communicate about other messages. Let's look at each of these functions.

**TO COMMUNICATE MEANING**

Nonverbal messages may communicate the exact same meanings as verbal messages. The same purposes that were identified for communication in general are served by nonverbal signals as well. First, nonverbal messages help us to discover- to learn, to acquire information about the world and about other people. Nonverbal messages-the smile, the focused eye contact, the leaning forward, and of course the kiss-also help us to establish and maintain relationships.

We signal that we like another person first though nonverbal signals; then, usually at least, we follow up with verbal messages. At the same time, of course, our nonverbal messages can help destroy and dissolve interpersonal relationships. When you avoid eye contact and touching, when you frown more than smile, and when your voice is without warmth, you're using nonverbal signals to distance yourself from the other person.

You can also use nonverbal messages to help. Gently touching an ill person's face, hugging someone who's in pain, or helping an old person walk are common examples. You use nonverbal messages to persuade; for example, when your posture and clothing communicate your self-confidence, when your steady gaze communicates conviction that you're right, or when your facial expression communicates that the advertised product tastes great. Nonverbal messages may also be used to play. Tickling or playing patty-cake with a young child, making funny faces, and drawing cartoons are simple examples.

**To Metacommunicate**

Much of nonverbal communication, however, occurs in combination with verbal messages and serves a metacommunication function. That is, nonverbal messages often comment on or communicate something about other messages (often verbal messages). Six general ways in which nonverbal communication blends with verbal communication have been identified and will illustrate the wide variety of metacommunication functions that nonverbal messages may serve. Nonverbal messages are often used to accent or emphasize some part of the verbal message.

You might, for example, raise your voice to underscore a particular word or phrase, bang your fist on the desk to stress your commitment, or look longingly into someone's eyes when saying"I love you." You use nonverbal communication to complement, to add nuances of meaning not communicated by your verbal message.

Thus, you might smile when telling a story (to suggest that you find it humorous) or frown and shake your head when recounting someone's deceit (to suggest your disapproval). You may deliberately contradict your verbal messages with nonverbal movements-for example, by crossing your fingers or winking to indicate that you're lying. Movements may be used to regulate or control the flow of verbal messages, as when you purse your lips, lean forward, or make hand gestures to indicate that you want to speak. You might also put up your hand or vocalize your pauses (for example, with"um" or"ah") to indicate that you've not finished and aren't ready to relinquish the floor to the next speaker.

You can repeat or restate the verbal message nonverbally. You can, for example, follow your verbal"Is that all right?" with raised eyebrows and a questioning look, or motion with your head or hand to repeat your verbal"Let's go." You may also use nonverbal communication to substitute for or take the place of verbal messages. For instance, you can signal"OK" with a hand gesture. You can nod your head to indicate yes or shake your head to indicate no.

***Communicating Power Nonverbally***

I f you want to signal power nonverbally, try these suggestions.

- Walk slowly and deliberately.To appear hurried is to appear powerless, as if you were rushing to meet the expectations of those who have power over you.
- Use facial expressions and gestures as appro-priate;these help you

express your concern for the other person and the interaction and help you communicate your comfort and control of the situation.
- Consider standing relatively close to your listeners (even in public speaking);it will create greater immediacy and is likely to be more persuasive.
- Other things being equal, dress relatively conser-vatively if you want to influence others;conser vative clothing is associated with wpoer and status.
- Select chairs you can get in and out of easily;a void deep plush chairs that you will sink into and have trouble getting out of.
- To communicate dominance with your handshake, exert more pressure than usual and hold the grip a bit longer than normal.
- Use consistent packaging;be careful that your verbal and nonverbal messages do not contradict each other, a signal of uncertainty and a lack of conviction.
- Be sure to respond in kind to another's eyebrow flash (raising the eyebrow as a way of acknowledging another person).
- When you break eye contact, direct your gaze downward;otherwise you will communicate a lack of interest in the other person.

## The Channels of Nonverbal Communication

Nonverbal communication is probably most easily explained in terms of the various channels through which messages pass. Here we'll survey 10 channels: body, face, eye, space, artifactual, touch, paralanguage, silence, time, and smell.

### The Body

Two areas of the body are especially important in communicating messages. First, the movements you make with your body communicate; second, the general appearance of your body communicates.

### Body Movements

Researchers in kinesics, or the study of nonverbal communication through face and body movements, identify five major types of movements: emblems, illustrators, affect displays, regulators, and adaptors. Emblems are body gestures that directly translate into words or phrases; for example, the OK sign, the thumbs-up for"good job," and the V for victory. You use these consciously and purposely to communicate the same meaning as the words. But emblems are culture specific, so be careful when using your culture's emblems in other cultures.

For example, when President Nixon visited Latin America and gestured with the OK sign, intending to communicate something positive, he was quickly informed that this gesture was not universal. In Latin America the gesture has a far more negative meaning.

*Here are a few cultural differences in the emblems you may commonly use*:

- In the United States, to say"hello" you wave with your whole hand moving from side to side, but in a large part of Europe that same signal means"no." In Greece such a gesture would be considered insulting.
- The V for victory is common throughout much of the world; but if you make this gesture in England with the palm facing your face, it's as insulting as the raised middle finger is in the United States.
- In Texas the raised fist with little finger and index finger held upright is a positive expression of support, because it represents the Texas longhorn steer. But in Italy it's an insult that means"Your spouse is having an affair with someone else." In parts of South America it's a gesture to ward off evil, and in parts of Africa it's a curse:"May you experience bad times."
- In the United States and in much of Asia, hugs are rarely exchanged among acquaintances; but among Latins and southern Europeans, hugging is a common greeting gesture, and failing to hug someone may communicate unfriendliness.

Illustrators enhance (literally"illustrate") the verbal messages they accompany. For example, when referring to something to the left, you might gesture toward the left. Most often you illustrate with your hands, but you can also illustrate with head and general body movements. You might, for example, turn your head or your entire body toward the left. You might also use illustrators to communicate the shape or size of objects you're talking about.

Affect displays are movements of the face (smiling or frowning, for example) but also of the hands and general body (body tension or relaxation, for example) that communicate emotional meaning. Affect displays are often unconscious; you smile or frown, for example, without awareness. At other times, however, you may smile consciously, trying to convey your pleasure or satisfaction. Regulators are behaviors that monitor, control, coordinate, or maintain the speaking of another individual. When you nod your head, for example, you tell the speaker to keep on speaking; when you lean forward and open your mouth, you tell the speaker that you would like to say something.

Adaptors are gestures that satisfy some personal need, such as scratching to relieve an itch or moving your hair out of your eyes. Self-adaptors are selftouching movements (for example, rubbing your nose). Alter-adaptors are movements directed at the person with whom you're speaking, such as removing lint from someone's jacket or straightening a person's tie or folding your arms in front of you to keep others a comfortable distance from you. Objectadaptors are gestures focused on objects, such as doodling on or shredding a Styrofoam coffee cup.

**Body Appearance**

Your general body appearance also communicates. Height, for example, has been shown to be significant in a wide v ariety of situations. Tall presidential candidates have a much better record of winning the election than do their shorter opponents. Tall people seem to be paid more and are favored by interviewers over shorter applicants. Your body also reveals your race (through skin colour and tone) and may also give clues as to your more specific nationality.

Your weight in proportion to your height will also communicate messages to others, as will the length, colour, and style of your hair. Your general attractiveness is also a part of body communication. Attractive people have the advantage in just about every activity you can name. They get better grades in school, are more valued as friends and lovers, and are preferred as coworkers. Although we normally think that attractiveness is culturally determined- and to some degree it is-research seems to indicate that definitions of attractiveness are becoming universal. A person rated as attractive in one culture is likely to be rated as attractive in other cultures-even in cultures whose people are widely different in appearance.

## LEGIBLE CLOTHING

L egible clothing is anything that you wear that contains some verbal message;it's clothing that literally can be read. In some instances the message proclaims status;it tells others thato uy are, for example, rich or stylish or youthful. The Gucci or Louis Vuitton logos on your luggage communicate your financial status.Your Bulls or Pirates sweatshirt communicates your interest in sports and your favourite team.

Items of legible clothing are being bought and worn in record numbers. Many designers and manufacturers have their names integrated into the design of the clothing: DKNY, Calvin Klein, Armani, L. L. Bean, the Gap, and Old Navy are just a few examples. At the same time that you're paying extra to buy the brand name, you're also providing free advertising. T-shirts and sweatshirts are especially popular as message senders. One study surveyed 600 male and female students as to the types of T-shirt messages they preferred. Four kinds of messages were cited most often:

- Affiliation messages, such as a club or school name, communicate that you're a part of a larger group.
- Trophy names, such as those of a high-status concert or perhaps a ski lodge, say that you were in the right place at the right time.
- Metaphorical expressions, such as pictures of rock groups or famous athletes, reveal that you're a part of the current trend.
- Personal messages, such as statements of beliefs or philosophies, tell others that you're willing to express your beliefs publicly.

### Follow-Up

Affiliation messages may create problems when they identify the wearer as a member of a gang, because wearing gang colors can contribute to violence, especially in schools. And personal messages may create conflict when they insult one gender, group, or popular and cherished belief. For example, the Wall Street Journal reports that boy-bashing slogans ("Boys are great. Every girl should own one" or"I make boys cry" or"Boys make good pets") are becoming increasingly popular with teenage girls, although they don't have the same sexual harassment connotations that girl-bashing slogans seem to have. How do you feel about these types of clothing messages? Do you feel that some clothing messages should be prohibited? If so, which ones? Or do you feel that such messages should be protected by the First Amendment guarantee of freedom of speech?

### Facial Communication

Throughout your interactions, your face communicates various messages, especially your emotions. Facial movements alone seem to communicate the degree of pleasantness, agreement, and sympathy felt; the rest of the body doesn't provide any additional information. But for other emotional messages-for example, the intensity with which an emotion is felt-both facial and bodily cues are used. So important are these cues in communicating your full meaning that graphic representations are now commonly used in Internet communication. In graphic user interface chat groups, buttons are available to help you encode your emotions graphically.

Some researchers in nonverbal communication claim that facial movements may express at least the following eight emotions: happiness, surprise, fear, anger, sadness, disgust, contempt, and interest. Facial expressions of these emotions are generally called primary affect displays: They indicate relatively pure, single emotions. Other emotional states and other facial displays are combinations of these various primary emotions and are called affect blends. You communicate these blended feelings with different parts of your face. Thus, for example, you may experience both fear and disgust at the same time. Your eyes and eyelids may signal fear, and movements of your nose, cheek, and mouth area may signal disgust.

### Facial Management Techniques

As you grew up, you learned your culture's nonverbal system of communication. You also learned certain facial management techniques; for example, to hide certain emotions and to emphasize others. Here are four facial management techniques that you will quickly recognize:

- Intensifying helps you to exaggerate a feeling; for example, to exaggerate your surprise when friends throw you a party, so as to make your friends feel better.
- Deintensifying helps you to underplay a feeling; for example, to cover up your own joy in the presence of a friend who didn't receive such good news.

- Neutralizing helps you to hide feelings; for example, to cover up your sadness so as not to depress others.
- Masking helps you to replace or substitute the expression of one emotion for the emotion you're really feeling; for example, to express happiness in order to cover up your disappointment about not receiving the gift you had expected.

These facial management techniques are learned along with display rules, which tell you what emotions to express when; they're the rules of appropriateness. For example, when someone gets bad news in which you may secretly take pleasure, the display rule dictates that you frown and otherwise nonverbally signal your displeasure. If you violate this kind of display rule, you'll be judged insensitive.

## EXPRESSIONS AND ATTITUDES

T he facial feedback hypothesis holds that your facial expressions influence physiological arousal. In one study, for example, participants held a pen in their teeth to simulate a sad expression and then rated a series of photographs. Results showed that mimicking sad expressions actually increased the degree of sadness the subjects reported feeling when viewing the photographs.

*Further support for this hypothesis comes from a study that compared:*

- Participants who felt emotions such as happiness and anger with
- Participants who both felt and expressed these emotions.

In support of the facial feedback hypothesis, subjects who felt and expressed the emotions became emotionally aroused faster than did those who only felt the emotions. Generally, research finds that facial expressions can produce or heighten feelings of sadness, fear, disgust, and anger. But this effect does not occur with all emotions; smiling, for example, doesn't seem to make us feel happier. Further, it has not been demonstrated that facial expressions can eliminate one feeling and replace it with another: If you're feeling sad, smiling will not eliminate the sadness and replace it with gladness. A reasonable conclusion seems to be that your facial expressions can influence some feelings but not all.

### Encoding-Decoding Accuracy

One popular question concerns the accuracy with which people can encode and decode emotions through facial expressions. One problem confronting us as we try to answer this question is that it's difficult to separate the ability of the encoder from the ability of the decoder. Thus, a person may be quite adept at communicating emotions nonverbally, but the receiver may prove insensitive.

On the other hand, the receiver may be good at deciphering emotions, but the sender may be inept. For example, introverts are not as accurate at decoding nonverbal cues as are extroverts. Research in 11 different countries shows that women are better than men at both encoding and decoding nonverbal cues.

It may be argued that because men and women play different roles in society, they've learned different adaptive techniques and skills to help them perform these roles. Thus, in most societies women are expected to be more friendly, nurturing, and supportive and so learn these skills. Accuracy also varies with the emotions themselves. Some emotions are easier to encode and decode than others. In one study, for example, people judged facial expressions of happiness with an accuracy ranging from 55 to 100 per cent, surprise from 38 to 86 per cent, and sadness from 19 to 88 per cent.

**Eye Communication**

Research on the messages communicated by the eyes (a study known technically as oculesis) shows that these messages vary depending on the duration, direction, and quality of the eye behaviour. For example, in every culture there are strict, though unstated, rules for the proper duration for eye contact. In U.S. culture the average length of gaze is 2.95 seconds. The average length of mutual gaze (two persons gazing at each other) is 1.18 seconds. When eye contact falls short of this amount, you may think the person is uninterested, shy, or preoccupied. When the appropriate amount of time is exceeded, you may perceive the person as showing unusually high interest.

The direction of the eye also communicates. In much of the United States, you're expected to glance alternately at the other person's face, then away, then again at the face, and so on. The rule for the public speaker is to scan the entire audience, not focusing for too long on or ignoring any one area of the audience. When you break these directional rules, you communicate different meanings- abnormally high or low interest, self-consciousness, nervousness over the interaction, and so on. The quality of eye behaviour-how wide or how narrow your eyes get during interaction-also communicates meaning, especially interest level and such emotions as surprise, fear, and disgust.

**The Functions of Eye Contact and Eye Avoidance**

Eye contact can serve a variety of functions. One such function is to seek feedback. In talking with someone, we look at her or him intently, as if to say,"Well, what do you think?" As you might predict, listeners gaze at speakers more than speakers gaze at listeners. In public speaking, you may scan hundreds of people to secure this feedback. A second function is to inform the other person that the channel of communication is open and that he or she should now speak. You see this regularly in conversation, when one person asks a question or finishes a thought and then looks to you for a response.

And one study found that eye contact was the most frequently noted nonverbal behaviour used to tell library users that the librarian was approachable. Eye movements may also signal the nature of a relationship, whether positive (an attentive glance) or negative (eye avoidance). You can also signal your power through visual dominance behaviour. The average speaker, for example, maintains a high level of eye contact while listening and a lower level while speaking. When people want to signal dominance, they may reverse this pattern-maintaining a high level of eye contact while talking but a much lower level while listening.

By making eye contact you psychologically lessen the physical distance between yourself and another person. When you catch someone's eye at a party, for example, you become psychologically close though physically far apart. Eye avoidance can also serve several different functions. When you avoid eye contact or avert your glance, you may help others maintain their privacy.

For example, you may do this when you see a couple arguing in public. You turn your eyes away (though your eyes may be wide open) as if to say,"I don't mean to intrude; I respect your privacy," a behaviour referred to as civil inattention. Eye avoidance can also signal lack of interest-in a person, a conversation, or some visual stimulus. At times, too, you may hide your eyes to block out unpleasant stimuli (a particularly gory or violent scene in a movie, for example) or close your eyes to block out visual stimuli and thus heighten other senses. For example, you may listen to music with your eyes closed. Lovers often close their eyes while kissing, and many prefer to make love in a dark or dimly lit room.

**Pupil Dilation**

In the fifteenth and sixteenth centuries, Italian women put drops of belladonna (which literally means"beautiful woman") into their eyes to enlarge the pupils so that they would look more attractive. Contemporary pupillometrics research supports the intuitive logic of these women; dilated pupils are judged more attractive than constricted ones. In one study, researchers retouched photographs of women; in half they enlarged the pupils, and in the other half they made them smaller. Men were then asked to judge the women's personalities from the photographs.

The photos of women with small pupils drew responses such as"cold,""hard," and"selfish"; those with dilated pupils drew responses such as"feminine" and"soft." Interestingly, the male observers could not verbalize the reasons for their different perceptions. Pupil dilation and our reactions to changes in the pupil size of others may function below the level of conscious awareness.

Pupil size also reveals your interest and level of emotional arousal. Your pupils enlarge when you're interested in something or when you are emotionally aroused. When homosexuals and heterosexuals were shown pictures of nude bodies, the homosexuals' pupils dilated more when they viewed same-sex bodies, whereas the heterosexuals' pupils dilated more when they viewed opposite-sex bodies. These pupillary responses are also observed in persons with profound mental retardation. Perhaps we judge dilated pupils as more attractive because we respond to them as indicative of a person's interest in us. And that may be the reason why both models and fuzzy beanbag toys have exceptionally large pupils.

## SPACE COMMUNICATION

Your use of space to communicate-an area of study known technically as proxemics-speaks as surely and as loudly as words and sentences. Speakers who stand close to their listener, with their hands on the listener's shoulders and their eyes focused directly on those of the listener, communicate something very different from speakers who stand in a corner with arms folded and eyes downcast.

### Spatial Distances

Edward Hall distinguishes four proxemic distances: types of spatial distances that define the types of relationships between people and the types of communication in which they're likely to engage. In intimate distance, ranging from actual touching to 18 inches, the presence of the other individual is unmistakable. Each person experiences the sound, smell, and feel of the other's breath.

You use intimate distance for lovemaking, comforting, and protecting. This distance is so short that most people don't consider it proper in public. Personal distance refers to the protective"bubble" that defines your personal space, ranging from 18 inches to 4 feet.

This imaginary bubble keeps you protected and untouched by others. You can still hold or grasp another person at this distance, but only by extending your arms; this allows you to take certain individuals such as loved ones into your protective bubble. At the outer limit of personal distance, you can touch another person only if both of you extend your arms.

This is the distance at which you conduct most of your interpersonal interactions; for example, talking with friends and family. At social distance, ranging from 4 to 12 feet, you lose the visual detail you have at personal distance. You conduct impersonal business and interact at a social gathering at this social distance.

The more distance you maintain in your interactions, the more formal they appear. In offices of high officials, the desks are positioned so the official is assured of at least this distance from clients. Public distance, from 12 to more than 25 feet, protects you. At this distance you could take defensive action if threatened. On a public bus or train, for example, you might keep at least this distance from a drunken passenger. Although at this distance you lose fine details of the face and eyes, you're still close enough to see what is happening.

### Influences on Space Communication

Several factors influence the way you relate to and use space in communicating. Here are a few examples of how status, culture, subject matter, gender, and age influence space communication. People of equal status maintain shorter distances between themselves than do people of unequal status. When status is unequal, the higher-status person may approach the lower-status person more closely than the lower-status person would approach the higher-status person.

Members of different cultures treat space differently. For example, people from northern European cultures and many Americans stand fairly far apart when conversing; those from southern European and Middle Eastern cultures stand much closer. It's easy to see how people who normally stand far apart may interpret the close distances of others as pushy and overly intimate. It's equally easy to appreciate how those who normally stand close may interpret the far distances of others as cold and unfriendly. When discussing personal subjects you maintain shorter distances than with impersonal subjects.

## BUILDING COMMUNICATION SKILLS

### How Can You Choose a Seat

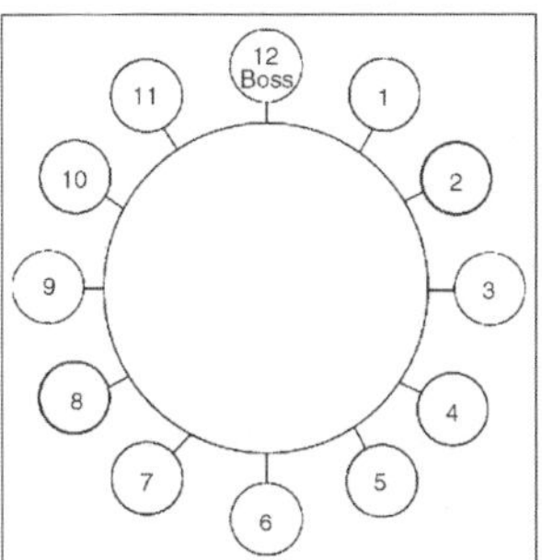


With your recently acquired sensitivity to nonverbal cues, where would you sit in each of the following situations to best achieve the purposes identified? What would be your first choice? Your second choice?

- You want to polish the apple and ingratiate yourself with your boss.
- You aren't prepared and want to be ignored.
- You want to challenge your boss on a certain policy that will come up for a vote.
- You want to be accepted as a new (but important) member of the company.
- You want to get to know the person already seated at position number 5.

After making your choices, consider why you made them. Do you normally make choices based on such factors as these? What interpersonal factors-for example, the desire to talk to or get a closer look at someone-influence your day-to-day seating behaviour?. Also, you stand closer to someone who is praising you than to someone criticizing you. Your gender also influences your spatial relationships. Women generally stand closer to each other than men do. Similarly, when someone approaches another person, he or she will come closer to a woman than to a man. With increasing age there's a tendency for the spaces to become larger. Children stand much closer to each other than do adults.

These research findings provide some evidence that maintaining distance is a learned behaviour. The evaluation you make of a person (whether positive or negative) will also influence your space. For example, you stand farther from enemies, authority figures, and higher-status individuals than from friends and peers. You maintain a greater distance from people you see as different from yourself; for example, different in race or in physical condition. Typically, you maintain more distance between yourself and people you may unconsciously evaluate negatively.

## TERRITORIALITY

One of the most interesting concepts in ethology (the study of animals in their natural surroundings) is territoriality, a possessive or ownership reaction to an area of space or to particular objects. Two interesting dimensions of territoriality are territorial types and territorial markers.

### Territory Types

Three types of territory are often distinguished: primary, secondary, and public. Primary territories are your exclusive preserve: your desk, room, house, or backyard, for example. In these areas you're in control. The effect is similar to the home field advantage that a sports team has when playing in its own ballpark. When you're in these home territories, you generally have greater influence over others than you would in someone else's territory.

For example, in their own home or office people generally take on a kind of leadership role; they initiate conversations, fill in silences, assume relaxed and comfortable postures, and maintain their positions with greater conviction. Because the territorial owner is dominant, you stand a better chance of getting your raise approved, your point accepted, or a contract resolved in your favour if you're in your own primary territory (home, office) rather than in someone else's. Secondary territories, although they don't belong to you, are associated with you-perhaps because you've occupied them for a long time or they were assigned to you.

For example, your desk in a classroom may become a secondary territory if it is assigned to you or if you regularly occupy it and others treat it as yours. Your neighborhood turf, a cafeteria table where you usually sit, or a favourite corner of a local coffee shop may be secondary territories. You feel a certain"ownership-like" attachment to the place, even though it's really not yours in any legal sense. Public territories are areas that are open to all people, such as a park, movie house, restaurant, or beach.

European cafés, food courts in suburban malls, and the open areas in large city office buildings are public spaces that bring people together and stimulate communication. The electronic revolution, however, may well change the role of public space in stimulating communication. For example, home shopping clubs make it less necessary for people to go downtown or to the mall, and shoppers consequently have less opportunity to run into other people and to talk and exchange news.

Similarly, electronic mail permits us to communicate without talking and without even leaving the house to mail a letter. Perhaps the greatest change is telecommuting, in which workers can go to work without even leaving their homes. The face-to-face communication that normally takes place in an office is replaced by communication via computer.

Territoriality is closely linked to status. Generally, the size and location of your territories signal your status within your social group. For example, male animals will stake out a particular territory and consider it their own. They will allow prospec- tive mates to enter but will defend the territory against entrance by others, especially by other males of the same species. The larger the animal's territory, the higher the animal is in status within the herd. The size and location of human territories also say something about status.

An apartment or office in midtown Manhattan or downtown Tokyo, for example, is extremely high-status territory. The cost of the territory restricts it to those who have lots of money.

### Territorial Markers

Much as animals mark their territory, humans mark theirs with three types of markers: central markers, boundary markers, and earmarkers. Central markers are items you place in a territory to reserve it.

For example, you place a drink at the bar, books on your desk, or a sweater over the chair to let others know that these territories belong to you. Boundary markers set boundaries that divide your territory from"theirs." In the supermarket checkout line, the bar placed between your groceries and those of the person behind you is a boundary marker. Similarly, the armrests separating your seat from those of the people on either side at a movie theater and the molded plastic seats on a bus or train are boundary markers. Earmarkers-a term taken from the practice of branding animals on their ears-are those identifying marks that indicate your possession of a territory or object. Trademarks, nameplates, and initials on a shirt or attaché case are all examples of earmarkers.

## ARTIFACTUAL COMMUNICATION

Artifactual communication is communication via objects made by human hands. Thus, colour, clothing, jewelry, and the decoration of space would be considered artifactual. Let's look at each of these briefly.

**Colour Communication**

There is some evidence that colors affect us physiologically. For example, respiratory movements increase with red light and decrease with blue light. Similarly, eye blinks increase in frequency when eyes are exposed to red light and decrease when exposed to blue. These responses seem consistent with our intuitive feelings about blue being more soothing and red more arousing. When a school changed the colour of its walls from orange and white to blue, the blood pressure of the students decreased and their academic performance increased. Colour communication also influences perceptions and behaviors.

People's acceptance of a product, for example, is largely determined by its packaging, especially its colour. In one study the very same coffee taken from a yellow can was described as weak, from a dark brown can as too strong, from a red can as rich, and from a blue can as mild. Even your acceptance of a person may depend on the colors he or she wears. Consider, for example, the comments of one colour expert:"If you have to pick the wardrobe for your defence lawyer heading into court and choose anything but blue, you deserve to lose the case." Black is so powerful it could work against the lawyer with the jury. Brown lacks sufficient authority. Green would probably elicit a negative response.

## UNDERSTANDING THEORY AND RESEARCH

### SPACE VIOLATIONS

Expectancy violations theory explains what happens when you increase or decrease the distance between yourself and another person in an interpersonal interaction. Each culture has certain expectancies about the distance that people should normally maintain in their conversations. And, of course, each person has certain idiosyncrasies.

Together these determine"expected distance." If you violate the expected distance to a great extent (small violations most often go unnoticed), then the relationship itself comes into focus. Then the other person begins to turn attention away from the topic of conversation and toward you and your relationship with him or her. If this other person perceives you positively-for example, if you're a high-status person or you're particularly attractive-then you'll be perceived even more positively if you violate the expected distance. If, on the other hand, you're perceived negatively and you violate the norm, you'll be perceived even more negatively.

**Clothing and Body Adornment**

People make inferences about who you are, at least in part, from the way you dress. Whether these inferences are accurate or not, they will influence what people think of you and how they react to you. Your socioeconomic class, your seriousness, your attitudes (for example, whether you're conservative or liberal), your concern for convention, your sense of style, and perhaps even your creativity will all be judged in part by the way you dress. Similarly, college students will perceive an instructor dressed informally as friendly, fair, enthusiastic, and flexible; they will see the same instructor dressed formally as prepared, knowledgeable, and organized.

The way you wear your hair says something about your attitudes-from a concern about being up to date to a desire to shock to perhaps a lack of interest in appearances. Men with long hair will generally be judged as less conservative than those with shorter hair. Your jewelry also communicates about you. Wedding and engagement rings are obvious examples that communicate specific messages. College rings and political buttons likewise communicate specific messages.

If you wear a Rolex watch or large precious stones, others are likely to infer that you're rich. Men who wear earrings will be judged differently from men who don't. What judgments are made will depend on who the receiver is, the communication context, and all the factors identified throughout this text.

### Space Decoration

The way you decorate your private spaces also communicates about you. The office with a mahogany desk and bookcases and oriental rugs communicates your importance and status within an organization, just as a metal desk and bare floor indicate a worker much farther down in the hierarchy. Similarly, people will make inferences about you based on the way you decorate your home. The expensiveness of the furnishings may communicate your status and wealth; their coordination may convey your sense of style.

The magazines may reflect your interests, and the arrangement of chairs around a television set may reveal how important watching television is to you. The contents of bookcases lining the walls reveal the importance of reading in your life. In fact, there's probably little in your home that would not send messages from which others would draw inferences about you. Computers, wide-screen televisions, well-equipped kitchens, and oil paintings of great grandparents, for example, all say something about the people who live in the home. Similarly, the absence of certain items will communicate something about you. Consider what messages you'd get from a home where no television, phone, or books could be seen.

## TOUCH COMMUNICATION

The study of touch communication, technically referred to as haptics, suggests that touch is perhaps the most primitive form of communication.

Developmentally, touch is probably the first sense to be used. Even in the womb the child is stimulated by touch. Soon after birth the child is fondled, caressed, patted, and stroked. In turn, the child explores its world through touch. In a short time the child learns to communicate a wide variety of meanings through touch.

### The Meanings of Touch

*Touch communicates a wide variety of messages. Here are five major ones that will illustrate this great variety.*

- Touch communicates positive feelings; for example, support, appreciation, inclusion, sexual interest or intent, composure, immediacy, affection, trust, similarity and quality, and informality. Touch also stimulates self-disclosure.
- Touch often communicates your intention to play, either affectionately or aggressively.
- Touch may control the behaviors, attitudes, or feelings of the other person. To obtain compliance, for example, you touch the other person to communicate"move over,""hurry,""stay here," or"do it." You might also touch a person to gain his or her attention, as if to say"look at me" or"look over here." In some situations touching can even amount to a kind of nonverbal dominace behaviour.
- Ritualistic touching centers on greetings and departures; examples are shaking hands to say"hello" or"good-bye," hugging, kissing, or putting your arm around another's shoulder when greeting or saying farewell.
- Task-related touching is associated with the performance of some function, as when you remove a speck of dust from another person's coat, help someone out of a car, or check someone's forehead for fever.

### Judgments about People

Paralanguage cues are often used as a basis for judgments about people; for example, evaluations of their emotional state or even their personality. A listener can accurately judge the emotional state of a speaker from vocal expression alone, if both speaker and listener speak the same language. Paralanguage cues are not so accurate when used to communicate emotions to those who speak a different language. Also, some emotions are easier to identify than others; it's easy to distinguish between hate and sympathy but more difficult to distinguish between fear and anxiety. And, of course, listeners vary in their ability to decode, and speakers in their ability to encode emotions.

### Judgments about Communication Effectiveness

In one-way communication (when one person is doing all or most of the speaking and the other person is doing all or most of the listening), those who talk fast (about 50 per cent faster than normal) are more persuasive. People agree more with a fast speaker than with a slow speaker and find the fast speaker more intelligent and objective. When we look at comprehension, rapid speech shows an interesting effect. When the speaking rate is increased by 50 per cent, the comprehension level drops by only 5 per cent. When the rate is doubled, the comprehension level drops only 10 per cent. These 5 and 10 per cent losses are more than offset by the increased speed; thus the faster rates are much more efficient in communicating information. If speeds are more than twice the rate of normal speech, however, comprehension begins to fall dramatically. Do exercise caution in applying this research to all forms of communication. For example, if you increase your rate to increase efficiency, you may create an impression so unnatural that others will focus on your speed instead of your meaning.

## SILENCE

Like words and gestures, silence, too, communicates important meanings and serves important functions. Silence allows the speaker time to think, time to formulate and organize his or her verbal communications. Before messages of intense conflict, as well as before those confessing undying love, there's often silence. Again, silence seems to prepare the receiver for the importance of these future messages. Some people use silence as a weapon to hurt others. We often speak of giving someone"the silent treatment." After a conflict, for example, one or both individuals may remain silent as a kind of punishment.

Silence used to hurt others may also take the form of refusing to acknowledge the presence of another person, as in disconfirmation; here silence is a dramatic demonstration of the total indifference one person feels toward the other. Sometimes silence is used as a response to personal anxiety, shyness, or threats.

You may feel anxious or shy among new people and prefer to remain silent. By remaining silent you preclude the chance of rejection. Only when you break your silence and make an attempt to communicate with another person do you risk rejection. Silence may be used to prevent communication of certain messages. In conflict situations silence is sometimes used to prevent certain topics from surfacing and to prevent one or both parties from saying things they may later regret. In such situations silence often allows us time to cool off before expressing hatred, severe criticism, or personal attacks- which, as we know, are irreversible.

Like the eyes, face, and hands, silence can also be used to communicate emotional responses. Sometimes silence communicates a determination to be uncooperative or defiant; by refusing to engage in verbal communication, you defy the authority or the legitimacy of the other person's position. Silence is often used to communicate annoyance, particularly when accompanied by a pouting expression, arms crossed in front of the chest, and nostrils flared. Silence may express affection or love, especially when coupled with long and longing stares into each other's eyes. Of course, you may also use silence when you simply have nothing to say, when nothing occurs to you, or when you don't want to say anything. James Russell Lowell expressed this best:"Blessed are they who have nothing to say, and who cannot be persuaded to say it." Silence may also be used to avoid responsibility for any wrongdoing.

## BUILDING COMMUNICATION SKILLS

### How Can You Praise and Criticize

Consider how paralanguage variations can communicate praise and criticism by reading each of the following 10 statements aloud-first to communicate praise in each case and second, criticism. Then consider what paralanguage cues you used to convey the praise and criticism. Did you read the statements with different facial expressions, eye movements, and body postures depending on your desire to communicate praise or criticism?

- Now that looks good on you.
- You lost weight.
- You look younger than that.
- You're gonna make it.
- That was some meal.
- You really know yourself.
- You're an expert.
- You're so sensitive. I'm amazed.
- Your parents are really something.
- Are you ready? Already?

## UNDERSTANDING THEORY AND RESEARCH

### The Social Clock

Your culture or, more specifically, your society maintains a schedule of the right times for doing a variety of important things; for example, the right times to start dating, to finish college, to buy your own home, or to have a child. This unwritten schedule provides you with a"social clock"-a clock that will tell you if you're keeping pace with your peers, are ahead of them, or are falling behind. And although the social clock is becoming more flexible and more tolerant of deviations from the standard timetable, it still exerts pressure on you to keep pace with your peers.

On the basis of this social clock, which you learned as you grew up, you evaluate your own social and professional development. If you're in step with the rest of your peers-for example, you started dating at the"appropriate" age or you're finishing college at the"appropriate" age-then you'll feel well adjusted, competent, and a part of the group. If you're late, you'll probably experience feelings of dissatisfaction.

### Smell Communication

Smell communication, or olfactory communication, is extremely important in a wide variety of situations and is now big business. For example, there's some evidence (though clearly not very conclusive evidence) that the smell of lemon contributes to a perception of heath, the smells of lavender and eucalyptus increase alertness, and the smell of rose oil reduces blood pressure. Findings such as these have contributed to the growth of aromatherapy and to a new profession of aromatherapists. Because humans possess"denser skin concentrations of scent glands than almost any other mammal," it has been argued that it only remains for us to discover how we use scent to communicate a wide variety of messages. Here are some of the most important messages scent seems to communicate.

- *Attraction messages*: Humans use perfumes, colognes, after-shave lotions, powders, and the like to enhance their attractiveness to others and to themselves. After all, you also smell yourself. When the smells are pleasant, you feel better about yourself.
- *Taste messages*: Without smell, taste would be severely impaired. For example, without smell it would be extremely difficult to taste the difference between a raw potato and an apple. Street vendors selling hot dogs, sausages, and similar foods are aided greatly by the smells, which stimulate the appetites of passersby.
- *Memory messages*: Smell is a powerful memory aid; you often recall situations from months and even years ago when you encounter a similar smell.
- *Identification messages*: Smell is often used to create an image or an identity for a product. Advertisers and manufacturers spend millions of dollars each year creating scents for cleaning products and toothpastes, for example, which have nothing to do with their cleaning power. There's also evidence that we can identify specific significant others by smell. For example, young children were able to identify the T-shirts of their brothers and sisters solely on the basis of smell.

## CULTURE AND NONVERBAL COMMUNICATION

Not surprisingly, nonverbal communication is heavily influenced by culture. Consider a variety of differences. At the sight of unpleasant pictures, members of some cultures (American and European, for example) will facially express disgust. Members of other cultures (Japanese, for example) will avoid facially expressing disgust. Although Americans consider direct eye contact an expression of honesty and forthrightness, the Japanese often view this as showing a lack of respect. The Japanese will glance at the other person's face rarely and then only for very short periods.

Among some Latin Americans and Native Americans, direct eye contact between, say, a student and a teacher is considered inappropriate, perhaps aggressive; appropriate student behaviour is to avoid eye contact with the teacher.

Folding your arms over your chest is considered disrespectful in Fiji; pointing with the index finger is considered impolite in many Middle Eastern countries; and waving your hand can be considered insulting in Greece and Nigeria. In the United States living next door to someone means that you're expected to be friendly and to interact with that person. This cultural expectation seems so natural that Americans and members of many other cultures probably don't even consider that it is not shared by all cultures. In Japan, the fact that your house is next to another's does not imply that you should become close or visit each other. Consider, therefore, the situation in which a Japanese person buys a house next to an American. The Japanese may see the American as overly familiar and as taking friendship for granted. The American may see the Japanese as distant, unfriendly, and unneighborly.

Yet each person is merely fulfilling the expectations of his or her own culture. Different cultures also assign different meanings to colors. Touching varies greatly from one culture to another. For example, African Americans touch one another more than do whites. Similarly, touching declines from kindergarten to the sixth grade for white but not for African American children. Japanese people touch one another much less than do Anglo- Saxons, who in turn touch one another much less than do southern Europeans.

In one study students in the United States reported being touched twice as much as did students from Japan. In Japan there's a strong taboo against touching between strangers. The Japanese are therefore especially careful to maintain sufficient distance. Another obvious cross-cultural contrast is presented by the Middle East, where same-sex touching in public is extremely common. Middle Easterners, Latin Americans, and southern Europeans touch one another while talking a great deal more than do people from"noncontact cultures" such as those of Asia and northern Europe. Even such seemingly minor nonverbal differences as these can create difficulties when members of different cultures interact.

Southern Europeans may perceive northern Europeans or Japanese, for example, as cold, distant, and uninvolved. Southern Europeans in turn may be perceived as pushy, aggressive, and inappropriately intimate. In the study of touch avoidance discussed earlier, women said that they avoid touching members of the opposite sex more than do men. This male-female difference, however, seems to conflict with a study by Jones, who reported that women initiated more opposite-sex touching than did men (especially more opposite-sex touching designed to control).

Yet women also report feeling less positive about opposite-sex touching than do men. Opposite-sex friends touch more than do samesex friends. Both male and female college students report that they touch and are touched more by their opposite-sex friends than by their same-sex friends. The strong societal bias against same-sex touching may have influenced these self-reports; people may have reported as they did in order to conform to what they saw as culturally accepted and expected. Not surprisingly, the role of silence is seen differently in different cultures.

Among the Apache, for example, mutual friends don't feel the need to introduce strangers who may be working in the same area or on the same project. The strangers may remain silent for several days. During this time they're looking each other over, trying to determine if the other person is all right. Only after this period do the individuals talk. When courting, especially during the initial stages, the Apache remain silent for hours; if they do talk, they generally talk very little. Only after a couple has been dating for several months will they have lengthy conversations. These periods of silence are generally attributed to shyness or self-consciousness; but the use of silence is explicitly taught to Apache women, who are especially discouraged from engaging in long discussions with their dates.

To many Apache, silence during courtship is a sign of modesty. In Iranian culture there's an expression, qahr, which means not being on speaking terms with someone, giving someone the silent treatment. For example, when children disobey their parents, are disrespectful, or fail to do their chores as they should, they're given this silent treatment.

With adults qahr may be instituted when one person insults or injures another. After a cooling-off period, ashti (making up after qahr) may be initiated. Qahr lasts for a relatively short time between parents and children, but longer when between adults.

Qahr is more frequently initiated between two women than between two men, but when men experience qahr it lasts much longer and often requires the intercession of a mediator to establish ashti. An interesting cultural difference in time orientation is that between monochronic and polychronic time orientations. Monochronic people or cultures (the United States, Germany, Scandinavia, and Switzerland are good examples) schedule one thing at a time.

Time is compartmentalized; there's a time for everything, and everything has its own time. Polychronic people or cultures (Latin Americans, Mediterranean people, and Arabs are good examples), on the other hand, schedule a number of things at the same time.

Eating, conducting business with several different people, and taking care of family matters may all be conducted at the same time. No culture is entirely monochronic or polychronic; rather, these are general tendencies that are found across a large part of the culture. Some cultures combine both time orientations; for example, in Japan and in some areas of American culture, both orientations are found.

## ON ETHICS IN HUMAN COMMUNICATION

### Interpersonal Silence

Often, though not always, you have the right to remain silent in order to maintain your privacy-to withhold information that has no bearing on the matter at hand. Thus, for example, your previous relationship history, affectional orientation, or religion is usually irrelevant to your ability to function in a job, and thus may be kept private in most job-related situations.

On the other hand, these issues may be relevant when, for example, you're about to enter a new relationship-and then there may be an obligation to reveal your relationship history, affectional orientation, or religion.

In court, of course, you have the right to refuse to incriminate yourself or to reveal information about yourself that could be used against you. But you don't generally have the right to refuse to reveal information about the criminal activities of others (although psychiatrists, clergy, and lawyers are often exempt from this rule).

### What would you do

You're the assistant manager of a store that sells high-tech equipment. You discover that over the last several weeks your brother-in-law, who also works in the store, has stolen equipment worth well over $20,000.

You wonder if you should say something or remain silent. Would your answer be different depending on whether the store owner or the insurance company had to cover the loss? What would you do in this situation? More generally, what obligation do you have to reveal wrongdoing that you've witnessed?

# 8

# Nonverbal Communication

Nonverbal communication (NVC) is usually understood as the process of communication through sending and receiving wordless messages. i.e, language is not the only source of communication, there are other means also. NVC can be communicated through gestures and touch (Haptic communication), by body language or posture, by facial expression and eye contact. NVC can be communicated through object communication such as clothing, hairstyles or even architecture, symbols and infographics. Speech contains nonverbal elements known as paralanguage, including voice quality, emotion and speaking style, as well as prosodic features such as rhythm, intonation and stress. Dance is also regarded as a nonverbal communication. Likewise, written texts have nonverbal elements such as handwriting style, spatial arrangement of words, or the use of emoticons.

However, much of the study of nonverbal communication has focused on face-to-face interaction, where it can be classified into three principal areas: environmental conditions where communication takes place, the physical characteristics of the communicators, and behaviors of communicators during interaction.

## Verbal vs. oral Communication

Scholars in this field usually use a strict sense of the term"verbal", meaning"of or concerned with words," and do not use"verbal communication" as a synonym for oral or spoken communication. Thus, vocal sounds that are not considered to be words, such as a grunt, or singing a wordless note, are nonverbal. Sign languages and writing are generally understood as forms of verbal communication, as both make use of words - although like speech, both may contain para-linguistic elements and often occur alongside nonverbal messages. Nonverbal communication can occur through any <

"When we speak (or listen), our attention is focused on words rather than body language. But our judgement includes both. An audience is simultaneously processing both verbal and nonverbal cues. Body movements are not usually positive or negative in and of themselves; rather, the situation and the message will determine the appraisal."

The first scientific study of nonverbal communication was Charles Darwin's book The Expression of the Emotions in Man and Animals. He argued that all mammals show emotion reliably in their faces. Studies now range across a number of fields, including, linguistics, semiotics and social psychology.

## ARBITRARINESS

While much nonverbal communication is based on arbitrary symbols, which differ from culture to culture, a large proportion is also to some extent iconic and may be universally understood. Paul Ekman's influential 1960s studies of facial expression determined that expressions of anger, disgust, fear, joy, sadness and surprise are universal.

### Clothing and Bodily Characteristics

Uniforms have both a functional and a communicative purpose. This man's clothes identify him as male and a police officer; his badges and shoulder sleeve insignia give information about his job and rank.

Elements such as physique, height, weight, hair, skin colour, gender, odors, and clothing send nonverbal messages during interaction. For example, a study, carried out in Vienna, Austria, of the clothing worn by women attending discotheques showed that in certain groups of women (especially women which were in town without their partners) motivation for sex, and levels of sexual hormones, were correlated with aspects of the clothing, especially the amount of skin displayed, and the presence of sheer clothing, e.g. at the arms. Thus, to some degree, clothing sent signals about interest in courtship.

Research into height has generally found that taller people are perceived as being more impressive. Melamed & Bozionelos studied a sample of managers in the UK and found that height was a key factor affecting who was promoted. Often people try to make themselves taller, for example, standing on a platform, when they want to make more of an impact with their speaking.

### Physical Environment

Environmental factors such as furnifur, architectural style, interior decorating, lighting conditions, colors, temperature, noise, and music affect the behaviour of communicators during interaction. The furniture itself can be seen as a nonverbal message.

#### *Proxemics: Physical Space in Communication*

Proxemics is the study of how people use and perceive the physical space around them. The space between the sender and the receiver of a message influences the way the message is interpreted.

The perception and use of space varies significantly across cultures and different settings within cultures. Space in nonverbal communication may be divided into four main categories: intimate, social, personal, and public space.

The term territoriality is still used in the study of proxemics to explain human behaviour regarding personal space.

*Hargie and Dickson identify 4 such territories*:

1. Primary territory: this refers to an area that is associated with someone who has exclusive use of it. For example, a house that others cannot enter without the owner's permission.
2. Secondary territory: unlike the previous type, there is no"right" to occupancy, but people may still feel some degree of ownership of a particular space. For example, someone may sit in the same seat on train every day and feel aggrieved if someone else sits there.
3. Public territory: this refers to an area that is available to all, but only for a set period, such as a parking space or a seat in a library. Although people have only a limited claim over that space, they often exceed that claim. For example, it was found that people take longer to leave a parking space when someone is waiting to take that space.
4. Interaction territory: this is space created by others when they are interacting. For example, when a group is talking to each other on a footpath, others will walk around the group rather than disturb it.

## Chronemics: Time in Communication

Chronemics is the study of the use of time in nonverbal communication. The way we perceive time, structure our time and react to time is a powerful communication tool, and helps set the stage for communication. Time perceptions include punctuality and willingness to wait, the speed of speech and how long people are willing to listen. The timing and frequency of an action as well as the tempo and rhythm of communications within an interaction contributes to the interpretation of nonverbal messages. Gudykunst & Ting-Toomey) identified 2 dominant time patterns:

### *Monochronic Time*

A monochronic time system means that things are done one at a time and time is segmented into precise, small units. Under this system time is scheduled, arranged and managed.

The United States is considered a monochronic society. This perception of time is learned and rooted in the Industrial Revolution, where"factory life required the labour force to be on hand and in place at an appointed hour". For Americans, time is a precious resource not to be wasted or taken lightly."We buy time, save time, spend time and make time. Our time can be broken down into years, months, days, hours, minutes, seconds and even milliseconds. We use time to structure both our daily lives and events that we are planning for the future. We have schedules that we must follow: appointments that we must go to at a certain time, classes that start and end at certain times, work schedules that start and end at certain times, and even our favourite TV shows, that start and end at a certain time."

As communication scholar Edward T. Hall wrote regarding the American's viewpoint of time in the business world,"the schedule is sacred." Hall says that for monochronic cultures, such as the American culture,"time is tangible" and viewed as a commodity where"time is money" or"time is wasted." The result of this perspective is that Americans and other monochronic cultures, such as the German and Swiss, place a paramount value on schedules, tasks and"getting the job done." These cultures are committed to regimented schedules and may view those who do not subscribe to the same perception of time as disrespectful.

Monochronic cultures include Germany, Canada, Switzerland, United States, and Scandinavia. Polychronic Time Main article: Polychronicity

A polychronic time system is a system where several things can be done at once, and a more fluid approach is taken to scheduling time. Unlike Americans and most northern and western European cultures, Latin American and Arabic cultures use the polychronic system of time.

These cultures are much less focused on the preciseness of accounting for each and every moment. As Raymond Cohen notes, polychronic cultures are deeply steeped in tradition rather than in tasks-a clear difference from their monochronic counterparts. Cohen notes that"Traditional societies have all the time in the world. The arbitrary divisions of the clock face have little saliency in cultures grounded in the cycle of the seasons, the invariant pattern of rural life, and the calendar of religious festivities".

Instead, their culture is more focused on relationships, rather than watching the clock. They have no problem being"late" for an event if they are with family or friends, because the relationship is what really matters. As a result, polychronic cultures have a much less formal perception of time. They are not ruled by precise calendars and schedules. Rather,"cultures that use the polychronic time system often schedule multiple appointments simultaneously so keeping on schedule is an impossibility." Polychronic cultures include Saudi Arabia, Egypt, Mexico, Philippines, India, and many in Africa.

## MOVEMENT AND BODY POSITION

### Kinesics

The term was first used by Ray Birdwhistell, an anthropologist who wished to study how people communicate through posture, gesture, stance, and movement. Part of Birdwhistell's work involved making film of people in social situations and analyzing them to show different levels of communication not clearly seen otherwise. The study was joined by several other anthropologists, including Margaret Mead and Gregory Bateson.

## Posture

Posture can be used to determine a participant's degree of attention or involvement, the difference in status between communicators, and the level of fondness a person has for the other communicator. Studies investigating the impact of posture on interpersonal relationships suggest that mirror-image congruent postures, where one person's left side is parallel to the other's right side, leads to favorable perception of communicators and positive speech; a person who displays a forward lean or a decrease in a backwards lean also signify positive sentiment during communication. Posture is understood through such indicators as direction of lean, body orientation, arm position, and body openness.

## Gesture

A gesture is a non-vocal bodily movement intended to express meaning. They may be articulated with the hands, arms or body, and also include movements of the head, face and eyes, such as winking, nodding, or rolling ones' eyes. The boundary between language and gesture, or verbal and nonverbal communication, can be hard to identify.

Although the study of gesture is still in its infancy, some broad categories of gestures have been identified by researchers. The most familiar are the so-called emblems or quotable gestures. These are conventional, culture-specific gestures that can be used as replacement for words, such as the handwave used in the US for"hello" and"goodbye". A single emblematic gesture can a have very different significance in different cultural contexts, ranging from complimentary to highly offensive. The page List of gestures discusses emblematic gestures made with one hand, two hands, hand and other body parts, and body and facial gestures.

Another broad category of gestures comprises those gestures used spontaneously when we speak. These gestures are closely coordinated with speech. The so-called beat gestures are used in conjunction with speech and keep time with the rhythm of speech to emphasize certain words or phrases. These types of gestures are integrally connected to speech and thought processes. Other spontaneous gestures used when we speak are more contentful and may echo or elaborate the meaning of the co-occurring speech.For example, a gesture that depicts the act of throwing may be synchronous with the utterance,"He threw the ball right into the window."

Gestural languages such as American Sign Language and its regional siblings operate as complete natural languages that are gestural in modality. They should not be confused with finger spelling, in which a set of emblematic gestures are used to represent a written alphabet.

Gestures can also be categorised as either speech-independent or speech-related. Speech-independent gestures are dependent upon culturally accepted interpretation and have a direct verbal translation. A wave hello or a peace sign are examples of speech-independent gestures. Speech related gestures are used in parallel with verbal speech; this form of nonverbal communication is used to emphasize the message that is being communicated. Speech related gestures are intended to provide supplemental information to a verbal message such as pointing to an object of discussion.

Gestures such as Mudra (Sanskrit) encode sophisticated information accessible to initiates that are privy to the subtlety of elements encoded in their tradition.

**Haptics: Touching in Communication**

Haptic communication is the means by which people and other animals communicate via touching. Touch is an extremely important sense for humans; as well as providing information about surfaces and textures it is a component of nonverbal communication in interpersonal relationships, and vital in conveying physical intimacy. It can be both sexual (such as kissing) and platonic (such as hugging or tickling).

Touch is the earliest sense to develop in the fetus. The development of an infant's haptic senses and how it relates to the development of the other senses such as vision has been the target of much research. Human babies have been observed to have enormous difficulty surviving if they do not possess a sense of touch, even if they retain sight and hearing. Babies who can perceive through touch, even without sight and hearing, tend to fare much better. Touch can be thought of as a basic sense in that most life forms have a response to being touched, while only a subset have sight and hearing.

In chimpanzees the sense of touch is highly developed. As newborns they see and hear poorly but cling strongly to their mothers. Harry Harlow conducted a controversial study involving rhesus monkeys and observed that monkeys reared with a"terry cloth mother", a wire feeding apparatus wrapped in softer terry cloth which provided a level of tactile stimulation and comfort, were considerably more emotionally stable as adults than those with a mere wire mother.

Touching is treated differently from one country to another. Socially acceptable levels of touching varies from one culture to another. In the Thai culture, touching someone's head may be thought rude. Remland and Jones studied groups of people communicating and found that in England (8%), France (5%) and the Netherlands (4%) touching was rare compared to their Italian (14%) and Greek (12.5%) sample.

Striking, pushing, pulling, pinching, kicking, strangling and hand-to-hand fighting are forms of touch in the context of physical abuse. In a sentence like"I never touched him/her" or"Don't you dare to touch him/her" the term touch may be meant as euphemism for either physical abuse or sexual touching. To'touch oneself' is a euphemism for masturbation. The word touch has many other metaphorical uses. One can be emotionally touched, referring to an action or object that evokes an emotional response. To say"I was touched by your letter" implies the reader felt a strong emotion when reading it. Usually does not include anger, disgust or other forms of emotional rejection unless used in a sarcastic manner.

Stoeltje wrote about how Americans are'losing touch' with this important communication skill. During a study conduced by University of Miami School of Medicine, Touch Research Institutes, American children were said to be more aggressive than their French counterparts while playing at a playground. It was noted that French women touched their children more

**Paralanguage: Nonverbal cues of the Voice**

Paralanguage (sometimes called vocalics) is the study of nonverbal cues of the voice. Various acoustic properties of speech such as tone, pitch and accent, collectively known as prosody, can all give off nonverbal cues. Paralanguage may change the meaning of words.

*The linguist George L. Trager developed a classification system which consists of the voice set, voice qualities, and vocalization*:

- The voice set is the context in which the speaker is speaking. This can include the situation, gender, mood, age and a person's culture.
- The voice qualities are volume, pitch, tempo, rhythm, articulation, resonance, nasality, and accent. They give each individual a unique"voice print".
- Vocalization consists of three subsections: characte-rizers, qualifiers and segregates. Characterizers are emotions expressed while speaking, such as laughing, crying, and yawning. A voice qualifier is the style of delivering a message - for example, yelling"Hey stop that!", as opposed to whis-pering"Hey stop that". Vocal segregates such as"uh-huh" notify the speaker that the listener is listening.

**Functions of Nonverbal communication**

Argyle put forward the hypothesis that whereas spoken language is normally used for communicating information about events external to the speakers, non-verbal codes are used to establish and maintain interpersonal relationships. It is considered more polite or nicer to communicate attitudes towards others non-verbally rather than verbally, for instance in order to avoid embarrassing situations.

*Argyle concluded there are five primary functions of nonverbal bodily behaviour in human communication*:

- Express emotions
- Express interpersonal attitudes

- To accompany speech in managing the cues of interaction between speakers and listeners
- Self-presentation of one's personality
- Rituals (greetings)

### Concealing Deception

Nonverbal communication makes it easier to lie without being revealed. This is the conclusion of a study where people watched made-up interviews of persons accused of having stolen a wallet. The interviewees lied in about 50 per cent of the cases. People had access to either written transcripts of the interviews, or audio tape recordings, or video recordings.

The more clues that were available to those watching, the larger was the trend that interviewees who actually lied were judged to be truthful. That is, people that are clever at lying can use voice tone and face expression to give the impression that they are truthful

### The Relation Between Verbal and Nonverbal Communication

An interesting question is: When two people are communicating face-to-face, how much of the meaning is communicated verbally, and how much is communicated non-verbally? This was investigated by Albert Mehrabian and reported in two papers.

The latter paper concluded:"It is suggested that the combined effect of simultaneous verbal, vocal, and facial attitude communications is a weighted sum of their independent effects - with coefficients of.07.38, and.55, respectively." This"rule" that clues from spoken words, from the voice tone, and from the facial expression, contribute 7 per cent, 38 per cent, and 55 per cent respectively to the total meaning, is widely cited. It is presented on all types of popular courses with statements like"scientists have found out that...". In reality, however, it is extremely weakly founded. First, it is based on the judgment of the meaning of single taperecorded words, i.e. a very artificial context.

Second, the figures are obtained by combining results from two different studies which maybe cannot be combined. Third, it relates only to the communication of positive versus negative emotions. Fourth, it relates only to women, as men did not participate in the study. Since then, other studies have analysed the relative contribution of verbal and nonverbal signals under more naturalistic situations. Argyle, using video tapes shown to the subjects, analysed the communication of submissive/dominant attitude and found that non-verbal cues had 4.3 times the effect of verbal cues.

The most important effect was that body posture communicated superior status in a very efficient way. On the other hand, a study by Hsee et al. had subjects judge a person on the dimension happy/sad and found that words spoken with minimal variation in intonation had an impact about 4 times larger than face expressions seen in a film without sound. Thus, the relative importance of spoken words and facial expressions may be very different in studies using different set-ups.

## Interaction of Verbal and Nonverbal Communication

When communicating, nonverbal messages can interact with verbal messages in six ways: repeating, conflicting, complementing, substituting, regulating and accenting/moderating.

### *Repeating*

"Repeating" consists of using gestures to strengthen a verbal message, such as pointing to the object of discussion.

### *Conflicting*

Verbal and nonverbal messages within the same interaction can sometimes send opposing or conflicting messages. A person verbally expressing a statement of truth while simultaneously fidgeting or avoiding eye contact may convey a mixed message to the receiver in the interaction. Conflicting messages may occur for a variety of reasons often stemming from feelings of uncertainty, ambivalence, or frustration. When mixed messages occur, nonverbal communication becomes the primary tool people use to attain additional information to clarify the situation; great attention is placed on bodily movements and positioning when people perceive mixed messages during interactions.

### *Complementing*

Accurate interpretation of messages is made easier when nonverbal and verbal communication complement each other. Nonverbal cues can be used to elaborate on verbal messages to reinforce the information sent when trying to achieve communicative goals; messages have been shown to be remembered better when nonverbal signals affirm the verbal exchange.

### *Substituting*

Nonverbal behaviour is sometimes used as the sole channel for communication of a message. People learn to identify facial expressions, body movements, and body positioning as corresponding with specific feelings and intentions. Nonverbal signals can be used without verbal communication to convey messages; when nonverbal behaviour does not effectively communicate a message, verbal methods are used to enhance understanding.

### *Regulating*

Nonverbal behaviour also regulates our conversations. For example, touching someone's arm can signal that you want to talk next or interrupt.

### *Accenting/Moderating*

Nonverbal signals are used to alter the interpretation of verbal messages. Touch, voice pitch, and gestures are some of the tools people use to accent or amplify the message that is sent; nonverbal behaviour can also be used to moderate or tone down aspects of verbal messages as well. For example, a person who is verbally expressing anger may accent the verbal message by shaking a fist.

## Dance and Nonverbal Communication

Dance is a form of nonverbal communication that requires the same underlying faculty in the brain for conceptualization, creativity and memory as does verbal language in speaking and writing. Means of self-expression, both forms have vocabulary (steps and gestures in dance), grammar (rules for putting the vocabulary together) and meaning. Dance, however, assembles (choreographs) these elements in a manner that more often resembles poetry, with its ambiguity and multiple, symbolic and elusive meanings.

### *Clinical Studies of Nonverbal Communication*

From 1977 to 2004, the influence of disease and drugs on receptivity of nonverbal communication was studied by teams at three separate medical schools using a similar paradigm..Researchers at the University of Pittsburgh, Yale University and Ohio State University had subjects observe gamblers at a slot machine awaiting payoffs.

The amount of this payoff was read by nonverbal transmission prior to reinforcement. This technique was developed by and the studies directed by psychologist, Dr. Robert E. Miller and psychiatrist, Dr. A. James Giannini. These groups reported diminished receptive ability in heroin addicts and phencyclidine abusers was contrasted with increased receptivity in cocaine addicts. Men with major depression manifested signicantly decreased ability to read nonverbal cues when compared with euthymic men. Freitas-Magalhaes studied the effect of smile in the treatment of depression and concluded that depressive states decrease when you smile more often.

Obese women and women with premenstrual syndrome were found to also possess diminished abilities to read these cues. In contradistinction, men with bipolar disorder possessed increased abilities.. A woman with total paralysis of the nerves of facial expression was found unable to transmit any nonverbal facial cues whatsoever.. Because of the changes in levels of accuracy on the levels of nonverbal receptivity, the members of the research team hypothesized a biochemical site in the brain which was operative for reception of nonverbal cues.

Because certain drugs enhanced ability while others diminished it, the neurotransmitters dopamine and endorphin were considered to be likely etiological candidate. Based on the available data, however, the primary cause and primary effect could not be sorted out on the basis of the paradigm employed. A byproduct of the work of the Pittsburgh/Yale/ Ohio State team was an investigation of the role of nonverbal facial cues in heterosexual nondate rape. Males who were serial rapists of adult women were studied for nonverbal receptive abilities.

Their scores were the highest of any subgroup. Rape victims were next tested. It was reported that women who had been raped on at least two occasions by different perpetrators had a highly significant impairment in their abilities to read these cues in either male or female senders. These results were troubling, indicating a predator-prey model. The authors did note that whatever the nature of these preliminary findings the responsibility of the rapist was in no manner or level,diminished.

The final target of study for this group was the medical students they taught. Medical students at Ohio State University, Ohio University and Northest Ohio Medical College were invited to serve as subjects. Students indicating a preference for the specialties of family practice, psychiatry, pediatrics and obstetrics-gynecology achieved significantly higher levels of accuracy than those students who planned to train as surgeons, radiologists, or pathologists. Internal medicine and plastic surgery candidates scored at levels near the mean.

### *Difficulties with Nonverbal Communication*

People vary in their ability to send and receive nonverbal communication. Thus, on average, to a moderate degree, women are better at nonverbal communication than are men. Measurements of the ability to communicate nonverbally and the capacity to feel empathy have shown that the two abilities are independent of each other. For people who have relatively large difficulties with nonverbal communication, this can pose significant challenges, especially in interpersonal relationships. There exist resources that are tailored specifically to these people, which attempt to assist those in understanding information which comes more easily to others. A specific group of persons that face these challenges are those with autism spectrum disorders, including Asperger syndrome.

## NON-VERBAL COMMUNICATION

When Demosthenes was asked what was the first part of oratory he answered,"'action"; and which was the second, he replied,"action"; and which was third he still answered," action." People tend to believe actions more than words! Have you ever heard anyone say,"His actions spoke so loudly I couldn't hear what he said?" Have you ever wondered whether anyone has said this about you? What we do is a means of communication, subject to interpretation by others. Did you ever stop to think that even failure to act is a way of communicating?

Today, many researchers are concerned with the information sent by communication that is independent of and different from verbal information; namely, the non-verbal communication. Verbal communication is organized by language; non-verbal communication is not.

Communication is the transfer of information from one person to another. Most of us spend about 75 per cent of our waking hours communicating our knowledge, thoughts, and ideas to others. However, most of us fail to realise that a great deal of our communication is of a non-verbal form as opposed to the oral and written forms. Non-verbal communication includes facial expressions, eye contact, tone of voice, body posture and motions, and positioning within groups. It may also include the way we wear our clothes or the silence we keep.

In person-to-person communications our messages are sent on two levels simultaneously. If the nonverbal cues and the spoken message are incongruous, the flow of communication is hindered. Right or wrong, the receiver of the communication tends to base the intentions of the sender on the non- verbal cues he receives.

## Categories and Features

*G. W. Porter divides non-verbal communication into four broad categories*:

- *Physical*: This is the personal type of communication. It includes facial expressions, tone of voice, sense of touch, sense of smell, and body motions.
- *Aesthetic*: This is the type of communication that takes place through creative expressions: playing instru-mental music, dancing, painting and sculpturing.
- *Signs*: This is the mechanical type of communication, which includes the use of signal flags, the 21-gun salute, horns, and sirens.
- *Symbolic*: This is the type of communication that makes use of religious, status, or ego-building symbols.

Our concern here will be with what Porter has called the physical method of non-verbal communication.

*Knowledge of non-verbal communication is important managers who serve as leaders of organizational"teams," for at least two reasons*:

- To function effectively as a team leader the manager must interact with the other members successfully. Non-verbal cues, when interpreted correctly, provide him with one means to do so.
- The team members project attitudes and feelings through non-verbal communication. Some personal needs such as approval, growth, achievement, and recognition may be met in effective teams. The extent to which these needs are met is closely related to how perceptive the team leader and team members are to non-verbal communication in themselves and in others on the team.

If the team members show a true awareness to non-verbal cues, the organization will have a better chance to succeed, for it will be an open, honest, and confronting unit. Argyle and his associates have been studying the features of nonverbal communication that provide information to managers and their team members. The following summarizes their findings:

*Static Features*:

- *Distance*: Distance. The distance one stands from another frequently conveys a non-verbal message. In some cultures it is a sign of attraction, while in others it may reflect status or the intensity of the exchange.
- *Orientation*: People may present themselves in various ways: face-to-face, side-to-side, or even back-to-back. For example, cooperating people are likely to sit side-by-side while competitors frequently face one another.
- *Posture*: Obviously one can be lying down, seated, or standing. These are not the elements of posture that convey messages. Are we slouched or erect ? Are our legs crossed or our arms folded ? Such postures convey a degree of formality and the degree of relaxation in the communication exchange.
- *Physical Contact*: Shaking hands, touching, holding, embracing, pushing, or patting on the back all convey messages. They reflect an element of intimacy or a feeling of (or lack of) attraction.

*Dynamic Features*:

- *Facial Expressions*: Facial Expressions. A smile, frown, raised eyebrow, yawn, and sneer all convey information. Facial expressions continually change during interaction and are monitored constantly by the recipient. There is evidence that the meaning of these expressions may be similar across cultures.
- *Gestures*: One of the most frequently observed, but least understood, cues is a hand movement. Most people use hand movements regularly when talking. While some gestures (e.g., a clenched fist) have universal meanings, most of the others are individually learned and idiosyncratic.
- *Looking*: A major feature of social communication is eye contact. It can convey emotion, signal when to talk or finish, or aversion. The frequency of contact may suggest either interest or boredom.

The above list shows that both static features and dynamic features transmit important information from the sender to the receiver.

### *Kinesics*

Lamb believes the best way to access an executive's managerial potential is not to listen to what he has to say, but to observe what he does when he is saying it. He calls this new behavioral science"movement analysis."

*Some of the movements and gestures he has analysed follow:*

- Forward and Backward Movements. If you extend a hand straight forward during an interview or tend to lean forward, Lamb considers you to be an"operator"- good for an organization requiring an infusion of energy or dramatic change of course.
- Vertical Movements. If you tend to draw yourself up to your tallest during the handshake, Lamb considers you to be a"presenter." You are a master at selling yourself or the organization in which you are employed.
- Side-to-Side Movements. If you take a lot of space while talking by moving your arms about, you are a good informer and good listener. You are best suited for an organization seeking a better sense of direction. Lamb believes there is a relationship between positioning of the body and movements of the limbs and facial expressions. He has observed harmony between the two. On the other hand, if certain gestures are rehearsed, such as those made to impress others, there is a tendency to separate the posture and the movements. The harmony disappears.

Studies by Lamb also indicate that communication comes about through our degree of body flexibility. If you begin a movement with considerable force and then decelerate, you are considered a"gentle-touch." By contrast, if you are a"pressurizer," you are firm from beginning to end. The accuracy of Lamb's analyses is not fully known. However, it is important that corporation executives are becoming so sensitive to the importance of non-verbal messages that they are hiring consultants, such as Lamb, to analyse non-verbal communications in their organizations.

### Facial Expressions

Facial expressions usually communicate emotions. The expressions tell the attitudes of the communicator. Researchers have discovered that certain facial areas reveal our emotional state better than others. For example, the eyes tend to reveal happiness or sadness, and even surprise. The lower face also can reveal happiness or surprise; the smile, for example, can communicate friendliness and cooperation. The lower face, brows, and forehead can also reveal anger. Mehrabian believes verbal cues provide 7 per cent of the meaning of the message; vocal cues, 38 per cent; and facial expressions, 55 per cent. This means that, as the receiver of a message, you can rely heavily on the facial expressions of the sender because his expressions are a better indicator of the meaning behind the message than his words.

### Eye Contact

Eye contact is a direct and powerful form of non-verbal communication. The superior in the organization generally maintains eye contact longer than the subordinate. The direct stare of the sender of the message conveys candor and openness. It elicits a feeling of trust. Downward glances are generally associated with modesty. Eyes rolled upward are associated with fatigue.

## Tactile Communication

Communication through touch is obviously non-verbal. Used properly it can create a more direct message than dozens of words; used improperly it can build barriers and cause mistrust. You can easily invade someone's space through this type of communication. If it is used reciprocally, it indicates solidarity; if not used reciprocally, it tends to indicate differences in status. Touch not only facilitates the sending of the message, but the emotional impact of the message as well.

## Personal Space

Personal space is your"bubble" - the space you place between yourself and others. This invisible boundary becomes apparent only when someone bumps or tries to enter your bubble. How you identify your personal space and use the environment in which you find yourself influences your ability to send or receive messages.

How close do you stand to the one with whom you are communicating ? Where do you sit in the room ? How do you position yourself with respect to others at a meeting ? All of these things affect your level of comfort, and the level of comfort of those receiving your message. Goldhaber says there are three basic principles that summarize the use of personal space in an organization.

*The higher your position (status) in the organization*:

- The more and better space you will have,
- The better protected your territory will be, and
- The easier it will be to invade the territory of lower-status personnel.

The impact of use of space on the communication process is related directly to the environment in which the space is maintained.

## Environment

How do you arrange the objects in your environment - the desks, chairs, tables, and bookcases? The design of your office, according to researchers, can greatly affect the communications within it. Some managers divide their offices into personal and impersonal areas. This can improve the communication process if the areas are used for the purposes intended. Your pecking-order in the organization is frequently determined by such things as the size of your desk, square feet in your office, number of windows in the office, quality of the carpet, and type of paintings (originals or copies) on the wall. It is obvious that your personal space and environment affect the level of your comfort and your status and facilitate or hinder the communication process.

## Paralanguage

Is the content of your message contradicted by the attitude with which you are communicating it? Researchers have found that the tone, pitch, quality of voice, and rate of speaking convey emotions that can be accurately judged regardless of the content of the message. The important thing to gain from this is that the voice is important, not just as the conveyor of the message, but as a complement to the message. As a communicator you should be sensitive to the influence of tone, pitch, and quality of your voice on the interpretation of your message by the receiver.

## Silence and Time

Silence can be a positive or negative influence in the communications process. It can provide a link between messages or sever relationships. It can create tension and uneasiness or create a peaceful situation. Silence can also be judgmental by indicating favour or disfavor - agreement or disagreement.

For example, suppose a manager finds a couple of his staff members resting. If he believes these staff members are basically lazy, the idleness conveys to him that they are"goofing off" and should be given additional assignments. If he believes these staff members are self-motivated and good workers, the idleness conveys to him that they are taking a well-deserved"break." If he is personally insecure, the idleness conveys to him that they are threatening his authority.

Time can be an indicator of status. How long will you give the staff member who wishes to speak to you ? How long will you make him wait to see you ? Do you maintain a schedule? Is your schedule such that your subordinates must arrange their schedules to suit yours ? In a healthy organization, the manager and his subordinates use time to communicate their mutual respect to each other.

## Closing Thoughts

Regardless of your position in the organization it is important for you to develop some sensitivity to nonverbal messages. Cooperation improves as we recognize and respond appropriately to non-verbal cues. Of course you have been aware of non-verbal communications all of your life, but how much thought have you given them?

# NONVERBAL COMMUNICATION SKILLS

## The Power of Nonverbal Communication and Body Language

Good communication is the foundation of successful relationships, both personally and professionally. But we communicate with much more than words. In fact, research shows that the majority of our communication is nonverbal. Nonverbal communication, or body language, includes our facial expressions, gestures, eye contact, posture, and even the tone of our voice.

The ability to understand and use nonverbal communi-cation is a powerful tool that will help you connect with others, express what you really mean, navigate challenging situations, and build better relationships at home and work.

Nonverbal communication, or body language, is a vital form of communication. When we interact with others, we continuously give and receive countless wordless signals. All of our nonverbal behaviors-the gestures we make, the way we sit, how fast or how loud we talk, how close we stand, how much eye contact we make-send strong messages.

The way you listen, look, move, and react tell the other person whether or not you care and how well you're listening. The nonverbal signals you send either produce a sense of interest, trust, and desire for connection-or they generate disinterest, distrust, and confusion.

*Nonverbal communication cues can play five roles*:

- *Repetition*: they can repeat the message the person is making verbally
- *Contradiction*: they can contradict a message the individual is trying to convey
- *Substitution*: they can substitute for a verbal message. For example, a person's eyes can often convey a far more vivid message than words and often do
- *Complementing*: they may add to or complement a verbal message. A boss who pats a person on the back in addition to giving praise can increase the impact of the message
- *Accenting*: they may accent or underline a verbal message. Pounding the table, for example, can underline a message.

## Nonverbal Communication and Body Language in Relationships

It takes more than words to create fulfilling, strong relationships. Nonverbal communication has a huge impact on the quality of our relationships. Nonverbal communication skills improve relationships by helping you:

- Accurately read other people, including the emotions they're feeling and the unspoken messages they're sending.
- Create trust and transparency in relationships by sending nonverbal signals that match up with your words.
- Respond with nonverbal cues that show others that you understand, notice, and care.

Unfortunately, many people send confusing or negative nonverbal signals without even knowing it. When this happens, both connection and trust are lost in our relationships.

### Consider the Case of Arlene

Arlene is attractive and has no problem meeting eligible men - it's keeping them that is the problem! Arlene is funny and a good conversationalist, but even though she laughs and smiles constantly, she radiates tension. Arlene's shoulders and eyebrows are noticeably raised, her voice is shrill and her body stiff to touch.

Being around Arlene makes many people feel uncomfortable. Arlene has a lot going for her that is undercut by the discomfort she evokes in others. Arlene is articulate, attractive, and well-intentioned, but she struggles to connect with others because she isn't aware of the nonverbal messages she's communicating.

But she can break this pattern if she learns to pay attention to the wordless signals she sends and receives: Arlene notices that her date is tapping his fingers and that she has been swinging her leg and foot. He looks bored, and she feels tense all over.

Taking a long, deep breath and a swallow of wine, she feels her shoulders drop and her jaw relax. Arlene leans across the table and breaks into a warm smile. Her date smiles back, and their eyes meet and hold. She has also used her new observational skills at work and is now much more comfortable interacting with others in that setting.

### Types of Nonverbal Communication and Body Language

There are many different types of nonverbal communi-cation. Together, the following nonverbal signals and cues communicate your interest and investment in others.

#### *Facial Expressions*

The human face is extremely expressive, able to express countless emotions without saying a word. And unlike some forms of nonverbal communication, facial expressions are universal. The facial expressions for happiness, sadness, anger, surprise, fear, and disgust are the same across cultures.

#### *Body Movements and Posture*

Consider how your perceptions of people are affected by the way they sit, walk, stand up, or hold their head. The way you move and carry yourself communicates a wealth of information to the world. This type of nonverbal communication includes your posture, bearing, stance, and subtle movements.

#### *Gestures*

Gestures are woven into the fabric of our daily lives. We wave, point, beckon, and use our hands when we're arguing or speaking animatedly-

expressing ourselves with gestures often without thinking. However, the meaning of gestures can be very different across cultures and regions, so it's important to be careful to avoid misinterpretation.

***Eye contact***

Since the visual sense is dominant for most people, eye contact is an especially important type of nonverbal communication. The way you look at someone can communicate many things, including interest, affection, hostility, or attraction. Eye contact is also important in maintaining the flow of conversation and for gauging the other person's response.

***Touch***

We communicate a great deal through touch. Think about the messages given by the following: a firm handshake, a timid tap on the shoulder, a warm bear hug, a reassuring pat on the back, a patronizing pat on the head, or a controlling grip on your arm.

***Space***

Have you ever felt uncomfortable during a conversation because the other person was standing too close and invading your space? We all have a need for physical space, although that need differs depending on the culture, the situation, and the closeness of the relationship. You can use physical space to communicate many different nonverbal messages, including signals of intimacy, aggression, dominance, or affection.

***Voice***

We communicate with our voices, even when we are not using words. Nonverbal speech sounds such as tone, pitch, volume, inflection, rhythm, and rate are important communication elements. When we speak, other people"read" our voices in addition to listening to our words. These nonverbal speech sounds provide subtle but powerful clues into our true feelings and what we really mean. Think about how tone of voice, for example, can indicate sarcasm, anger, affection, or confidence.

*It's not what you say, it's how you say it*:

- Intensity. A reflection of the amount of energy you project is considered your intensity. Again, this has as much to do with what feels good to the other person as what you personally prefer.
- Timing and pace. Your ability to be a good listener and communicate interest and involvement is impacted by timing and pace.
- Sounds that convey understanding. Sounds such as"ahhh, ummm, ohhh," uttered with congruent eye and facial gestures, communicate understanding and emotional connection. More than words, these sounds are the language of interest, understanding and compassion.

## Using Body Language and Nonverbal Communication Successfully

### *A Nonverbal Role Play Exercise*

Nonverbal communication is a rapidly flowing back-and-forth process. Successful nonverbal communication depends on emotional self-awareness and an understanding of the cues you're sending, along with the ability to accurately pick up on the cues others are sending you. This requires your full concentration and attention. If you are planning what you're going to say next, daydreaming, or thinking about something else, you are almost certain to miss nonverbal cues and other subtleties in the conversation. You need to stay focused on the moment-to-moment experience in order to fully understand what's going on.

*Tips for successful nonverbal communication*:

- Take a time out if you're feeling overwhelmed by stress. Stress compromises your ability to communicate. When you're stressed out, you're more likely to misread other people, send off confusing or off-putting nonverbal signals, and lapse into unhealthy knee-jerk patterns of behaviour. Take a moment to calm down before you jump back into the conversation. Once you've regained your emotional equilibrium, you'll be better equipped to deal with the situation in a positive way.
- Pay attention to inconsistencies. Nonverbal communi-cation should reinforce what is being said. If you get the feeling that someone isn't being honest or that something is"off," you may be picking up on a mismatch between verbal and nonverbal cues. Is the person is saying one thing, and their body language something else? For example, are they telling you"yes" while shaking their head no?
- Look at nonverbal communication signals as a group. Don't read too much into a single gesture or nonverbal cue. Consider all of the nonverbal signals you are sending and receiving, from eye contact to tone of voice and body language. Are your nonverbal cues consistent-or inconsistent-with what you are trying to communicate?

*Nonverbal communication and body language: Common mistakes*:

- You're not subtle. Be objective about your own observations to make sure you aren't offending others by broadly mimicking their speech or behaviour. Remember, most people instinctively send and interpret nonverbal signals all the time, so don't assume you're the only one who's aware of nonverbal undercurrents. Finally, stay true to yourself. Be aware of your own natural style, and don't adopt behaviour that is incompatible with it.
- You bluff. Thinking you can bluff by deliberately altering your body language can do more harm than good. Unless you're a proficient

actor, it will be hard to overcome your body's inability to lie. There will always be mixed messages, signs that your channels of communication are not congruent. It's a prime example of leakage, and something others will detect, one way or another.

- You rush to accuse based on body language alone. Incorrect accusations based on erroneous observations can be embarrassing and damaging and take a long time to overcome. Always verify your interpretation with another communications channel before rushing in. You could say something like,"I get the feeling you're uncomfortable with this course of action. Would you like to add something to the discussion?" This should draw out the real message and force the individual to come clean or to adjust his or her body language.

## Improving your Nonverbal Communication Skills

Before you can improve your nonverbal communication skills, you need to figure out what you're doing right and where there is room for improvement. The most effective method is to observe yourself in action:

- *Video camera*: Videotape a conversation between you and a partner. Set the camera to record both of you at the same time, so you can observe the nonverbal back-and-forth. When you watch the recording, focus on any discrepancies between your verbal and nonverbal communication.
- *Digital camera*: Ask someone to take a series of photos of you while you're talking to someone else. As you look through the photos, focus on you and the other person's body language, facial expressions, and gestures.
- *Audio recorder*: Record a conversation between you and a friend or family member. As you listen to the recording afterwards, concentrate on the way things are said, rather than the words. Pay attention to tone, timing, pace, and other sounds.

*As you watch or listen to the recordings, ask yourself the following questions*:

- *Eye contact*: Is this source of connection missing, too intense, or just right in yourself or in the person you are looking at?
- *Facial expression*: What is your face showing? Is it masklike and unexpressive, or emotionally present and filled with interest? What do you see as you look into the faces of others?
- *Tone of voice*: Does your voice project warmth, confidence, and delight, or is it strained and blocked? What do you hear as you listen to other people?
- *Posture and gesture*: Does your body look still and immobile, or relaxed? Sensing the degree of tension in your shoulders and jaw answers this question. What do you observe about the degree of tension or relaxation in the body of the person you are speaking to?

- *Touch*: Remember, what feels good is relative. How do you like to be touched? Who do you like to have touching you? Is the difference between what you like and what the other person likes obvious to you?
- *Intensity*: Do you or the person you are communicating with seem flat, cool, and disinterested, or over-the-top and melodramatic? Again, this has as much to do with what feels good to the other person as it does with what you personally prefer.
- *Timing and pace*: What happens when you or someone you care about makes an important statement? Does a response-not necessarily verbal-come too quickly or too slowly? Is there an easy flow of information back and forth?
- *Sounds*: Do you use sounds to indicate that you are attending to the other person? Do you pick up on sounds from others that indicate their caring or concern for you?

The point of this exercise is to develop your nonverbal awareness. As you continue to pay attention to the nonverbal cues and signals you send and receive, your ability to communicate will improve.

## Nonverbal Communication is one of the Five Key Skills of Emotional Intelligence

### *The Five Skills of Emotional Intelligence*

- *Skill* 1: Quick Stress Relief
- *Skill* 2: Emotional Awareness
- *Skill* 3: Nonverbal Communication
- *Skill* 4: Playful Communication
- *Skill* 5: Conflict Resolution

The ability to communicate nonverbally is the third of five essential emotional intelligence skills. Together, the five skills of emotional intelligence help you build strong relationships, overcome challenges, and succeed at work and in life. The fourth key skill of emotional intelligence is the ability to use humour and play to deal with challenges. Playful communi-cation helps you bounce back from adversity, boost your energy and your spirits, come up with creative ways to solve problems, and keep your relationships fresh and exciting.

## Top 10 Nonverbal Communication Tips

Good communication skills can help you in both your personal and professional life. While verbal and written communication skills are important, research has shown that nonverbal behaviors make up a large percentage of our daily interpersonal communication. How can you improve your nonverbal communication skills?

The following top ten tips for nonverbal communication can help you learn to read the nonverbal signals of other people and enhance your own ability to communicate effectively.

- *Pay Attention to Nonverbal Signals*: People can communicate information in numerous ways; so pay attention to things like eye contact, gestures, posture, body movements, and tone of voice. All of these signals can convey important information that isn't put into words. By paying closer attention to other people's nonverbal behaviors, you will improve your own ability to communicate nonverbally.
- *Look for Incongruent Behaviors*: If someone's words do not match their nonverbal behaviors, you should pay careful attention. For example, someone might tell you they are happy while frowning and staring at the ground. Research has shown that when words fail to match up with nonverbal signals, people tend to ignore what has been said and focus instead on nonverbal expressions of moods, thoughts, and emotions.
- *Concentrate on Your Tone of Voice When Speaking*: Your tone of voice can convey a wealth of information, ranging from enthusiasm to disinterest to anger. Start noticing how your tone of voice affects how others respond to you and try using tone of voice to emphasize ideas that you want to communicate. For example, if you want to show genuine interest in something, express your enthusiasm by using an animated tone of voice.
- *Use Good Eye Contact*: When people fail to look others in the eye, it can seem as if they are evading or trying to hide something. On the other hand, too much eye contact can seem confrontational or intimidating. While eye contact is an important part of communication, it's important to remember that good eye contact does not mean staring fixedly into someone's eyes. How can you tell how much eye contact is correct? Some communication experts recommend intervals of eye contact lasting four to five seconds.
- *Ask Questions About Nonverbal Signals*: If you are confused about another person's nonverbal signals, don't be afraid to ask questions. A good idea is to repeat back your interpretation of what has been said and ask for clarification. An example of this might be,"So what you are saying is that..."
- *Use Signals to Make Communication More Effective and Meaningful*: Remember that verbal and nonverbal communication work together to convey a message. You can improve your spoken communication by using nonverbal signals and gestures that reinforce and support what you are saying. This can be especially useful when making presentations or when speaking to a large group of people.

- *Look at Signals as a Group*: A single gesture can mean any number of things, or maybe even nothing at all. The key to accurately reading nonverbal behaviour is to look for groups of signals that reinforce a common point. If you place too much emphasis on just one signal out of many, you might come to an inaccurate conclusion about what a person is trying to communicate.
- *Consider Context*: When you are communicating with others, always consider the situation and the context in which the communication occurs. Some situations require more formal behaviors that might be interpreted very differently in any other setting. Consider whether or not nonverbal behaviors are appropriate for the context. If you are trying to improve your own nonverbal communication, concentrate on ways to make your signals match the level of formality necessitated by the situation.
- *Be Aware That Signals Can be Misread*: According to some, a firm handshake indicates a strong personality while a weak handshake is taken as a lack of fortitude. This example illustrates an important point about the possibility of misreading nonverbal signals. A limp handshake might actually indicate something else entirely, such as arthritis. Always remember to look for groups of behaviour. A person's overall demeanor is far more telling than a single gesture viewed in isolation.
- *Practice, Practice, Practice*: Some people just seem to have a knack for using nonverbal communication effectively and correctly interpreting signals from others. These people are often described as being able to"read people." In reality, you can build this skill by paying careful attention to nonverbal behaviour and practicing different types of nonverbal communication with others. By noticing nonverbal behaviour and practicing your own skills, you can dramatically improve your communication abilities.

## NON-VERBAL COMMUICATION MODES

Definition (CBC):"nonverbal communication involves those nonverbal stimuli in a communication setting that are generated by both the source [speaker] and his or her use of the environment and that have potential message value for the source or receiver [listener] (Samovar et al). Basically it is sending and receiving messages in a variety of ways without the use of verbal codes (words). It is both intentional and unintentional. Most speakers/ listeners are not conscious of this.

*It includes - but is not limited to*:

- Touch
- Glance
- Eye contact (gaze)

- Volume
- Vocal nuance
- Proximity
- Gestures
- Facial expression ? pause (silence)
- Intonation
- Dress
- Posture
- Smell
- Word choice and syntax
- Sounds (paralanguage)

*Broadly speaking, there are two basic categories of non-verbal language*:

- Nonverbal messages produced by the body;
- Nonverbal messages produced by the broad setting (time, space, silence)

**Importance of Non-verbal Communication**

Basically, it is one of the key aspects of communication (and especially important in a high-context culture).

*It has multiple functions*:

- Used to repeat the verbal message (e.g. point in a direction while stating directions.
- Often used to accent a verbal message. (e.g. verbal tone indicates the actual meaning of the specific words).
- Often complement the verbal message but also may contradict. E.g.: a nod reinforces a positive message (among Americans); a"wink" may contradict a stated positive message.
- Regulate interactions (non-verbal cues covey when the other person should speak or not speak).
- May substitute for the verbal message (especially if it is blocked by noise, interruption, etc) - i.e. gestures (finger to lips to indicate need for quiet), facial expressions (i.e. a nod instead of a yes).

Note the implications of the proverb:"Actions speak louder than words." In essence, this underscores the importance of non-verbal communication. Non-verbal communication is especially significant in intercultural situations. Probably non-verbal differences account for typical difficulties in communicating.

**Cultural Differences in Non-verbal Communication**

***General Appearance and Dress***

All cultures are concerned for how they look and make judgements based on looks and dress. Americans, for instance, appear almost obsessed with dress and personal attractiveness. Consider differing cultural standards on what is attractive in dress and on what constitutes modesty. Note ways dress is used as a sign of status?

### *Body Movement*

We send information on attitude toward person (facing or leaning towards another), emotional statue (tapping fingers, jiggling coins), and desire to control the environment (moving towards or away from a person).

More than 700,000 possible motions we can make - so impossible to categorize them all! But just need to be aware the body movement and position is a key ingredient in sending messages.

### *Posture*

*Consider the following actions and note cultural differences*:

- Bowing (not done, criticized, or affected in US; shows rank in Japan)
- Slouching (rude in most Northern European areas)
- Hands in pocket (disrespectful in Turkey)
- Sitting with legs crossed (offensive in Ghana, Turkey)
- Showing soles of feet. (Offensive in Thailand, Saudi Arabia)
- Even in US, there is a gender difference on acceptable posture?

### *Gestures*

*Impossible to catalog them all. But need to recognize*:

- Incredible possibility and variety
- That an acceptable in one's own culture may be offensive in another.

In addition, amount of gesturing varies from culture to culture. Some cultures are animated; other restrained. Restrained cultures often feel animated cultures lack manners and overall restraint. Animated cultures often feel restrained cultures lack emotion or interest.

*Even simple things like using hands to point and count differ*:

- *Pointing*: US with index finger; Germany with little finger; Japanese with entire hand (in fact most Asians consider pointing with index finger to be rude)
- *Counting*: Thumb = 1 in Germany, 5 in Japan, middle finger for 1 in Indonesia.

### *Facial Expressions*

While some say that facial expressions are identical, meaning attached to them differs. Majority opinion is that these do have similar meanings world-wide with respect to smiling, crying, or showing anger, sorrow, or disgust. However, the intensity varies from culture to culture.

*Note the following*:

- Many Asian cultures suppress facial expression as much as possible.

- Many Mediterranean (Latino/ Arabic) cultures exaggerate grief or sadness while most American men hide grief or sorrow.
- Some see"animated" expressions as a sign of a lack of control.
- Too much smiling is viewed in as a sign of shallowness.
- Women smile more than men.

### *Eye Contact and Gaze*

In USA, eye contact indicates: degree of attention or interest, influences attitude change or persuasion, regulates interaction, communicates emotion, defines power and status, and has a central role in managing impressions of others.

- *Western cultures*: See direct eye to eye contact as positive (advise children to look a person in the eyes). But within USA, African-Americans use more eye contact when talking and less when listening with reverse true for Anglo Americans. This is a possible cause for some sense of unease between races in US. A prolonged gaze is often seen as a sign of sexual interest.
- *Arabic cultures make prolonged eye-contact*: Believe it shows interest and helps them understand truth-fulness of the other person. (A person who doesn't reciprocate is seen as untrustworthy)
- *Japan, Africa, Latin American, Caribbean*: Avoid eye contact to show respect.

### *Touch*

*Question*: Why do we touch, where do we touch, and what meanings do we assign when someone else touches us?

*Illustration*: An African-American male goes into a convenience store recently taken over by new Korean immigrants.

He gives a $20 bill for his purchase to Mrs Cho who is cashier and waits for his change. He is upset when his change is put down on the counter in front of him.

What is the problem? Traditional Korean (and many other Asian countries) don't touch strangers., especially between members of the opposite sex. But the African-American sees this as another example of discrimination (not touching him because he is black).

- *Basic answer*: Touch is culturally determined! But each culture has a clear concept of what parts of the body one may not touch. Basic message of touch is to affect or control - protect, support, disapprove (i.e. hug, kiss, hit, kick).
  - *USA*: Handshake is common (even for strangers), hugs, kisses for those of opposite gender or of family (usually) on an increasingly more intimate basis. Note differences between African-Americans and Anglos in USA. Most African Americans

touch on greeting but are annoyed if touched on the head (good boy, good girl overtones).
  - *Islamic and Hindu*: typically don't touch with the left hand. To do so is a social insult. Left hand is for toilet functions. Mannerly in India to break your bread only with your right hand (sometimes difficult for non-Indians)
  - Islamic cultures generally don't approve of any touching between genders (even hand shakes). But consider such touching (including hand holding, hugs) between same-sex to be appropriate.
  - Many Asians don't touch the head (Head houses the soul and a touch puts it in jeopardy).
- *Basic patterns*: Cultures (English, German, Scandinavian, Chinese, Japanese) with high emotional restraint concepts have little public touch; those which encourage emotion (Latino, Middle-East, Jewish) accept frequent touches.

### *Smell*

- *USA*: Fear of offensive natural smells (billion dollar industry to mask objectionable odors with what is perceived to be pleasant) - again connected with"attractiveness" concept.
- Many other cultures consider natural body odors as normal (Arabic).
- Asian cultures (Filipino, Malay, Indonesian, Thai, Indian) stress frequent bathing - and often criticize USA of not bathing often enough!

### *Paralanguage*

- Vocal characterizers (laugh, cry, yell, moan, whine, belch, yawn). These send different messages in different cultures (Japan - giggling indicates embarrassment; India - belch indicates satisfaction)
- Vocal qualifiers (volume, pitch, rhythm, tempo, and tone). Loudness indicates strength in Arabic cultures and softness indicates weakness; indicates confidence and authority to the Germans,; indicates impoliteness to the Thais; indicates loss of control to the Japanese. (Generally, one learns not to"shout" in Asia for nearly any reason!). Gender based as well: women tend to speak higher and more softly than men.
- Vocal segregates (un-huh, shh, uh, ooh, mmmh, humm, eh, mah, lah). Segregates indicate formality, acceptance, assent, uncertainty.

## CROSS-CULTURAL COMMUNICATION

11 communication is cultural — it draws on ways we have learned to speak and give nonverbal messages. We do not always communicate the same

way from day to day, since factors like context, individual personality, and mood interact with the variety of cultural influences we have internalized that influence our choices. Communication is interactive, so an important influence on its effectiveness is our relationship with others. Do they hear and understand what we are trying to say? Are they listening well? Are we listening well in response?

Do their responses show that they understand the words and the meanings behind the words we have chosen? Is the mood positive and receptive? Is there trust between them and us? Are there differences that relate to ineffective communication, divergent goals or interests, or fundamentally different ways of seeing the world? The answers to these questions will give us some clues about the effectiveness of our communication and the ease with which we may be able to move through conflict.

The challenge is that even with all the good will in the world, miscommunication is likely to happen, especially when there are significant cultural differences between communi-cators. Miscommunication may lead to conflict, or aggravate conflict that already exists. We make -- whether it is clear to us or not -- quite different meaning of the world, our places in it, and our relationships with others. In this module, cross-cultural communication will be outlined and demonstrated by examples of ideas, attitudes, and behaviors involving four variables:

- Time and Space
- Fate and Personal Responsibility
- Face and Face-Saving
- Nonverbal Communication

As our familiarity with these different starting points increases, we are cultivating cultural fluency -- awareness of the ways cultures operate in communication and conflict, and the ability to respond effectively to these differences.

**Time and Space**

Time is one of the most central differences that separate cultures and cultural ways of doing things. In the West, time tends to be seen as quantitative, measured in units that reflect the march of progress. It is logical, sequential, and present-focused, moving with incremental certainty toward a future the ego cannot touch and a past that is not a part of now. Novinger calls the United States a"chronocracy," in which there is such reverence for efficiency and the success of economic endeavors that the expression"time is money" is frequently heard. This approach to time is called monochronic -- it is an approach that favors linear structure and focus on one event or interaction at a time.

Robert's Rules of Order, observed in many Western meetings, enforce a monochronic idea of time. In the East, time feels like it has unlimited continuity, an unraveling rather than a strict boundary. Birth and death are not such absolute ends since the universe continues and humans, though changing form, continue as part of it. People may attend to many things happening at once in this approach to time, called polychronous. This may mean many conversations in a moment (such as a meeting in which people speak simultaneously,"talking over" each other as they discuss their subjects), or many times and peoples during one process (such as a ceremony in which those family members who have died are felt to be present as well as those yet to be born into the family).

A good place to look to understand the Eastern idea of time is India. There, time is seen as moving endlessly through various cycles, becoming and vanishing. Time stretches far beyond the human ego or lifetime. There is a certain timeless quality to time, an aesthetic almost too intricate and vast for the human mind to comprehend. Consider this description of an aeon, the unit of time which elapses between the origin and destruction of a world system:"Suppose there is a mountain, of very hard rock, much bigger than the Himalayas; and suppose that a man, with a piece of the very finest cloth of Benares, once every century should touch that mountain ever so slightly -- then the time it would take him to wear away the entire mountain would be about the time of an Aeon."

Differences over time can play out in painful and dramatic ways in negotiation or conflict-resolution processes. An example of differences over time comes from a negotiation process related to a land claim that took place in Canada. First Nations people met with representatives from local, regional, and national governments to introduce themselves and begin their work. During this first meeting, First Nations people took time to tell the stories of their people and their relationships to the land over the past seven generations. They spoke of the spirit of the land, the kinds of things their people have traditionally done on the land, and their sacred connection to it. They spoke in circular ways, weaving themes, feelings, ideas, and experiences together as they remembered seven generations into the past and projected seven generations forward.

When it was the government representatives' chance to speak, they projected flow charts showing internal processes for decision-making and spoke in present-focused ways about their intentions for entering the negotiation process. The flow charts were linear and spare in their lack of narrative, arising from the bureaucratic culture from which the government representatives came. Two different conceptions of time: in one, time stretches, loops forward and back, past and future are both present in this time. In the other, time begins with the present moment and extends into the horizon in which the matters at hand will be decided.

Neither side felt satisfied with this first meeting. No one addressed the differences in how time was seen and held directly, but everyone was aware that they were not"on the same page." Each side felt some frustration with the other. Their notions of time were embedded in their understandings of the world, and these understandings informed their common sense about how to proceed in negotiations. Because neither side was completely aware of these different notions of time, it was difficult for the negotiations to proceed, and difficult for each side to trust the other. Their different ideas of time made communication challenging.

This meeting took place in the early 1990s. Of course, in this modern age of high-speed communication, no group is completely disconnected from another. Each group -- government and First Nations representatives -- has had some exposure to the other's ideas of time, space, and ideas about appropriate approaches to negotiation. Each has found ways to adapt. How this adaptation takes place, and whether it takes place without one side feeling they are forced to give in to the other, has a significant impact on the course of the negotiations.

It is also true that cultural approaches to time or communication are not always applied in good faith, but may serve a variety of motives. Asserting power, superiority, advantage, or control over the course of the negotiations may be a motive wrapped up in certain cultural behaviors (for example, the government representatives' detailed emphasis on ratification procedures may have conveyed an implicit message of control, or the First Nations' attention to the past may have emphasized the advantages of being aware of history). Culture and cultural beliefs may be used as a tactic by negotiators; for this reason, it is important that parties be involved in collaborative-process design when addressing intractable conflicts.

As people from different cultural backgrounds work together to design a process to address the issues that divide them, they can ask questions about cultural preferences about time and space and how these may affect a negotiation or conflict-resolution process, and thus inoculate against the use of culture as a tactic or an instrument to advance power. Any one example will show us only a glimpse of approaches to time as a confounding variable across cultures. In fact, ideas of time have a great deal of complexity buried within them.

Western concepts of time as a straight line emanating from no one in particular obscure the idea that there are purposive forces at work in time, a common idea in indigenous and Eastern ways of thought. From an Eastern or indigenous perspective, Spirit operates within space and time, so time is alive with purpose and specific meanings may be discerned from events. A party to a negotiation who subscribes to this idea of time may also have ideas about fate, destiny, and the importance of uncovering"right relationship" and"right action." If time is a circle, an unraveling ball of twine, a spiral, an unfolding of stories already written, or a play in which much of the set is invisible, then relationships and meanings can be uncovered to inform current actions. Time, in this polychronic perspective, is connected to other peoples as well as periods of history. This is why a polychronic perspective is often associated with a communitarian starting point. The focus on the collective, or group, stretching forward and back, animates the polychronic view of time. In more monochronic settings, an individualist way of life is more easily accommodated. Individualists can more easily extract moments in time, and individuals themselves, from the networks around them. If time is a straight line stretching forward and not back, then fate or destiny may be less compelling.

**Fate and Personal Responsibility**

Another important variable affecting communication across cultures is fate and personal responsibility. This refers to the degree to which we feel ourselves the masters of our lives, versus the degree to which we see ourselves as subject to things outside our control. Another way to look at this is to ask how much we see ourselves able to change and maneuver, to choose the course of our lives and relationships. Some have drawn a parallel between the emphasis on personal responsibility in North American settings and the landscape itself. The North American landscape is vast, with large spaces of unpopulated territory.

The frontier mentality of"conquering" the wilderness, and the expansiveness of the land stretching huge distances, may relate to generally high levels of confidence in the ability to shape and choose our destinies. In this expansive landscape, many children grow up with an epic sense of life, where ideas are big, and hope springs eternal. When they experience setbacks, they are encouraged to redouble their efforts, to"try, try again." Action, efficacy, and achievement are emphasized and expected. Free will is enshrined in laws and enforced by courts.

Now consider places in the world with much smaller territory, whose history reflects repeated conquest and harsh struggles: Northern Ireland, Mexico, Israel, Palestine. In these places, there is more emphasis on destiny's role in human life. In Mexico, there is a legacy of poverty, invasion, and territorial mutilation. Mexicans are more likely to see struggles as inevitable or unavoidable. Their fatalistic attitude is expressed in their way of responding to failure or accident by saying"ni modo" ("no way" or"tough luck"), meaning that the setback was destined.

This variable is important to understanding cultural conflict. If someone invested in free will crosses paths with someone more fatalistic in orientation, miscommunication is likely. The first person may expect action and accountability. Failing to see it, they may conclude that the second is lazy, obstructionist, or dishonest. The second person will expect respect for the natural order of things. Failing to see it, they may conclude that the first is coercive or irreverent, inflated in his ideas of what can be accomplished or changed.

## Face and Face-Saving

Another important cultural variable relates to face and face-saving. Face is important across cultures, yet the dynamics of face and face-saving play out differently. Face is defined in many different ways in the cross-cultural communication literature. Novinger says it is"the value or standing a person has in the eyes of others...and that it relates to pride or self-respect." Others have defined it as"the negotiated public image, mutually granted each other by participants in communi-cation." In this broader definition, face includes ideas of status, power, courtesy, insider and outsider relations, humour, and respect. In many cultures, maintaining face is of great importance, though ideas of how to do this vary.

The starting points of individualism and communi-tarianism are closely related to face. If I see myself as a self-determining individual, then face has to do with preserving my image with others and myself. I can and should exert control in situations to achieve this goal. I may do this by taking a competitive stance in negotiations or confronting someone who I perceive to have wronged me. I may be comfortable in a mediation where the other party and I meet face to face and frankly discuss our differences.

If I see my primary identification as a group member, then considerations about face involve my group. Direct confrontation or problem-solving with others may reflect poorly on my group, or disturb overall community harmony. I may prefer to avoid criticism of others, even when the disappointment I have concealed may come out in other, more damaging ways later.

When there is conflict that cannot be avoided, I may prefer a third party who acts as a shuttle between me and the other people involved in the conflict. Since no direct confrontation takes place, face is preserved and potential damage to the relationships or networks of relationships is minimized.

## Nonverbal Communication

Nonverbal communication is hugely important in any interaction with others; its importance is multiplied across cultures. This is because we tend to look for nonverbal cues when verbal messages are unclear or ambiguous, as they are more likely to be across cultures (especially when different languages are being used). Since nonverbal behaviour arises from our cultural common sense -- our ideas about what is appropriate, normal, and effective as communication in relationships -- we use different systems of understanding gestures, posture, silence, spacial relations, emotional expression, touch, physical appearance, and other nonverbal cues. Cultures also attribute different degrees of importance to verbal and nonverbal behaviour.

Low-context cultures like the United States and Canada tend to give relatively less emphasis to nonverbal communication. This does not mean that nonverbal communi-cation does not happen, or that it is unimportant, but that people in these settings tend to place less importance on it than on the literal meanings of words themselves. In high-context settings such as Japan or Colombia, understanding the nonverbal components of communication is relatively more important to receiving the intended meaning of the communication as a whole.

Some elements of nonverbal communication are consistent across cultures. For example, research has shown that the emotions of enjoyment, anger, fear, sadness, disgust, and surprise are expressed in similar ways by people around the world. Differences surface with respect to which emotions are acceptable to display in various cultural settings, and by whom. For instance, it may be more social acceptable in some settings in the United States for women to show fear, but not anger, and for men to display anger, but not fear. At the same time, interpretation of facial expressions across cultures is difficult. In China and Japan, for example, a facial expression that would be recognized around the world as conveying happiness may actually express anger or mask sadness, both of which are unacceptable to show overtly.

These differences of interpretation may lead to conflict, or escalate existing conflict. Suppose a Japanese person is explaining her absence from negotiations due to a death in her family. She may do so with a smile, based on her cultural belief that it is not appropriate to inflict the pain of grief on others. For a Westerner who understands smiles to mean friendliness and happiness, this smile may seem incongruous and even cold, under the circumstances. Even though some facial expressions may be similar across cultures, their interpretations remain culture-specific. It is important to understand something about cultural starting-points and values in order to interpret emotions expressed in cross-cultural interactions.

Another variable across cultures has to do with proxemics, or ways of relating to space. Crossing cultures, we encounter very different ideas about polite space for conversations and negotiations. North Americans tend to prefer a large amount of space, perhaps because they are surrounded by it in their homes and countryside. Europeans tend to stand more closely with each other when talking, and are accustomed to smaller personal spaces. In a comparison of North American and French children on a beach, a researcher noticed that the French children tended to stay in a relatively small space near their parents, while U.S. children ranged up and down a large area of the beach. The difficulty with space preferences is not that they exist, but the judgments that get attached to them. If someone is accustomed to standing or sitting very close when they are talking with another, they may see the other's attempt to create more space as evidence of coldness, condescension, or a lack of interest. Those who are accustomed to more personal space may view attempts to get closer as pushy, disrespectful, or aggressive. Neither is correct -- they are simply different.

Also related to space is the degree of comfort we feel moving furniture or other objects. It is said that a German executive working in the United States became so upset with visitors to his office moving the guest chair to suit themselves that he had it bolted to the floor. Contrast this with U.S. and Canadian mediators and conflict-resolution trainers, whose first step in preparing for a meeting is not infrequently a complete rearrangement of the furniture.

Finally, line-waiting behaviour and behaviour in group settings like grocery stores or government offices is culturally-influenced. Novinger reports that the English and U.S. Americans are serious about standing in lines, in accordance with their beliefs in democracy and the principle of"first come, first served."

The French, on the other hand, have a practice of resquillage, or line jumping, that irritates many British and U.S. Americans. In another example, immigrants from Armenia report that it is difficult to adjust to a system of waiting in line, when their home context permitted one member of a family to save spots for several others. These examples of differences related to nonverbal communication are only the tip of the iceberg. Careful observation, ongoing study from a variety of sources, and cultivating relationships across cultures will all help develop the cultural fluency to work effectively with nonverbal communication differences.

Each of the variables discussed in this module -- time and space, personal responsibility and fate, face and face-saving, and nonverbal communication -- are much more complex than it is possible to convey. Each of them influences the course of communications, and can be responsible for conflict or the escalation of conflict when it leads to miscommunication or misinterpretation. A culturally-fluent approach to conflict means working over time to understand these and other ways communication varies across cultures, and applying these understandings in order to enhance relationships across differences.

## SIX WAYS TO IMPROVE YOUR NONVERBAL COMMUNICATIONS

It is not only what you say in the classroom that is important, but it's how you say it that can make the difference to students. Nonverbal messages are an essential component of communication in the teaching process.

*Teachers should be aware of nonverbal behaviour in the classroom for three major reasons*:

- An awareness of nonverbal behaviour will allow you to become better receivers of students' messages.
- You will become a better sender of signals that reinforce learning.
- This mode of communication increases the degree of the perceived psychological closeness between teacher and student.

*Some major areas of nonverbal behaviors to explore are*:

- Eye contact
- Facial expressions
- Gestures
- Posture and body orientation
- Proximity
- Paralinguistics
- Humour

## Eye contact

Eye contact, an important channel of interpersonal communication, helps regulate the flow of communication. And it signals interest in others. Furthermore, eye contact with audiences increases the speaker's credibility. Teachers who make eye contact open the flow of communication and convey interest, concern, warmth and credibility.

## Facial Expressions

*Smiling is a powerful cue that transmits*:

- Happiness
- Friendliness
- Warmth
- Liking
- Affiliation

Thus, if you smile frequently you will be perceived as more likable, friendly, warm and approachable. Smiling is often contagious and students will react favorably and learn more.

## Gestures

If you fail to gesture while speaking, you may be perceived as boring, stiff and unanimated. A lively and animated teaching style captures students' attention, makes the material more interesting, facilitates learning and provides a bit of entertainment. Head nods, a form of gestures, communicate positive reinforcement to students and indicate that you are listening.

## Posture and Body Orientation

You communicate numerous messages by the way you walk, talk, stand and sit. Standing erect, but not rigid, and leaning slightly forward communicates to students that you are approachable, receptive and friendly. Furthermore, interpersonal closeness results when you and your students face each other. Speaking with your back turned or looking at the floor or ceiling should be avoided; it communicates disinterest to your class.

## Proximity

Cultural norms dictate a comfortable distance for interaction with students. You should look for signals of discomfort caused by invading students' space.

*Some of these are*:

- Rocking
- Leg swinging
- Tapping
- Gaze aversion

Typically, in large college classes space invasion is not a problem. In fact, there is usually too much distance. To counteract this, move around the classroom to increase interaction with your students. Increasing proximity enables you to make better eye contact and increases the opportunities for students to speak.

**Paralinguistics**

*This facet of nonverbal communication includes such vocal elements as*:

- Tone
- Pitch
- Rhythm
- Timbre
- Loudness
- Inflection

For maximum teaching effectiveness, learn to vary these six elements of your voice. One of the major criticisms is of instructors who speak in a monotone. Listeners perceive these instructors as boring and dull. Students report that they learn less and lose interest more quickly when listening to teachers who have not learned to modulate their voices.

**Humour**

Humour is often overlooked as a teaching tool, and it is too often not encouraged in college classrooms. Laughter releases stress and tension for both instructor and student. You should develop the ability to laugh at yourself and encourage students to do the same. It fosters a friendly classroom environment that facilitates learning. (Lou Holtz wrote that when his players felt successful he always observed the presence of good humour in the locker room.)

Obviously, adequate knowledge of the subject matter is crucial to your success; however, it's not the only crucial element. Creating a climate that facilitates learning and retention demands good nonverbal and verbal skills. To improve your nonverbal skills, record your speaking on video tape. Then ask a colleague in communications to suggest refinements.

# 9

# Theory of Symbolic Interactionism

## SYMBOLIC INTERACTIONISM

Symbolic interactionism is a major sociological perspective that places emphasis on micro-scale social interaction, which is particularly important in subfields such as urban sociology and social psychology. Symbolic interactionism is derived from American pragmatism, especially the work of George Herbert Mead and Charles Cooley. Herbert Blumer, a student and interpreter of Mead, coined the term and put forward an influential summary of the perspective: people act toward things based on the meaning those things have for them; and these meanings are derived from social interaction and modified through interpretation. Sociologists working in this tradition have researched a wide range of topics using a variety of research methods. However, the majority of interactionist research uses qualitative research methods, like participant observation, to study aspects of:

- Social interaction
- Individuals' selves.

Sociological areas that have been particularly influenced by symbolic interactionism include the sociology of emotions, deviance/criminology, collective behaviour/social movements, and the sociology of sex. Interactionist concepts that have gained widespread usage include definition of the situation, emotion work, impression management, looking glass self, and total institution.

### Basic Premises and Approach

*Herbert Blumer, who coined the term"symbolic interactionism," set out three basic premises of the perspective:*

- "Human beings act toward things on the basis of the meanings they ascribe to those things."
- "The meaning of such things is derived from, or arises out of, the social interaction that one has with others and the society."
- "These meanings are handled in, and modified through, an interpretative process used by the person in dealing with the things he/she encounters."

Blumer, following Mead, claimed that people interact with each other by interpreting or'defining' each other's actions instead of merely reacting to each other's actions. Their'response' is not made directly to the actions of one another but instead is based on the meaning which they attach to such actions.

Thus, human interaction is mediated by the use of symbols and signification, by interpretation, or by ascertaining the meaning of one another's actions. Blumer contrasted this process, which he called"symbolic interaction," with behaviorist explanations of human behaviour, which don't allow for interpretation between stimulus and response.

Symbolic interactionist researchers investigate how people create meaning during social interaction, how they present and construct the self (or"identity"), and how they define situations of co-presence with others. One of the perspective's central ideas is that people act as they do because of how they define situations. Erving Goffman, although he claimed not to have been a symbolic interactionist, is recognized as one of the major contributors to the perspective.

### Society for the Study of Symbolic Interaction

The Society for the Study of Symbolic Interaction (SSSI) is the scholarly association for symbolic interactionists. SSSI holds a conference in conjunction with the meeting of the American Sociological Association in August and sponsors the Couch-Stone Symposium each spring. It also sponsors the journal Symbolic Interaction.

## CRITIQUE

Although symbolic interactionist concepts have gained widespread use among sociologists, the perspective has been criticized, particularly during the 1970s in the U.S. when quantitative approaches to sociology were dominant. Perhaps the best known of these is by Alvin Gouldner.

In addition to methodological criticisms, critics of symbolic interactionism have charged that it is unable to deal with social structure (a fundamental sociological concern) and macrosociological issues. A number of symbolic interactionists have addressed these topics, one of the best known being Negotiated Order Theory..

But their work has not gained as much recognition or influence as the work of those focusing on the interactional level.

## SYMBOLIC INTERACTIONISM

A leading American social psychological theory which focuses upon the ways in which meanings emerge through interaction. Its prime concern has been to analyse the meanings of everyday life, via close observational work and intimate familiarity, and from these to develop an understanding of the underlying forms of human interaction. Heavily influenced by pragmatism, the Chicago tradition of sociology and the philosophical writings of George Herbert Mead, the term itself was coined by Herbert Blumer in 1937.

The theory has four key foci. The first highlights the ways in which human beings are distinctly symbol-manipulating animals. It is through symbols that they, alone of all the animals, are capable of producing culture and transmitting a complex history. Interactionists are always concerned to study the ways in which people give meaning to their bodies, their feelings, their selves, their biographies, their situations, and indeed to the wider social worlds in which their lives exist. Research strategies such as participant observation are employed, which enable the researcher to gain access to these symbols and meanings, as in Howard S. Becker's Art Worlds and Arlie Hochschild's The Managed Heart. There is a broad affinity here to semiology, but unlike at least some positions in semiology which seek the structures of language, interactionists are more concerned with the ways in which meaning is always emergent, fluid, ambiguous, and contextually bound. R. S. Perinbanayagam has provided an important account of meaning in interactionism in his book Signifying Acts.

This leads to a second theme: that of process and emergence. For the interactionist, the social world is a dynamic and dialectical web, situations are always encounters with unstable outcomes, and lives and their biographies are always in the process of shifting and becoming, never fixed and immutable. Attention is fixed, not upon rigid structures (as in many other versions of sociology), but upon streams of activity with their adjustments and outcomes. Concepts such as career, negotiated order, becoming, encounters, and impression management are central to this approach.

A third focus of interactionism highlights the social world as precisely that-interactive. From this point of view there is no such thing as a solitary individual: humans are always connected to'others'. The most basic unit of interactionist analysis is that of the self, which stresses the ways in which people can (indeed must) come to view themselves as objects, and assume the role of others through a process of role-taking. This idea is clarified in Charles Horton Cooley's notion of the looking-glass self and Mead's more general idea of'the self'.

A fourth theme, derived from Georg Simmel, is that interactionism looks beneath these symbols, processes, and interactions in order to determine underlying patterns or forms of social life. Interactionists seek'generic social processes'. Thus, while they may study the life-experience of doctors, dance-band musicians, drug-users, and the dying, they can detect common processes at work in all such seemingly disparate groupings. A good example is Barney Glaser and Anselm Strauss's Status Passage, which provides a formal, interactionist theory of status changes.

Symbolic interactionism developed in the University of Chicago, in the first few decades of this century, and first achieved prominence when the

Chicago School came to dominate early American sociology. However, it again became very influential during the 1960s, as a challenge to the dominance of Talcott Parsons and Grand Theory (sometimes being referred to, during the heyday of functionalism, as'the loyal opposition').

It was particularly influential in the development of the labelling theory of deviance, but also in such fields as occupational research (Everett Hughes), medical sociology (Anselm Strauss), and in the study of classroom interaction. Strauss has pioneered a number of developments in interactionist theory.

From his early work on identity to his formulation of the concept of negotiated order, his work exemplifies a major methodological concern with qualitative research (usually, for him, in medical settings), the development of appropriate strategies for doing such research (the so-called grounded theory approach), and the building of case-study theory which moves beyond itself into a more formal sociology. His work on dying patients (with Barney Glaser) is an exemplary study of all these concerns.

In the 1970s interactionism attracted considerable criticism for its neglect of social structure, power, and history. More recent interactionist writings have shown this critique to be misguided; and, in the process, have revitalized the theory. For example, Sheldon Stryker has attempted to enunciate a version of symbolic interactionism which more clearly relates the conventionally microsociological concerns of that perspective to the organizational and societal levels of analysis, mainly by an imaginative restatement of role theory.

In particular, Stryker has been concerned with the idea of'role-making', the active creation of roles (rather than mere'taking' of them), where some social structures permit more such creativity than do others. In the 1990s interactionism has provided analyses of a range of new phenomena, and has become more theoretically sophisticated (some might say eclectic) in creating links to post-modernism (in the work of Norman Denzin), feminism, semiology, and cultural theory. The best collection of interactionist writings, and one which gives a good indication of the tradition's virtues and limitations, is Ken Plummer's Symbolic Interactionism.

## HERBERT BLUMER'S SYMBOLIC INTERACTIONISM

Symbolic Interactionism as thought of by Herbert Blumer, is the process of interaction in the formation of meanings for individuals. Blumer was a devotee of George H. Mead, and was influenced by John Dewey. Dewey insisted that human beings are best understood in relation to their environment . With this as his inspiration, Herbert Blumer outlined Symbolic Interactionism, a study of human group life and conduct. Blumer came up with three core principles to his theory. They are meaning, language, and thought. These core principles lead to conclusions about the creation of a person's self and socialization into a larger community. The first core principle of meaning states that humans act toward people and things based upon the meanings that they have given to those people or things. Symbolic Interactionism holds the principal of meaning as central in human behaviour.

The second core principle is language. Language gives humans a means by which to negotiate meaning through symbols. Mead's influence on Blumer becomes apparent here because Mead believed that naming assigned meaning, thus naming was the basis for human society and the extent of knowledge. It is by engaging in speech acts with others, symbolic interaction, that humans come to identify meaning, or naming, and develop discourse.

The third core principle is that of thought. Thought modifies each individual's interpretation of symbols. Thought, based-on language, is a mental conversation or dialogue that requires role taking, or imagining different points of view.

**The Case**

Last week, I received an exciting e-mail from an old flame named Jeremy. Jeremy and I have been getting to know each other again through the wonderful world of cyberspace. I like e-mall because it doesn't have the nervous element that phone calls do. Unfortunately, it doesn't have the personal touch of phone calls either. The biggest downfall of e-mail is that non-verbal cues are impossible to detect, because of the simple fact that e-mail is not verbal. It is very easy for misunderstanding to arise. Well, Jeremy's e-mail to me on Thursday said he was coming to Boulder the next day, and he was wondering if I wanted"to go out?" I accepted his offer"to go out." With the help of my friends, I picked out the perfect outfit for my date with Jeremy. The girls and I all assumed Jeremy and I would do dinner and a movie because that is pretty much standard date practice. The next night, Jeremy picked me up"to go out" to the bars with him and three of his buddies. I got very angry and he couldn't figure out why. After all, I told him we would"go out."

**Application of Theory to Case**

I can explain the problem between Jeremy and myself using the lens of the three core principles of Symbolic Interactionism as outlined by Herbert Blumer.

The first miscommunication that Jeremy and I had falls under the principal of meaning. Jeremy and I acted differently toward one another because we had different meanings of one another. Last year, Jeremy and I broke up under the heading"we're just friends." Therefore, Jeremy assigns"friend" as the meaning for me. For myself, however, when Jeremy and I started talking again, I reevaluated my meaning for him as"potential boyfriend." Jeremy was treating me like a friend, and I was treating him like a boyfriend because we act toward people based on the meanings we assign to them.

Our second miscommunication falls under the principle of language. The symbols"do you want to go out" are very ambiguous, especially without the luxury of non-verbal cues. After engaging in symbolic interaction with my group of friends, I decided that"going out" means a romantic evening of dinner and a movie. My girl friends asked where the two of us were going, what I was going to wear to impress him, would we kiss on the first date - even though it really wasn't our FIRST date, if the two of us were going to start dating again, and other things like that. Through my interaction with them, the language"going out" took on a specific meaning. Apparently for Jeremy, the language"going out" took on the specific meaning of hitting the bars for a night on the town. To put it another way, if the extent of knowledge is naming, I name a typical date as"going out," while Jeremy names being at the bars with friends"going out." Because we have two different situations with the same name, we fell upon a misunderstanding.

Our third miscommunication falls under the principal of thought. In my internal dialogue, the symbols"do you want to go out" were interpreted through my thought process based on my naming system. I read his e-mall, talked to my friends, and assigned meaning to the language through symbolic interaction. Based on that meaning from language, I had an internal dialogue, and ended up coming to the conclusion that Jeremy and I were going to spend some romantic time alone together. Jeremy's thought process also modified his interpretation of the language. Jeremy assigned the name of"just a friend" to me. That name was his meaning. He acted toward me based on that meaning. Through his internal dialogue, he used the language"going out" to be interpreted as time spent among friends.

While we ended up have a great time together, just the five of us, the focal point of the problem between Jeremy and myself is that each of us had different meanings with the same name which can account for our behaviour.

## CRITIQUE

The theory of Symbolic Interactionism is strong in that it provides a basis to understand the establishment of meaning. As I understand it, Symbolic Interactionism falls under the category of a Humanistic theory. It has creative meaning - interaction gives humans meaning. It has free will - every human has meanings which can change at any time. It has emancipation - individuals are free to find their own meaning. It has rules for interpretation meaning, language, and thought. And it uses a ethnography to find meaning.

Symbolic Interactionism also meets the five humanistic standards that make a good theory. There is a new understanding of the people where we get meaning. There is a clarification of values. Meaning comes from interaction, so interaction is important to human society. There is aesthetic appeal - the theory is in three, easy-to-understand parts. There is a community of agreement - Blumer's ideas are adopted by people in the academic community. And there is a reform of society - because meaning comes from interaction, interaction must not be taken for granted. Although Symbolic Interactionism is a good theory by the five humanistic standards, there is a critique of the whole basis for it.

While Blumer insists that the interpretive process and the context in which it is done are a vital element in the person's use of meaning and formation thereof, others view the use of meaning as simply the calling upon and application to specific situations of previously held meanings. That is, a social interactionist believes that meaning arises out of the interaction between people, while a contradicting point of view a asserts that meaning is already established in a person's psychological make-up.

## SYMBOLIC INTERACTIONISM

Symbolic interactionism, or interactionism for short, is one of the major theoretical perspectives in sociology. This perspective has a long intellectual history, beginning with the German sociologist and economist, Max Weber and the American philosopher, George H. Mead, both of whom emphasized the subjective meaning of human behaviour, the social process, and pragmatism.

Although there are a number of versions of interactionist thought, some deriving from phenomenological writings by philosophers, the following description offers a simplified amalgamation of these ideas, concentrating on points of convergence. Herbert Blumer, who studied with Mead at the University of Chicago, is responsible for coining the term,"symbolic interactionism," as well as for formulating the most prominent version of the theory.

Interactionists focus on the subjective aspects of social life, rather than on objective, macro-structural aspects of social systems. One reason for this focus is that interactionists base their theoretical perspective on their image of humans, rather than on their image of society (as the functionalists do). For interactionists, humans are pragmatic actors who continually must adjust their behaviour to the actions of other actors. We can adjust to these actions only because we are able to interpret them, i.e., to denote them symbolically and treat the actions and those who perform them as symbolic objects.

This process of adjustment is aided by our ability to imaginatively rehearse alternative lines of action before we act. The process is further aided by our ability to think about and to react to our own actions and even our selves as symbolic objects. Thus, the interactionist theorist sees humans as active, creative participants who construct their social world, not as passive, conforming objects of socialization.

For the interactionist, society consists of organized and patterned interactions among individuals. Thus, research by interactionists focuses on easily observable face-to-face interactions rather than on macro-level structural relationships involving social institutions. Furthermore, this focus on interaction and on the meaning of events to the participants in those events (the definition of the situation) shifts the attention of interactionists away from stable norms and values toward more changeable, continually readjusting social processes.

Whereas for functionalists socialization creates stability in the social system, for interactionists negotiation among members of society creates temporary, socially constructed relations which remain in constant flux, despite relative stability in the basic framework governing those relations. These emphases on symbols, negotiated reality, and the social construction of society lead to an interest in the roles people play.

Erving Goffman, a prominent social theorist in this tradition, discusses roles dramaturgically, using an analogy to the theater, with human social behaviour seen as more or less well scripted and with humans as role-taking actors. Role-taking is a key mechanism of interaction, for it permits us to take the other's perspective, to see what our actions might mean to the other actors with whom we interact.

At other times, interactionists emphasize the improvisational quality of roles, with human social behaviour seen as poorly scripted and with humans as role-making improvisers. Role-making, too, is a key mechanism of interaction, for all situations and roles are inherently ambiguous, thus requiring us to create those situations and roles to some extent before we can act. Ethnomethodology, an offshoot of symbolic intera-ctionism, raises the question of how people who are interacting with each other can create the illusion of a shared social order even when they don't understand each other fully and in fact have different points of view.

Harold Garfinkel, a pioneer in these investigations, demonstrated the problem by sending his students out to perform"experiments in trust," called breaching experiments, in which they brought ordinary conversations to an abrupt halt by refusing to take for granted that they knew what the other person was saying, and so demanded explanations and then explanations of the explanations.

More recently, ethnomethodologist researchers have performed minutely detailed analyses of ordinary conversations in order to reveal the methods by which turn-taking and other conversational maneuvers are managed. Interactionists tend to study social interaction through participant observation, rather than surveys and interviews.

They argue that close contact and immersion in the everyday lives of the participants is necessary for understanding the meaning of actions, the definition of the situation itself, and the process by which actors construct the situation through their interaction.

Given this close contact, interactionists could hardly remain free of value commitments, and, in fact, interactionists make explicit use of their values in choosing what to study but strive to be objective in the conduct of their research. Symbolic interactionists are often criticized by other sociologists for being overly impressionistic in their research methods and somewhat unsystematic in their theories.

These objections, combined with the fairly narrow focus of interactionist research on small-group interactions and other social psychological issues, have relegated the interactionist camp to a minority position among sociologists, although a fairly substantial minority.

# 10

# Human-computer Interaction

Human-computer interaction (HCI) is the study of interaction between people (users) and computers. It is often regarded as the intersection of computer science, behavioral sciences, design and several other fields of study. Interaction between users and computers occurs at the user interface (or simply interface), which includes both software and hardware; for example, characters or objects displayed by software on a personal computer's monitor, input received from users via hardware peripherals such as keyboards and mice, and other user interactions with large-scale computerized systems such as aircraft and power plants.

The Association for Computing Machinery defines human-computer interaction as"a discipline concerned with the design, evaluation and implementation of interactive computing systems for human use and with the study of major phenomena surrounding them." An important facet of HCI is the securing of user satisfaction (see Computer user satisfaction).

Because human-computer interaction studies a human and a machine in conjunction, it draws from supporting knowledge on both the machine and the human side. On the machine side, techniques in computer graphics, operating systems, programming languages, and development environments are relevant.

On the human side, communication theory, graphic and industrial design disciplines, linguistics, social sciences, cognitive psychology, and human factors are relevant. Engineering and design methods are also relevant. Due to the multidisciplinary nature of HCI, people with different backgrounds contribute to its success. HCI is also sometimes referred to as man-machine interaction (MMI) or computer-human interaction (CHI).

Attention to human-machine interaction is important, because poorly designed human-machine interfaces can lead to many unexpected problems. A classic example of this is the Three Mile Island accident where investigations concluded that the design of the human-machine interface was at least partially responsible for the disaster. Similarly, accidents in aviation have resulted from manufacturers' decisions to use non-standard flight instrument and/or throttle quadrant layouts: even though the new designs were proposed to be superior in regards to basic human-machine interaction, pilots had already ingrained the"standard" layout and thus the conceptually good idea actually had undesirable results. Thus, human-machine interaction is a complex field.

Human-computer interaction (HCI) is the study of interaction between people (users) and computers. It is often regarded as the intersection of computer science, behavioral sciences, design and several other fields of study. Interaction between users and computers occurs at the user interface (or simply interface), which includes both software and hardware; for example, characters or objects displayed by software on a personal computer's monitor, input received from users via hardware peripherals such as keyboards and mice, and other user interactions with large-scale computerized systems such as aircraft and power plants.

The Association for Computing Machinery defines human-computer interaction as"a discipline concerned with the design, evaluation and implementation of interactive computing systems for human use and with the study of major phenomena surrounding them." An important facet of HCI is the securing of user satisfaction.

Because human-computer interaction studies a human and a machine in conjunction, it draws from supporting knowledge on both the machine and the human side. On the machine side, techniques in computer graphics, operating systems, programming languages, and development environments are relevant. On the human side, communication theory, graphic and industrial design disciplines, linguistics, social sciences, cognitive psychology, and human factors are relevant. Engineering and design methods are also relevant. Due to the multidisciplinary nature of HCI, people with different backgrounds contribute to its success. HCI is also sometimes referred to as man-machine interaction (MMI) or computer-human interaction (CHI).

Attention to human-machine interaction is important, because poorly designed human-machine interfaces can lead to many unexpected problems. A classic example of this is the Three Mile Island accident where investigations concluded that the design of the human-machine interface was at least partially responsible for the disaster.

Similarly, accidents in aviation have resulted from manufacturers' decisions to use non-standard flight instrument and/or throttle quadrant layouts: even though the new designs were proposed to be superior in regards to basic human-machine interaction, pilots had already ingrained the"standard" layout and thus the conceptually good idea actually had undesirable results. Thus, human-machine interaction is a complex field.

## GOALS

A basic goal of HCI is to improve the interactions between users and computers by making computers more usable and receptive to the user's needs.

*Specifically, HCI is concerned with*:

- Methodologies and processes for designing interfaces (i.e., given a task and a class of users, design the best possible interface within given constraints, optimizing for a desired property such as learning ability or efficiency of use)
- Methods for implementing interfaces (e.g. software toolkits and libraries; efficient algorithms)
- Techniques for evaluating and comparing interfaces
- Developing new interfaces and interaction techniques
- Developing descriptive and predictive models and theories of interaction

A long term goal of HCI is to design systems that minimize the barrier between the human's cognitive model of what they want to accomplish and the computer's under-standing of the user's task.

Professional practitioners in HCI are usually designers concerned with the practical application of design methodologies to real-world problems. Their work often revolves around designing graphical user interfaces and web interfaces.

Researchers in HCI are interested in developing new design methodologies, experimenting with new hardware devices, prototyping new software systems, exploring new paradigms for interaction, and developing models and theories of interaction.

## DIFFERENCES WITH RELATED FIELDS

HCI differs from human factors in that with HCI the focus is more on users working specifically with computers, rather than other kinds of machines or designed artifacts. There is also a focus in HCI on how to implement the computer software and hardware mechanisms to support human-computer interaction. Thus, human factors is a broader term; HCI could be described as the human factors of computers - although some experts try to differentiate these areas.

According to some experts, HCI also differs from ergonomics in that there is less of a focus on repetitive work-oriented tasks and procedures, and much less emphasis on physical stress and the physical form or industrial design of the user interface, such as keyboards and mice.

However, this does not take a full account of ergonomics, the oldest areas of which were mentioned above, but which more recently has gained a much broader focus (equivalent to human factors). Cognitive ergonomics, for example, is a part of ergonomics, of which software ergonomics (an older term, essentially the same as HCI) is a part.

Three areas of study have substantial overlap with HCI even as the focus of inquiry shifts. In the study of personal information management (PIM), human interactions with the computer are placed in a larger informational context - people may work with many forms of information, some computer-based, many not (e.g., whiteboards, notebooks, sticky notes, refrigerator magnets) in order to understand and effect desired changes in their world.

In computer supported cooperative work (CSCW), emphasis is placed on the use of computing systems in support of the collaborative work of a group of people.

The principles of human interaction management (HIM) extend the scope of CSCW to an organizational level and can be implemented without use of computer systems.

## DESIGN PRINCIPLES

When evaluating a current user interface, or designing a new user interface, it is important to keep in mind the following experimental design principles:

- *Early focus on users and tasks*: Establish how many users are needed to perform the tasks and determine who the appropriate users should be; someone that has never used the interface, and will not use the interface in the future, is most likely not a valid user. In addition, define the tasks the users will be performing and how often the tasks need to be performed.
- Empirical measurement: Test the interface early on with real users who come in contact with the interface on an everyday basis. Keep in mind that results may be altered if the performance level of the user is not an accurate depiction of the real human-computer interaction. Establish quantitative usability specifics such as: the number of users performing the tasks, the time to complete the tasks, and the number of errors made during the tasks.
- Iterative design: After determining the users, tasks, and empirical measurements to include, perform the following iterative design steps:
  - Design the user interface
  - Test
  - Analyse results
  - Repeat

Repeat the iterative design process until a sensible, user-friendly interface is created.

## DESIGN METHODOLOGIES

A number of diverse methodologies outlining techniques for human-computer interaction design have emerged since the rise of the field in the 1980s. Most design methodologies stem from a model for how users, designers, and technical systems interact. Early methodologies, for example, treated users' cognitive processes as predictable and quantifiable and encouraged design practitioners to look to cognitive science results in areas such as memory and attention when designing user interfaces.

Modern models tend to focus on a constant feedback and conversation between users, designers, and engineers and push for technical systems to be wrapped around the types of experiences users want to have, rather than wrapping user experience around a completed system.

- User-centered design: user-centered design (UCD) is a modern, widely practiced design philosophy rooted in the idea that users must take centre-stage in the design of any computer system. Users, designers and technical practitioners work together to articulate the wants, needs and limitations of the user and create a system that addresses these elements. Often, user-centered design projects are informed by ethnographic studies of the environments in which users will be interacting with the system. This practice is similar but not identical to Participatory Design, which emphasizes the possibility for end-users to contribute actively through shared design sessions and workshops.
- Principles of User Interface Design: these are seven principles that may be considered at any time during the design of a user interface in any order, namely Tolerance, Simplicity, Visibility, Affordance, Consistency, Structure and Feedback.

## DISPLAY DESIGNS

Displays are human-made artifacts designed to support the perception of relevant system variables and to facilitate further processing of that information. Before a display is designed, the task that the display is intended to support must be defined (e.g. navigating, controlling, decision making, learning, entertaining, etc.). A user or operator must be able to process whatever information that a system generates and displays; therefore, the information must be displayed according to principles in a manner that will support perception, situation awareness, and understanding.

### Thirteen Principles of Display Design

These principles of human perception and information processing can be utilized to create an effective display design. A reduction in errors, a reduction in required training time, an increase in efficiency, and an increase in user satisfaction are a few of the many potential benefits that can be achieved through utilization of these principles.

Certain principles may not be applicable to different displays or situations. Some principles may seem to be conflicting, and there is no simple solution to say that one principle is more important than another. The principles may be tailored to a specific design or situation. Striking a functional balance among the principles is critical for an effective design.

## Perceptual Principles

### *Make Displays Legible (or Audible)*

A display's legibility is critical and necessary for designing a usable display. If the characters or objects being displayed cannot be discernible, then the operator cannot effectively make use of them.

### *Avoid Absolute Judgment Limits*

Do not ask the user to determine the level of a variable on the basis of a single sensory variable (e.g. colour, size, loudness). These sensory variables can contain many possible levels.

### *Top-down processing*

Signals are likely perceived and interpreted in accordance with what is expected based on a user's past experience. If a signal is presented contrary to the user's expectation, more physical evidence of that signal may need to be presented to assure that it is understood correctly.

### *Redundancy gain*

If a signal is presented more than once, it is more likely that it will be understood correctly. This can be done by presenting the signal in alternative physical forms (e.g. colour and shape, voice and print, etc.), as redundancy does not imply repetition. A traffic light is a good example of redundancy, as colour and position are redundant.

### *Similarity Causes Confusion: Use Discriminable Elements*

Signals that appear to be similar will likely be confused. The ratio of similar features to different features causes signals to be similar. For example, A423B9 is more similar to A423B8 than 92 is to 93. Unnecessary similar features should be removed and dissimilar features should be highlighted.

## Mental Model Principles

### *Principle of Pictorial Realism*

A display should look like the variable that it represents (e.g. high temperature on a thermometer shown as a higher vertical level). If there are multiple elements, they can be configured in a manner that looks like it would in the represented environment.

### *Principle of the Moving Part*

Moving elements should move in a pattern and direction compatible with the user's mental model of how it actually moves in the system. For example, the moving element on an altimeter should move upward with increasing altitude.

## Principles Based on Attention

### *Minimizing Information Access Cost*

When the user's attention is diverted from one location to another to access necessary information, there is an associated cost in time or effort. A display design should minimize this cost by allowing for frequently accessed sources to be located at the nearest possible position. However, adequate legibility should not be sacrificed to reduce this cost.

### *Proximity Compatibility Principle*

Divided attention between two information sources may be necessary for the completion of one task. These sources must be mentally integrated and are defined to have close mental proximity. Information access costs should be low, which can be achieved in many ways (e.g. close proximity, linkage by common colors, patterns, shapes, etc.). However, close display proximity can be harmful by causing too much clutter.

### *Principle of Multiple Resources*

A user can more easily process information across different resources. For example, visual and auditory information can be presented simultaneously rather than presenting all visual or all auditory information.

## Memory Principles

### *Replace Memory with Visual Information: Knowledge in the World*

A user should not need to retain important information solely in working memory or to retrieve it from long-term memory. A menu, checklist, or another display can aid the user by easing the use of their memory. However, the use of memory may sometimes benefit the user by eliminating the need to reference some type of knowledge in the world (e.g. an expert computer operator would rather use direct commands from memory than refer to a manual). The use of knowledge in a user's head and knowledge in the world must be balanced for an effective design.

### *Principle of Predictive Aiding*

Proactive actions are usually more effective than reactive actions. A display should attempt to eliminate resource-demanding cognitive tasks and replace them with simpler perceptual tasks to reduce the use of the user's mental resources.

This will allow the user to not only focus on current conditions, but also think about possible future conditions. An example of a predictive aid is a road sign displaying the distance from a certain destination.

### *Principle of Consistency*

Old habits from other displays will easily transfer to support processing of new displays if they are designed in a consistent manner. A user's long-term memory will trigger actions that are expected to be appropriate. A design must accept this fact and utilize consistency among different displays.

## HUMAN-COMPUTER INTERFACE

The human-computer interface can be described as the point of communication between the human user and the computer. The flow of information between the human and computer is defined as the loop of interaction.

*The loop of interaction has several aspects to it including*:

- *Task Environment*: The conditions and goals set upon the user.
- *Machine Environment*: The environment that the computer is connected to, i.e a laptop in a college student's dorm room.
- *Areas of the Interface*: Non-overlapping areas involve processes of the human and computer not pertaining to their interaction. Meanwhile, the overlapping areas only concern themselves with the processes pertaining to their interaction.
- *Input Flow*: The flow of information that begins in the task environment, when the user has some task that requires using their computer.
- *Output*: The flow of information that originates in the machine environment.
- *Feedback*: Loops through the interface that evaluate, moderate, and confirm processes as they pass from the human through the interface to the computer and back.

## ACADEMIC CONFERENCES

One of the top academic conferences for new research in human-computer interaction, especially within computer science, is the annually held ACM's Conference on Human Factors in Computing Systems, usually referred to by its short name CHI (pronounced kai, or khai). CHI is organized by ACM SIGCHI Special Interest Group on Computer-Human Interaction. CHI is a large, highly competitive conference, with thousands of attendants, and is quite broad in scope. There are also dozens of other smaller, regional or specialized HCI-related conferences held around the world each year, the most important of which include:

# USABILITY

In design, Usability is the study of the ease with which people can employ a particular tool or other human-made object in order to achieve a particular goal. This can include endevours as varied as consumer electronics, communication, and knowledge transfer objects (such as a cookbook, a document or online help) and mechanical objects such as a door handles or a hammer. Usability includes the methods of measuring usability and the study of the principles behind an object's perceived efficiency or elegance.

In human-computer interaction and computer science, usability studies the elegance and clarity with which the interaction with a computer programme or a web site is designed. Usability differs from user satisfaction insofar as the former also embraces usefulness (see Computer user satisfaction).

*The primary notion of usability is that an object designed with a generalized users' psychology and physiology in mind is, for example*:

- More efficient to use-it takes less time to accomplish a particular task
- Easier to learn-operation can be learned by observing the object
- More satisfying to use

Complex computer systems are finding their way into everyday life, and at the same time the market is becoming saturated with competing brands. This has led to usability becoming more popular and widely recognized in recent years as companies see the benefits of researching and developing their products with user-oriented instead of technology-oriented methods. By understanding and researching the interaction between product and user, the usability expert can also provide insight that is unattainable by traditional company-oriented market research.

For example, after observing and interviewing users, the usability expert may identify needed functionality or design flaws that were not anticipated. A method called"contextual inquiry" does this in the naturally occurring context of the users own environment.

In the user-centered design paradigm, the product is designed with its intended users in mind at all times. In the user-driven or participatory design paradigm, some of the users become actual or de facto members of the design team.

The term user friendly is often used as a synonym for usable, though it may also refer to accessibility. Usability is also used to describe the quality of user experience across websites, software, products and environments.

There is no consensus about the relation of the terms ergonomics (or human factors) and usability. Some think of usability as the software specialization of the larger topic of ergonomics. Others view these topics as tangential, with ergonomics focusing on physiological matters (e.g., turning a door handle) and usability focusing on psychological matters (e.g., recognizing that a door can be opened by turning its handle).

Usability is also very important in website development. According to Jakob Nielsen,"Studies of user behaviour on the Web find a low tolerance for difficult designs or slow sites. People don't want to wait. And they don't want to learn how to use a home page. There's no such thing as a training class or a manual for a Web site. People have to be able to grasp the functioning of the site immediately after scanning the home page-for a few seconds at most." Otherwise, most casual users will simply leave the site and continue browsing-or shopping-somewhere else.

**Definition**

Usability is a qualitative attribute that assesses how easy user interfaces are to use. The word"usability" also refers to methods for improving ease-of-use during the design process. Usability consultant Jakob Nielsen and computer science professor Ben Shneiderman have written (separately) about a framework of system acceptability, where usability is a part of"usefulness" and is composed of:

- Learnability: How easy is it for users to accomplish basic tasks the first time they encounter the design?
- Efficiency: Once users have learned the design, how quickly can they perform tasks?
- Memorability: When users return to the design after a period of not using it, how easily can they re establish proficiency?
- Errors: How many errors do users make, how severe are these errors, and how easily can they recover from the errors?
- Satisfaction: How pleasant is it to use the design?

Usability is often associated with the functionalities of the product , in addition to being solely a characteristic of the user interface . For example, in the context of mainstream consumer products, an automobile lacking a reverse gear could be considered unusable according to the former view, and lacking in utility according to the latter view.

When evaluating user interfaces for usability, the definition can be as simple as"the perception of a target user of the effectiveness (fit for purpose) and efficiency (work or time required to use) of the Interface". Each component may be measured subjectively against criteria e.g. Principles of User Interface Design, to provide a metric, often expressed as a percentage.

It is important to distinguish between usability testing and usability engineering. Usability testing is the measurement of ease of use of a product or piece of software. In contrast, usability engineering (UE) is the research and design process that ensures a product with good usability.

Usability is an example of a non-functional requirement. As with other non-functional requirements, usability cannot be directly measured but must be quantified by means of indirect measures or attributes such as, for example, the number of reported problems with ease-of-use of a system.

***Intuitive interfaces***

The term intuitive is often listed as a desirable trait in usable interfaces, often used as a synonym for learnable. Some experts such as Jef Raskin have discouraged using this term in user interface design, claiming that easy to use interfaces are often easy because of the user's exposure to previous similar systems, thus the term'familiar' should be preferred.

As an example: Two vertical lines"||" on media player buttons do not intuitively mean"pause" - they do so by convention. Aiming for"intuitive" interfaces (based on reusing existing skills with interaction systems) could lead designers to discard a better design solution only because it would require a novel approach.

This position is sometimes illustrated with the remark that"the only intuitive interface is the nipple; everything else is learned." Bruce Tognazzini even denies the existence of"intuitive" interfaces, since such interfaces must be able to intuit, i.e."perceive the patterns of the user's behaviour and draw inferences."). Instead, he advocates the term"intuitable", i.e."that users could intuit the workings of an application by seeing it and using it." He continues, however,"But even that is a less than useful goal since only 25 per cent of the population depends on intuition to perceive anything."

## INVESTIGATION

The key principle for maximizing usability is to employ iterative design, which progressively refines the design through evaluation from the early stages of design. The evaluation steps enable the designers and developers to incorporate user and client feedback until the system reaches an acceptable level of usability.

The preferred method for ensuring usability is to test actual users on a working system. Although, there are many methods for studying usability, the most basic and useful is user testing, which has three components:

- Get some representative users.
- Ask the users to perform representative tasks with the design.
- Observe what the users do, where they succeed, and where they have difficulties with the user interface.

It's important to test users individually and let them solve any problems on their own. If you help them or direct their attention to any particular part of the screen, you will bias the test. Rather than running a big, expensive study, it's better to run many small tests and revise the design between each one so you can fix the usability flaws as you identify them. Iterative design is the best way to increase the quality of user experience. The more versions and interface ideas you test with users, the better.

Usability plays a role in each stage of the design process. The resulting need for multiple studies is one reason to make individual studies fast and cheap, and to perform usability testing early in the design process.

*Here are the main steps*:

- Before starting the new design, test the old design to identify the good parts that you should keep or emphasize, and the bad parts that give users trouble.

- Test competitors' designs to get data on a range of alternative designs.
- Conduct a field study to see how users behave in their natural habitat.
- Make paper prototypes of one or more new design ideas and test them. The less time you invest in these design ideas the better, because you'll need to change them all based on the test results.
- Refine the design ideas that test best through multiple iterations, gradually moving from low-fidelity prototyping to high-fidelity representations that run on the computer. Test each iteration.
- Inspect the design relative to established usability guidelines, whether from your own earlier studies or published research.
- Once you decide on and implement the final design, test it again. Subtle usability problems always creep in during implementation.

Don't defer user testing until you have a fully implemented design. If you do, it will be impossible to fix the vast majority of the critical usability problems that the test uncovers.

Many of these problems are likely to be structural, and fixing them would require major rearchitecting. The only way to a high-quality user experience is to start user testing early in the design process and to keep testing every step of the way.

## ISO STANDARDS

"Ergonomics of human-system interaction -- Usability methods supporting human-centered design". This standard provides information on human-centred usability methods which can be used for design and evaluation.

It details the advantages, disadvantages and other factors relevant to using each usability method. It explains the implications of the stage of the life cycle and the individual project characteristics for the selection of usability methods and provides examples of usability methods in context. The main users of ISO/TR 16982:2002 will be project managers. It therefore addresses technical human factors and ergonomics issues only to the extent necessary to allow managers to understand their relevance and importance in the design process as a whole.

The guidance in ISO/TR 16982:2002 can be tailored for specific design situations by using the lists of issues characterizing the context of use of the product to be delivered. Selection of appropriate usability methods should also take account of the relevant life-cycle process.

ISO/TR 16982:2002 is restricted to methods that are widely used by usability specialists and project managers.

It does not specify the details of how to implement or carry out the usability methods described.

## ISO 9241

ISO 9241 is a multi-part standard covering a number of aspects for people working with computers. Although originally titled Ergonomic requirements for office work with visual display terminals (VDTs) it is being retitled to the more generic Ergonomics of Human System Interaction by ISO. As part of this change, ISO is renumbering the standard so that it can include many more topics. The first part to be renumbered was part 10.

Part 1 is a general introduction to the rest of the standard. Part 2 addresses task design for working with computer systems. Parts 3-9 deal with physical characteristics of computer equipment. Parts 110 and parts 11-19 deal with usability aspects of software, including Part 110 (a general set of usability heuristics for the design of different types of dialogue) and Part 11 (general guidance on the specification and measurement of usability).

## Usability Considerations

*Usability includes considerations such as*:

- Who are the users, what do they know, and what can they learn?
- What do users want or need to do?
- What is the general background of the users?
- What is the context in which the user is working?
- What has to be left to the machine?

Answers to these can be obtained by conducting user and task analysis at the start of the project.

*Other considerations*:

- Can users easily accomplish their intended tasks? For example, can users accomplish intended tasks at their intended speed?
- How much training do users need?
- What documentation or other supporting materials are available to help the user? Can users find the solutions they seek in these materials?
- What and how many errors do users make when interacting with the product?
- Can the user recover from errors? What do users have to do to recover from errors? Does the product help users recover from errors? For example, does software present comprehensible, informative, non-threatening error messages?
- Are there provisions for meeting the special needs of users with disabilities? (accessibility)
- Are there substantial differences between the cognitive approaches of various users that will affect the design or can a one size fits all approach be used?

Examples of ways to find answers to these and other questions are: user-focused requirements analysis, building user profiles, and usability testing.

**Discoverability**

Even if software is usable as per the above considerations, it may still be hard to learn to use.

*Other questions that must be asked are*:

- Is the user ever expected to do something that is not obvious? (e.g. Are important features only accessible by right-clicking on a menu header, on a text box, or on an unusual GUI element?)
- Are there hints and tips and shortcuts that appear as the user is using the software?
- Should there be instructions in the manual that actually belong as contextual tips shown in the programme?
- Is the user at a disadvantage for not knowing certain keyboard shortcuts? A user has the right to know all major and minor keyboard shortcuts and features of an application.
- Is the learning curve (of hints and tips) skewed towards point-and-click users rather than keyboard users?
- Are there any"hidden" or undocumented keyboard shortcuts, that would better be revealed in a"Keyboard Shortcuts" Help-Menu item? A strategy to prevent this"undocumented feature disconnect" is to automatically generate a list of keyboard shortcuts from their definitions in the code.

**Lund, 1997 Usability Maxims**

*When evaluating the design and usability of a website, one must consider the following*:

- Know the user, and YOU are not the user.
- Things that look the same should act the same.
- The information for the decision needs to be there when the decision is needed.
- Error messages should actually mean something to the user and tell the user how to fix the problem.
- Every action should have a reaction.
- Everyone makes mistakes, so every mistake should be fixable.
- Don't overload the user's buffers.
- Consistency, consistency, consistency.
- Minimize the need for a mighty memory.
- Keep it simple.
- The user should always know what is happening.
- The more you do something, the easier it should be to do.
- The user should control the system. The system should not control the user. The user is the boss and the system should show it.
- Eliminate unnecessary decisions and illuminate the rest.
- The best journey is the one with fewest steps. Shorten the distance between the user and the goal.

- The user should be able to do what the user wants to do.
- If I made an error, let me know about it before I get into REAL trouble.
- You should always know how to find out what to do next.
- The idea is to empower the user, not speed up the system.
- Things that look different should act different.

Also note that these are presented in a descending order determined by their mean rating of importance.

## DESIGNING FOR USABILITY

Any system that is designed for people should be easy to use, easy to learn, and useful for the users. Therefore, when designing for usability, three principles of design, as identified by John Gould and Clayton Lewis, should be followed: early focus on users and tasks, empirical measurement, and Iterative Design.

### *Early Focus on Users and Tasks*

The design team should be user driven and direct contact with potential users is recommended. Several evaluation methods including personas, cognitive modeling, inspection, inquiry, prototyping, and testing methods may be used to gain an understanding of the potential users.

Usability considerations such as who the users are and their experience with similar systems must be examined. As part of understanding users, this knowledge must"be played against the tasks that the users will be expected to perform." This includes the analysis of what tasks the users will perform, which are most important, and what decisions the users will make while using your system.

Designers must understand how cognitive and emotional characteristics of users will relate to a proposed system. One way to stress the importance of these issues in the designers' minds is to use personas, which are made-up representative users.

### *Empirical Measurement*

Two important factors of empirical measurement are stressed: testing the system early on, and testing the system on real users using behavioral measurements. This includes testing the system for both learnability and usability. (See Evaluation Methods). It is important in this stage to use quantitative usability specs such as time and errors to complete tasks and number of users to test, as well as examine performance and attitudes of the users testing the system.

]Finally,"reviewing or demonstrating" a system before the user tests it can result in misleading results. The emphasis of empirical measurement is on measurement, both informal and formal, which can be carried out through a variety of evaluation methods.

### *Iterative Design*

Iterative Design is a design methodology based on a cyclic process of prototyping, testing, analyzing, and refining a product or process. Based on the results of testing the most recent iteration of a design, changes and refinements are made.This process is intended to ultimately improve the quality and functionality of a design.

In iterative design, interaction with the designed system is used as a form of research for informing and evolving a project, as successive versions, or iterations of a design are implemented. The key requirements for Iterative Design are: identification of required changes, an ability to make changes, and a willingness to make changes.

When a problem is encountered, there is no set method to determine the correct solution. Rather, there are empirical methods that can be used during system development or after the system is delivered, usually a more inopportune time. Ultimately, iterative design works towards meeting goals such as making the system user friendly, easy to use, easy to operate, simple, etc.

## EVALUATION METHODS

There are a variety of methods currently used to evaluate usability. Certain methods make use of data gathered from users, while others rely on usability experts. There are usability evaluation methods that apply to all stages of design and development, from product definition to final design modifications. When choosing a method you must consider the cost, time constraints, and appropriateness of the method.

### Cognitive Modeling Methods

Cognitive modeling involves creating a computational model to estimate how long it takes people to perform a given task. Models are based on psychological principles and experimental studies to determine times for cognitive processing and motor movements. Cognitive models can be used to improve user interfaces or predict problem errors and pitfalls during the design process. A few examples of cognitive models include:

### *Parallel Design*

With parallel design, several people create an initial design from the same set of requirements. Each person works independently, and when finished, shares his/her concepts with the group.

The design team considers each solution, and each designer uses the best ideas to further improve their own solution. This process helps to generate many different, diverse ideas and ensures that the best ideas from each design are integrated into the final concept. This process can be repeated several times until the team is satisfied with the final concept.

### *GOMS*

GOMS is an acronym that stands for Goals, Operator, Methods, and Selection Rules. It is a family of techniques that analyses the user complexity of interactive systems. Goals are what the user has to accomplish. An operator is an action performed in service of a goal. A method is a sequence of operators that accomplish a goal. Selection rules specify which method should be used to satisfy a given goal, based on the context.

### *Human Processor Model*

Sometimes it is useful to break a task down and analyse each individual aspect separately. This allows the tester to locate specific areas for improvement. To do this, it is necessary to understand how the human brain processes information.

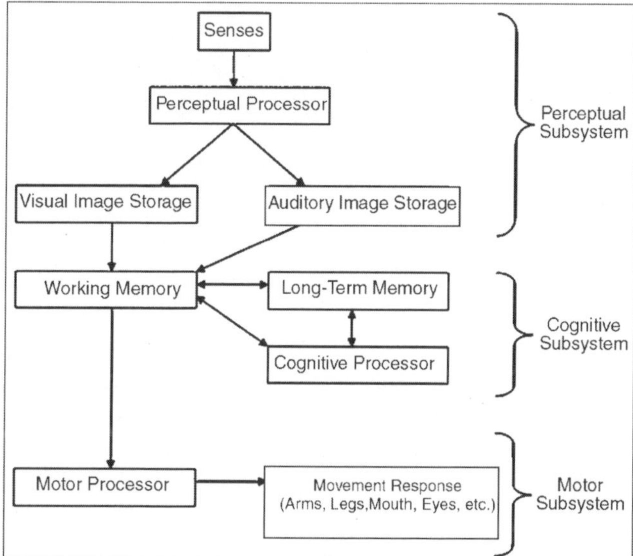


Many studies have been done to estimate the cycle times, decay times, and capacities of each of these processors. Variables that affect these can include subject age, aptitudes, ability, and the surrounding environment. For a younger adult, reasonable estimates are:

| Parameter | Mean | Range |
|---|---|---|
| Eye movement time | 230 ms | 70-700 ms |
| Decay half-life of visual image storage | 200 ms | 90-1000 ms |
| Perceptual processor cycle time | 100 ms | 50-200 ms |
| Cognitive processor cycle time | 70 ms | 25-170 ms |
| Motor processor cycle time | 70 ms | 30-100 ms |
| Effective working memory capacity | 7 items | 5-9 items |

Long-term memory is believed to have an infinite capacity and decay time.

## Keystroke Level Modeling

Keystroke level modeling is essentially a less comprehensive version of GOMS that makes simplifying assumptions in order to reduce calculation time and complexity. See Keystroke level model for more information.

## Inspection Methods

These usability evaluation methods involve observation of users by an experimenter, or the testing and evaluation of a programme by an expert reviewer. They provide more quantitative data as tasks can be timed and recorded.

### *Card Sorting*

Card sorting is a way to involve users in grouping information for a website's usability review. Participants in a card sorting session are asked to organize the content from a Web site in a way that makes sense to them. Participants review items from a Web site and then group these items into categories. Card sorting helps to learn how users think about the content and how they would organize the information on the Web site. Card sorting helps to build the structure for a Web site, decide what to put on the home page, and label the home page categories. It also helps to ensure that information is organized on the site in a way that is logical to users.

### *Tree Testing*

Tree testing is a way to evaluate the effectiveness of a website's top-down organization. Participants are given"find it" tasks, then asked to drill down through successive text lists of topics and subtopics to find a suitable answer. Tree testing evaluates the findability and labeling of topics in a site, separate from its navigation controls or visual design.

### *Ethnography*

Ethnographic analysis is derived from anthropology. Field observations are taken at a site of a possible user, which track the artifacts of work such as Post-It notes, items on desktop, shortcuts, and items in trash bins. These observations also gather the sequence of work and interruptions that determine the user's typical day.

### *Heuristic Evaluation*

Heuristic evaluation is a usability engineering method for finding and assessing usability problems in a user interface design as part of an iterative design process. It involves having a small set of evaluators examining the interface and using recognized usability principles (the"heuristics"). It is the most popular of the usability inspection methods, as it is quick, cheap, and easy.

Heuristic evaluation was developed to aid in the design of computer user-interface design. It relies on expert reviewers to discover usability problems and then categorize and rate them by a set of principles (heuristics.) It is widely used based on its speed and cost-effectiveness. Jakob Nielsen's list of ten heuristics is the most commonly used in industry. These are ten general principles for user interface design. They are called"heuristics" because they are more in the nature of rules of thumb than specific usability guidelines.

- *Visibility of system status*: The system should always keep users informed about what is going on, through appropriate feedback within reasonable time.
- *Match between system and the real world*: The system should speak the users' language, with words, phrases and concepts familiar to the user, rather than system-oriented terms. Follow real-world conven-tions, making information appear in a natural and logical order.
- *User control and freedom*: Users often choose system functions by mistake and will need a clearly marked"emergency exit" to leave the unwanted state without having to go through an extended dialogue. Support undo and redo.
- *Consistency and standards*: Users should not have to wonder whether different words, situations, or actions mean the same thing. Follow platform conventions.
- *Error prevention*: Even better than good error messa-ges is a careful design which prevents a problem from occurring in the first place. Either eliminate error-prone conditions or check for them and present users with a confirmation option before they commit to the action.
- *Recognition rather than recall*: Minimize the user's memory load by making objects, actions, and options visible. The user should not have to remember information from one part of the dialogue to another. Instructions for use of the system should be visible or easily retrievable whenever appropriate.
- *Flexibility and efficiency of use*: Accelerators-unseen by the novice user-may often speed up the interaction for the expert user such that the system can cater to both inexperienced and experienced users. Allow users to tailor frequent actions.
- *Aesthetic and minimalist design*: Dialogues should not contain information which is irrelevant or rarely needed. Every extra unit of information in a dialogue competes with the relevant units of information and diminishes their relative visibility.
- *Help users recognize, diagnose, and recover from errors*: Error messages should be expressed in plain language (no codes), precisely indicate the problem, and constructively suggest a solution.

- *Help and documentation*: Even though it is better if the system can be used without documentation, it may be necessary to provide help and documentation. Any such information should be easy to search, focused on the user's task, list concrete steps to be carried out, and not be too large.

Thus, by determining which guidelines are violated, the usability of a device can be determined.

### *Usability Inspection*

Usability inspection is a review of a system based on a set of guidelines. The review is conducted by a group of experts who are deeply familiar with the concepts of usability in design. The experts focus on a list of areas in design that have been shown to be troublesome for users.

### *Pluralistic Inspection*

Pluralistic Inspections are meetings where users, developers, and human factors people meet together to discuss and evaluate step by step of a task scenario. As more people inspect the scenario for problems, the higher the probability to find problems. In addition, the more interaction in the team, the faster the usability issues are resolved.

### *Consistency Inspection*

In consistency inspection, expert designers review products or projects to ensure consistency across multiple products to look if it does things in the same way as their own designs.

### *Activity Analysis*

Activity analysis is a usability method used in preliminary stages of development to get a sense of situation. It involves an investigator observing users as they work in the field. Also referred to as user observation, it is useful for specifying user requirements and studying currently used tasks and subtasks. The data collected is qualitative and useful for defining the problem. It should be used when you wish to frame what is needed, or"What do we want to know?"

## Inquiry Methods

The following usability evaluation methods involve collecting qualitative data from users. Although the data collected is subjective, it provides valuable information on what the user wants.

### *Task Analysis*

Task analysis means learning about users' goals and users' ways of working. Task analysis can also mean figuring out what more specific tasks users must do to meet those goals and what steps they must take to accomplish those tasks. Along with user and task analysis, we often do a third analysis: understanding users' environments (physical, social, cultural, and technological environments).

### *Focus Groups*

A focus group is a focused discussion where a moderator leads a group of participants through a set of questions on a particular topic. Although typically used as a marketing tool, Focus Groups are sometimes used to evaluate usability. Used in the product definition stage, a group of 6 to 10 users are gathered to discuss what they desire in a product. An experienced focus group facilitator is hired to guide the discussion to areas of interest for the developers. Focus groups are typically videotaped to help get verbatim quotes, and clips are often used to summarize opinions. The data gathered is not usually quantitative, but can help get an idea of a target group's opinion.

### *Questionnaires/Surveys*

Surveys have the advantages of being inexpensive, require no testing equipment, and results reflect the users' opinions. When written carefully and given to actual users who have experience with the product and knowledge of design, surveys provide useful feedback on the strong and weak areas of the usability of a design. This is a very common method and often does not appear to be a survey, but just a warranty card.

## Prototyping Methods

### *Rapid Prototyping*

Rapid prototyping is a method used in early stages of development to validate and refine the usability of a system. It can be used to quickly and cheaply evaluate user-interface designs without the need for an expensive working model. This can help remove hesitation to change the design, since it is implemented before any real programming begins. One such method of rapid prototyping is paper prototyping.

## Testing Methods

These usability evaluation methods involve testing of subjects for the most quantitative data. Usually recorded on video, they provide task completion time and allow for observation of attitude.

### *Remote Usability Testing*

Remote usability testing (also known as unmoderated or asynchronous usability testing) involves the use of a specially modified online survey, allowing the quantification of user testing studies by providing the ability to generate large sample sizes. Additionally, this style of user testing also provides an opportunity to segment feedback by demographic, attitudinal and behavioural type. The tests are carried out in the user's own environment (rather than labs) helping further simulate real-life scenario testing. This approach also provides a vehicle to easily solicit feedback from users in remote areas.

### *Thinking Aloud*

The Think aloud protocol is a method of gathering data that is used in both usability and psychology studies. It involves getting a user to verbalize their thought processes as they perform a task or set of tasks. Often an instructor is present to prompt the user into being more vocal as they work. Similar to the Subjects-in-Tandem method, it is useful in pinpointing problems and is relatively simple to set up. Additionally, it can provide insight into the user's attitude, which can not usually be discerned from a survey or questionnaire.

### *RITE Method*

Rapid Iterative Testing and Evaluation (RITE) is an iterative usability method similar to traditional"discount" usability testing. The tester and team must define a target population for testing, schedule participants to come in to the lab, decide on how the users behaviors will be measured, construct a test script and have participants engage in a verbal protocol (e.g. think aloud).

However it differs from these methods in that it advocates that changes to the user interface are made as soon as a problem is identified and a solution is clear. Sometimes this can occur after observing as few as 1 participant. Once the data for a participant has been collected the usability engineer and team decide if they will be making any changes to the prototype prior to the next participant. The changed interface is then tested with the remaining users.

### *Subjects-in-Tandem*

Subjects-in-tandem is pairing of subjects in a usability test to gather important information on the ease of use of a product. Subjects tend to think out loud and through their verbalized thoughts designers learn where the problem areas of a design are. Subjects very often provide solutions to the problem areas to make the product easier to use.

## Other Methods

### *Cognitive Walkthrough*

Cognitive walkthrough is a method of evaluating the user interaction of a working prototype or final product. It is used to evaluate the system's ease of learning. Cognitive walkthrough is useful to understand the user's thought processes and decision making when interacting with a system, specially for first-time or infrequent users.

***Benchmarking***

Benchmarking creates standardized test materials for a specific type of design. Four key characteristics are considered when establishing a benchmark: time to do the core task, time to fix errors, time to learn applications, and the functionality of the system. Once there is a benchmark, other designs can be compared to it to determine the usability of the system.

***Meta-Analysis***

Meta-Analysis is a statistical procedure to combine results across studies to integrate the findings. This phrase was coined in 1976 as a quantitative literature review. This type of evaluation is very powerful for determining the usability of a device because it combines multiple studies to provide very accurate quantitative support.

***Persona***

Personas are fictitious characters that are created to represent a site or product's different user types and their associated demographics and technographics. Alan Cooper introduced the concept of using personas as a part of interactive design in 1998 in his book The Inmates Are Running the Asylum, but had used this concept since as early as 1975.

Personas are a usability evaluation method that can be used at various design stages. The most typical time to create personas is at the beginning of designing so that designers have a tangible idea of who the users of their product will be.

Personas are the archetypes that represent actual groups of users and their needs, which can be a general description of person, context, or usage scenario. This technique turns marketing data on target user population into a few physical concepts of users to create empathy among the design team, with the final aim of tailoring a product more closely to how the personas will use it.

To gather the marketing data that personas require, several tools can be used, including online surveys, web analytics, customer feedback forms, and usability tests, and interviews with customer-service representatives.

**Evaluating with Tests and Metrics**

Regardless to how carefully a system is designed, all theories must be tested using usability tests. Usability tests involve typical users using the system (or product) in a realistic environment [see simulation]. Observation of the user's behaviour, emotions, and difficulties while performing different tasks, often identify areas of improvement for the system.

### *Prototypes*

It is often very difficult for designers to conduct usability tests with the exact system being designed. Cost constraints, size, and design constraints usually lead the designer to creating a prototype of the system. Instead of creating the complete final system, the designer may test different sections of the system, thus making several small models of each component of the system. The types of usability prototypes may vary from using paper models, index cards, hand drawn models, or storyboards.

Prototypes are able to be modified quickly, often are faster and easier to create with less time invested by designers and are more apt to change design; although sometimes are not an adequate representation of the whole system, are often not durable and testing results may not be parallel to those of the actual system.

### *Metrics*

While conducting usability tests, designers must use usability metrics to identify what it is they are going to measure, or the usability metrics. These metrics are often variable, and change in conjunction with the scope and goals of the project. The number of subjects being tested can also affect usability metrics, as it is often easier to focus on specific demographics. Qualitative design phases, such as general usability (can the task be accomplished?), and user satisfaction are also typically done with smaller groups of subjects. Using inexpensive prototypes on small user groups provides more detailed information, because of the more interactive atmosphere, and the designer's ability to focus more on the individual user.

As the designs become more complex, the testing must become more formalized. Testing equipment will become more sophisticated and testing metrics become more quantitative. With a more refined prototype, designers often test effectiveness, efficiency, and subjective satisfaction, by asking the user to complete various tasks. These categories are measured by the per cent that complete the task, how long it takes to complete the tasks, ratios of success to failure to complete the task, time spent on errors, the number of errors, rating scale of satisfactions, number of times user seems frustrated, etc. Additional observations of the users give designers insight on navigation difficulties, controls, conceptual models, etc. The ultimate goal of analyzing these metrics is to find/create a prototype design that users like and use to successfully perform given tasks.

After conducting usability tests, it is important for a designer to record what was observed, in addition to why such behaviour occurred and modify the model according to the results. Often it is quite difficult to distinguish the source of the design errors, and what the user did wrong. However, effective usability tests will not generate a solution to the problems, but provide modified design guidelines for continued testing.

**Benefits of Usability**

*The key benefits of usability are:*

- Higher revenues through increased sales
- Increased user efficiency and satisfaction
- Reduced development costs
- Reduced support costs

***Corporate Integration***

An increase in usability generally positively affects several facets of a company's output quality. In particular, the benefits fall into several common areas:

- Increased productivity
- Decreased training and support costs
- Increased sales and revenues
- Reduced development time and costs
- Reduced maintenance costs
- Increased customer satisfaction

Increased usability in the workplace fosters several responses from employees. Along with any positive feedback,"workers who enjoy their work do it better, stay longer in the face of temptation, and contribute ideas and enthusiasm to the evolution of enhanced productivity." In order to create standards, companies often implement experimental design techniques that create baseline levels. Areas of concern in an office environment include (though are not necessarily limited to):

- Working Posture
- Design of Workstation Furniture
- Screen Displays
- Input Devices
- Organizational Issues
- Office Environment
- Software Interface

By working to improve said factors, corporations can achieve their goals of increased output at lower costs, while potentially creating optimal levels of customer satisfaction. There are numerous reasons why each of these factors correlates to overall improvement. For example, making a piece of software's user interface easier to understand would reduce the need for extensive training.

The improved interface would also tend to lower the time needed to perform necessary tasks, and so would both raise the productivity levels for employees and reduce development time (and thus costs). It is important to note that each of the aforementioned factors are not mutually exclusive, rather should be understood to work in conjunction to form the overall workplace environment.

Usability is now recognized as an important software quality attribute, earning its place among more traditional attributes such as performance and robustness. Indeed, various academic programs focus on usability. Also several usability consultancy companies have emerged, and traditional consultancy and design firms are offering similar services.

### *Professional Development*

Usability practitioners are sometimes trained as industrial engineers, psychologists, kinesiologists, systems design engineers, or with a degree in information architecture, information or library science, or human-computer interaction (HCI). More often though they are people who are trained in specific applied fields who have taken on a usability focus within their organization. Anyone who aims to make tools easier to use and more effective for their desired function within the context of work or everyday living can benefit from studying usability principles and guidelines.

For those seeking to extend their training, the Usability Professionals' Association offers online resources, reference lists, courses, conferences, and local chapter meetings. The UPA also sponsors World Usability Day each November. Related professional organizations include the Human Factors and Ergonomics Society (HFES) and the Association for Computing Machinery's special interest groups in Computer Human Interaction (SIGCHI), and Computer Graphics and Interactive Techniques (SIGGRAPH).

The Society for Technical Communication also has a special interest group on Usability and User Experience (UUX). They publish a quarterly newsletter called Usability Interface.

## HUMAN FACTORS

Human factors science or human factors technologies is a multidisciplinary field incorporating contributions from psychology, engineering, industrial design, statistics, operations research and anthropometry. It is a term that covers:

- The science of understanding the properties of human capability (Human Factors Science).
- The application of this understanding to the design, development and deployment of systems and services (Human Factors Engineering).
- The art of ensuring successful application of Human Factors Engineering to a programme (sometimes referred to as Human Factors Integration). It can also be called ergonomics.

In general, a human factor is a physical or cognitive property of an individual or social behaviour which is specific to humans and influences functioning of technological systems as well as human-environment equilibriums.

In social interactions, the use of the term human factor stresses the social properties unique to or characteristic of humans.

Human factors involves the study of all aspects of the way humans relate to the world around them, with the aim of improving operational performance, safety, through life costs and/or adoption through improvement in the experience of the end user.

The terms human factors and ergonomics have only been widely used in recent times; the field's origin is in the design and use of aircraft during World War II to improve aviation safety. It was in reference to the psychologists and physiologists working at that time and the work that they were doing that the terms"applied psychology" and"ergonomics" were first coined.

Work by Elias Porter, Ph.D. and others within the RAND Corporation after WWII extended these concepts."As the thinking progressed, a new concept developed - that it was possible to view an organization such as an air-defence, man-machine system as a single organism and that it was possible to study the behaviour of such an organism. It was the climate for a breakthrough."

Specialisations within this field include cognitive ergonomics, usability, human computer/human machine interaction, and user experience engineering. New terms are being generated all the time. For instance,"user trial engineer" may refer to a human factors professional who specialises in user trials.

Although the names change, human factors professionals share an underlying vision that through application of an understanding of human factors the design of equipment, systems and working methods will be improved, directly affecting people's lives for the better.

Human factors practitioners come from a variety of backgrounds, though predominantly they are psychologists (engineering, cognitive, perceptual, and experimental) and physiologists. Designers (industrial, interaction, and graphic), anthropologists, technical communication scholars and computer scientists also contribute. Though some practitioners enter the field of human factors from other disciplines, both M.S. and Ph.D. degrees in Human Factors Engineering are available from several universities worldwide.

## THE FORMAL HISTORY OF AMERICAN HUMAN FACTORS ENGINEERING

The formal history describes activities in known chronological order.
*This can be divided into 5 markers*:

- Developments prior to World War I
- Developments during World War I
- Developments between World War I and World War II
- Developments during World War II
- Developments after World War II

### Developments Prior to World War I

Prior to WWI the only test of human to machine compatibility was that of trial and error. If the human functioned with the machine, he was accepted, if not he was rejected. There was a significant change in the concern for humans during the American civil war. The US patent office was concerned whether the mass produced uniforms and new weapons could be used by the infantry men. The next development was when the American inventor Simon Lake tested submarine operators for psychological factors, follow by the scientific study of the worker. This was an effort dedicated to improve the efficiency of humans in the work place. These studies were designed by F W Taylor. The next step was the derivation of formal time and motion study from the studies of Frank Gilbreth, Sr. and Lillian Gilbreth.

### Developments During World War I

With the onset of WWI, more sophisticated equipment was developed. The inability of the personnel to use such systems led to an increase in interest in human capability. Earlier the focus of aviation psychology was on the aviator himself. But as time progressed the focus shifted onto the aircraft, in particular, the design of controls and displays, the effects of altitude and environmental factors on the pilot. The war saw the emergence of aeromedical research and the need for testing and measurement methods.

Still, the war did not create a Human Factors Engineering (HFE) discipline, as such. The reasons attributed to this are that technology was not very advanced at the time and America's involvement in the war only lasting for 18 months.

### Developments Between World War I and World War II

This period saw relatively slow development in HFE. Although, studies on driver behaviour started gaining momentum during this period, as Henry Ford started providing millions of Americans with automobiles. Another major development during this period was the performance of aeromedical research.

By the end of WWI, two aeronautical labs were established, one at Brooks Airforce Base, Texas and the other at Wright field outside of Dayton, Ohio. Many tests were conducted to determine which characteristic differentiated the successful pilots from the unsuccessful ones.

During the early 1930s, Edwin Link developed the first flight simulator. The trend continued and more sophisticated simulators and test equipment were developed. Another significant development was in the civilian sector, where the effects of illumination on worker productivity were examined. This led to the identification of the'Hawthorne Effect', which suggested that motivational factors could significantly influence human performance.

### Developments During World War II

With the onset of the WW II, it was no longer possible to adopt the Tayloristic principle of matching individuals to preexisting jobs. Now the design of equipment had to take into account human limitations and take advantage of human capabilities. This change took time to come into place. There was a lot of research conducted to determine the human capabilities and limitations that had to be accomplished. A lot of this research took off where the aeromedical research between the wars had left off. An example of this is the study done by Fitts and Jones, who studied the most effective configuration of control knobs to be used in aircraft cockpits. A lot of this research transcended into other equipment with the aim of making the controls and displays easier for the operators to use. After the war, the Army Air Force published 19 volumes summarizing what had been established from research during the war.

### Developments after World War II

In the initial 20 years after the WW II, most activities were done by the founding fathers: Alphonse Chapanis, Paul Fitts, and Small. The beginning of cold war led to a major expansion of Defence supported research laboratories. Also, a lot of labs established during the war started expanding. Most of the research following the war was military sponsored. Large sums of money were granted to universities to conduct research. The scope of the research also broadened from small equipments to entire workstations and systems. Concurrently, a lot of opportunities started opening up in the civilian industry. The focus shifted from research to participation through advice to engineers in the design of equipment. After 1965, the period saw a maturation of the discipline. The field has expanded with the development of the computer and computer applications.

## THE CYCLE OF HUMAN FACTORS

Human Factors involves the study of factors and development of tools that facilitate the achievement of these goals. In the most general sense, the three goals of human factors are accomplished through several procedures in the human factors cycle, which depicts the human operator (brain and body) and the system with which he or she is interacting. First it is necessary to diagnose or identify the problems and deficiencies in the human-system interaction of an existing system. After defining the problems there are five different approaches that can be used in order to implement the solution.

*These are as follows*:

- *Equipment design*: Changes the nature of the physical equipment with which humans work.
- *Task design*: Focuses more on changing what operators do than on changing the devices they use. This may involve assigning part or all of tasks to other workers or to automated components.

- *Environmental design*: Implements changes, such as improved lighting, temperature control and reduced noise in the physical environment where the task is carried out.
- *Training the individuals*: Better preparing the worker for the conditions that he or she will encounter in the job environment by teaching and practicing the necessary physical or mental skills.
- *Selection of individuals*: Selection of individuals is a technique that recognizes the individual differences across humans in every physical and mental dimension that is relevant for good system performance. Such a performance can be optimized by selecting operators who possess the best profile of characteristics for the job.

## Human Factors Science

Human factors are sets of human-specific physical, cognitive, or social properties which either may interact in a critical or dangerous manner with technological systems, the human natural environment, or human organizations, or they can be taken under consideration in the design of ergonomic human-user oriented equipment. The choice or identification of human factors usually depends on their possible negative or positive impact on the functioning of human-organizations and human-machine systems.

### *The human-machine Model*

The simple human-machine model is a person interacting with a machine in some kind of environment. The person and machine are both modeled as information-processing devices, each with inputs, central processing, and outputs. The inputs of a person are the senses (e.g., eyes, ears) and the outputs are effectors (e.g., hands, voice). The inputs of a machine are input control devices (e.g., keyboard, mouse) and the outputs are output display devices (e.g., screen, auditory alerts). The environment can be characterized physically (e.g., vibration, noise, zero-gravity), cognitively (e.g., time pressure, uncertainty, risk), and/or organizationally (e.g., organizational structure, job design). This provides a convenient way for organizing some of the major concerns of human engineering: the selection and design of machine displays and controls; the layout and design of workplaces; design for maintainability; and the design of the work environment.

Example: Driving an automobile is a familiar example of a simple man-machine system. In driving, the operator receives inputs from outside the vehicle (sounds and visual cues from traffic, obstructions, and signals) and from displays inside the vehicle (such as the speedometer, fuel indicator, and temperature gauge). The driver continually evaluates this information, decides on courses of action, and translates those decisions into actions upon the vehicle's controls-principally the accelerator, steering wheel, and brake. Finally, the driver is influenced by such environmental factors as noise, fumes, and temperature. No matter how important it may be to match an individual operator to a machine, some of the most challenging and complex human problems arise in the design of large man-machine systems and in the integration of human operators into these systems.

Examples of such large systems are a modern jet airliner, an automated post office, an industrial plant, a nuclear submarine, and a space vehicle launch and recovery system. In the design of such systems, human-factors engineers study, in addition to all the considerations previously mentioned, three factors: personnel, training, and operating procedures.

Personnel are trained; that is, they are given appropriate information and skills required to operate and maintain the system. System design includes the development of training techniques and programs and often extends to the design of training devices and training aids. Instructions, operating procedures, and rules set forth the duties of each operator in a system and specify how the system is to function. Tailoring operating rules to the requirements of the system and the people in it contributes greatly to safe, orderly, and efficient operations.

**Human Factors Engineering**

Human Factors Engineering (HFE) is the discipline of applying what is known about human capabilities and limitations to the design of products, processes, systems, and work environments. It can be applied to the design of all systems having a human interface, including hardware and software. Its application to system design improves ease of use, system performance and reliability, and user satisfaction, while reducing operational errors, operator stress, training requirements, user fatigue, and product liability. HFE is distinctive in being the only discipline that relates humans to technology. Human factors engineering focuses on how people interact with tasks, machines (or computers), and the environment with the consideration that humans have limitations and capabilities. Human factors engineers evaluate"Human to Human,""Human to Group,""Human to Organizational," and"Human to Machine (Computers)" interactions to better understand these interactions and to develop a framework for evaluation.

*Human Factors engineering activities include*:

- Usability assurance
- Determination of desired user profiles
- Development of user documentation
- Development of training programs.

***Usability Assurance***

Usability assurance is an interdisciplinary concept, integrating system engineering with Human Factors engineering methodologies. Usability assurance is achieved through the system or service design, development, evaluation and deployment.

- User interface design comprises physical (ergonomic) design, interaction design and layout design.
- Usability development comprises integration of human factors in project planning and management, including system specification documents: require-ments, design and testing.
- Usability evaluation is a continuous process, starting with the operational requirements specification, through prototypes of the user interfaces, through usability alpha and beta testing, and through manual and automated feedback after the system has been deployed.

**User Interface Design**

Human-computer interaction is a discipline concerned with the design, evaluation and implementation of interactive computing systems for human use and with the study of major phenomena surrounding them. This is a well known subject of Human Factors within the Engineering field. There are many different ways to determine human computer interaction at the user interface by usability testing.

**Human Factors Evaluation Methods**

Human Factors evaluation methods are part of Human Factors methodology, which is part of Human Factors Engineering. Besides evaluation, Human Factors Engineering also deals with methods for usability assurance, for assessing desired user profiles, for developing user documentation and training programs, etc.

Until recently, methods used to evaluate human factors ranged from simple questionnaires to more complex and expensive usability labs. Recently, new methods were proposed, based on analysis of logs of the activity of the system users. Actually, the work in usability labs and that of the new methods is part of Usability Engineering, which is part of Human Factors Engineering.

**Brief Summary of Human Factors Evaluation Methods**

- *Ethnographic analysis*: Using methods derived from ethnography, this process focuses on observing the uses of technology in a practical environment. It is a qualitative and observational methods that focuses on"real-world" experience and pressures, and the usage of technology or environments in the workplace. Best used early in the design process
- *Focus Groups*: Focus groups are another form of qualitative research in which one individual will facilitate discussion and elicit opinions about the technology or process under investigation. This can be on a one to one interview basis, or in a group session. Can be used to gain a large quantity of deep qualitative data, though due to the

small sample size, can be subject to a higher degree of individual bias. Can be used at any point in the design process, as it is largely dependent on the exact questions to be pursued, and the structure of the group. Can be extremely costly.

- *Iterative design*: Also known as prototyping, the iterative design process seeks to involve users at several stages of design, in order to correct problems as they emerge. As prototypes emerge from the design process, these are subjected to other forms of analysis as outlined in this article, and the results are then taken and incorporated into the new design. Trends amongst users are analysed, and products redesigned. This can become a costly process, and needs to be done as soon as possible in the design process before designs become too concrete.
- *Meta-analysis*: A supplementary technique used to examine a wide body of already existing data or literature in order to derive trends or form hypotheses in order to aid design decisions. As part of a literature survey, a meta-analysis can be performed in order to discern a collective trend from individual variables.
- *Subjects-in-tandem*: Two subjects are asked to work concurrently on a series of tasks while vocalizing their analytical observations. This is observed by the researcher, and can be used to discover usability difficulties. This process is usually recorded.
- *Surveys and questionnaires*: A commonly used technique outside of Human Factors as well, surveys and questionnaires have an advantage in that they can be administered to a large group of people for relatively low cost, enabling the researcher to gain a large amount of data. The validity of the data obtained is, however, always in question, as the questions must be written and interpreted correctly, and are, by definition, subjective. Those who actually respond are in effect self-selecting as well, widening the gap between the sample and the population further.
- *Task analysis*: A process with roots in activity theory, task analysis is a way of systematically describing human interaction with a system or process to understand how to match the demands of the system or process to human capabilities. The complexity of this process is generally proportional to the complexity of the task being analysed, and so can vary in cost and time involvement. It is a qualitative and observational process. Best used early in the design process.
- *Think aloud protocol*: Also known as"concurrent verbal protocol", this is the process of asking a user to execute a series of tasks or use technology, while continuously verbalizing their thoughts so that a researcher can gain insights as to the users' analytical process. Can be useful for finding design flaws that do not affect task

performance, but may have a negative cognitive affect on the user. Also useful for utilizing experts in order to better understand procedural knowledge of the task in question. Less expensive than focus groups, but tends to be more specific and subjective.
- *User analysis*: This process is based around designing for the attributes of the intended user or operator, establishing the characteristics that define them, creating a persona for the user. Best done at the outset of the design process, a user analysis will attempt to predict the most common users, and the characteristics that they would be assumed to have in common. This can be problematic if the design concept does not match the actual user, or if the identified are too vague to make clear design decisions from. This process is, however, usually quite inexpensive, and commonly used.
- *"Wizard of Oz"*: This is a comparatively uncommon technique but has seen some use in mobile devices. Based upon the Wizard of Oz experiment, this technique involves an operator who remotely controls the operation of a device in order to imitate the response of an actual computer programme. It has the advantage of producing a highly changeable set of reactions, but can be quite costly and difficult to undertake.

## Problems with Human Factors Methods

*Problems in how usability measures are employed include*:
- Measures of learning and retention of how to use an interface are rarely employed during methods and
- Some studies treat measures of how users interact with interfaces as synonymous with quality-in-use, despite an unclear relation.

### *Weakness of Usability Lab Testing*

Although usability lab testing is believed to be the most influential evaluation method, it does have some limitations.

*These limitations include*:
- Additional resources and time than other methods
- Usually only examines a fraction of the entire market segment
- Test scope is limited to the sample tasks chosen
- Long term ease-of-use problems are difficult to identify
- May reveal only a fraction of total problems
- Laboratory setting excludes factors that the operational environment places on the products usability

### *Weakness of Inspection Methods*

Inspection methods (expert reviews and walkthroughs) can be accomplished quickly, without resources from outside the development team, and does not require the research expertise that usability tests need.

*However, inspection methods do have limitations, which include*:

- Do not usually directly involve users
- Often do not involve developers
- Set up to determine problems and not solutions
- Do not foster innovation or creative solutions
- Not good at persuading developers to make product improvements

### *Weakness of Surveys, Interviews, and Focus Groups*

These traditional human factors methods have been adapted, in many cases, to assess product usability. Even though there are several surveys that are tailored for usability and that have established validity in the field, these methods do have some limitations, which include:

- Reliability of all surveys is low with small sample sizes
- Interview lengths restricts use to a small sample size
- Use of focus groups for usability assessment has highly debated value
- All of these methods are highly dependent on the respondents

### *Weakness of Field Methods*

Although field methods can be extremely useful because they are conducted in the users natural environment, they have some major limitations to consider.

*The limitations include*:

- Usually take more time and resources than other methods
- Very high effort in planning, recruiting, and executing than other methods
- Much longer study periods and therefore requires much goodwill among the participants
- Studies are longitudinal in nature, therefore, attrition can become a problem.

## Application of Human Factors Engineering

### *An Example: Human Factors Engineering Applied to the Military*

Before World War II, HFE had no significance in the design of machines. Consequently, many fatal human errors during the war were directly or indirectly related to the absence of comprehensive HFE analyses in the design and manufacturing process. One of the reasons for so many costly errors was the fact that the capabilities of the human were not clearly differentiated from those of the machine.

Furthermore, human performance capabilities, skill limitation, and response tendencies were not adequately considered in the designs of the new systems that were being produced so rapidly during the war. For example, pilots were often trained on one generation of aircraft, but by the time they got to the war zone, they were required to fly a newer model. The newer model was usually more complex than the older one and, even more detrimental, the controls may have had opposing functions assigned to them. Some aircraft required that the control stick be pulled back toward the pilot in order to pull the nose up. In other aircraft the exact opposite was required; namely, in order to ascend you would push the stick away from you. Needless to say, in an emergency situation many pilots became confused and performed the incorrect maneuver, with disastrous results.

Along the same line, pilots were subject to substitution errors due mostly to lack of uniformity of control design, inadequate separation of controls, or the lack of a coding system to help the pilot identify controls by the sense of touch alone. For example, in the early days of retractable landing gear, pilots often grabbed the wrong lever and mistakenly raised the landing gear instead of the flaps. Sensory overload also became a problem, especially in cockpit design. The 1950's brought a strong programme of standardizing control shapes, locations and overload management.

The growth of human factors engineering during the mid- to late-forties was evidenced by the establishment of several organizations to conduct psychological research on equipment design. Toward the end of 1945, Paul Fitts established what came to be known as the Behavioral Sciences Laboratory at the Army Corps Aeromedical Laboratory in Dayton, Ohio.

Around the same time, the U.S. Navy established the Naval Research Laboratory at Anacostia, Maryland (headed by Frank V. Taylor), and the Navy Special Devices Centre at Port Washington, New York (headed by Leonard C. Mead). The Navy Electronics Laboratory in San Diego, California, was established about a year later with Arnold M. Small as head.

In addition to the establishment of these military organizations, the human factors discipline expanded within several civilian activities. Contract support was provided by the U.S. Navy and the U.S. Air Force for research at several noted universities, specifically Johns Hopkins, Tufts, Harvard, Maryland, Holyoke, and California (Berkeley). Paralleling this growth was the establishment of several private corporate ventures. Thus, as a direct result of the efforts of World War II, a new industry known as engineering psychology or human factors engineering was born.

### Why is HFE important to the Military

Until today, many project managers and designers are still slow to consider Human Factors Engineering (HFE) as an essential and integral part of the design process. This is mostly due to their lack of education on the purpose of HFE. Nevertheless, progress is being made as HFE is becoming more and more accepted and is now implemented in a wide variety of applications and processes.

The U.S. military is particularly concerned with the implementation of HFE in every phase of the acquisition process of its systems and equipment. Just about every piece of gear, from a multi-billion dollar aircraft carrier to the boots that Servicemembers wear, goes at least in part through some HFE analyses before procurement and throughout its lifecycle.

Lessons learned in the aftermath of World War II prompted the U.S. War Department (now U.S. Department of Defence) to take some steps in improving safety in military operations. U.S. Department of Defence regulations require a comprehensive management and technical strategy for human systems integration (HSI) be initiated early in the acquisition process to ensure that human performance is considered throughout the system design and development process.

## HFE Applications in the U.S. Army

In the U.S. Army, the term MANPRINT is used as the programme designed to implement HSI. The programme was established in 1984 with a primary objective to place the human element (functioning as individual, crew/ team, unit and organization) on an equal footing with other design criteria such as hardware and software. The entry point of MANPRINT in the acquisition process is through requirements documents and studies.

## What is Manprint

MANPRINT (Manpower and Personnel Integration) is a comprehensive management and technical programme that focuses attention on human capabilities and limitations throughout the system's life cycle: concept development, test and evaluation, documentation, design, development, fielding, post-fielding, operation and modernization of systems. It was initiated in recognition of the fact that the human is an integral part of the total system. If the human part of the system can't perform efficiently, the entire system will function sub-optimally.

MANPRINT's goal is to optimize total system performance at acceptable cost and within human constraints. This is achieved by the continuous integration of seven human-related considerations (known as MANPRINT domains) with the hardware and software components of the total system and with each other, as appropriate. The seven MANPRINT domains are: Manpower (M), Personnel (P), Training (T), Human Factors Engineering (HFE), System Safety (SS), Health Hazards (HH), Soldier Survivability (SSv).

## Manpower (M)

Manpower addresses the number of military and civilian personnel required and potentially available to operate, maintain, sustain, and provide training for systems. It is the number of personnel spaces (required or authorized positions) and available people (operating strength). It considers these requirements for peacetime, conflict, and low intensity operations. Current and projected constraints on the total size of the Army/organization/ unit are also considered. The MANPRINT practitioner evaluates the manpower required and/or available to support a new system and subsequently considers these constraints to ensure that the human resource demands of the system do not exceed the projected supply.

**Personnel (P)**

Manpower and personnel are closely related. While manpower looks at numbers of spaces and people, the domain of personnel addresses the cognitive and physical characteristics and capabilities required to be able to train for, operate, maintain, and sustain materiel and information systems. Personnel capabilities are normally reflected as knowledge, skills, abilities, and other characteristics (KSAOs). The availability of personnel and their KSAOs should be identified early in the acquisition process and may result in specific thresholds. On most systems, emphasis is placed on enlisted personnel as the primary operators, maintainers, and supporters of the system. Personnel characteristics of enlisted personnel are easier to quantify since the Armed Services Vocational Aptitude Battery (ASVAB) is administered to potential enlistees.

While normally enlisted personnel are operators and maintainers; that is not always the case, especially in aviation systems. Early in the requirements determination process, identification of the target audience should be accomplished and used as a baseline for assessment. Cognitive and physical demands of the system should be assessed and compared to the projected supply. MANPRINT also takes into consideration personnel factors such as availability, recruitment, skill identifiers, promotion, and assignment.

**Training (T)**

Training is defined as the instruction or education, on-the-job, or self development training required to provide all personnel and units with their essential job skills, and knowledge. Training is required to bridge the gap between the target audiences' existing level of knowledge and that required to effectively operate, deploy/employ, maintain and support the system. The MANPRINT goal is to acquire systems that meet the Army's training thresholds for operation and maintenance. Key considerations include developing an affordable, effective and efficient training strategy (which addresses new equipment, training devices, institutional, sustainment, and unit collective tactical training); determining the resources required to implement it in support of fielding and the most efficient method for dissemination (contractor, distance learning, exportable packages, etc.); and evaluating the effectiveness of the training. Training is particularly crucial in the acquisition and employment of a new system. New tasks may be introduced into a duty position; current processes may be significantly changed; existing job responsibilities may be redefined, shifted, or eliminated; and/or entirely new positions may be required. It is vital to consider the total training impact of the system on both the individuals and the organization as a whole.

### Human Factors Engineering (HFE)

The goal of HFE is to maximize the ability of an individual or crew to operate and maintain a system at required levels by eliminating design-induced difficulty and error. Human factors engineers work with systems engineers to design and evaluate human-system interfaces to ensure they are compatible with the capabilities and limitations of the potential user population. HFE is conducted during all phases of system development, to include requirements specification, design and testing and evaluation.

HFE activities during requirements specification include: evaluating predecessor systems and operator tasks; analyzing user needs; analyzing and allocating functions; and analyzing tasks and associated workload. During the design phase, HFE activities include: evaluating alternative designs through the use of equipment mockups and software prototypes; evaluating software by performing usability testing; refining analysis of tasks and workload; and using modeling tools such as human figure models to evaluate crew station and workplace design and operator procedures. During the testing and evaluation phase, HFE activities include: confirming the design meets HFE specification requirements; measuring operator task performance; and identifying any undesirable design or procedural features.

### System Safety (SS)

System Safety is the design features and operating characteristics of a system that serve to minimize the potential for human or machine errors or failures that cause injurious accidents. Safety considerations should be applied in system acquisition to minimize the potential for accidental injury of personnel and mission failure.

### Health Hazards (HH)

Health Hazards addresses the design features and operating characteristics of a system that create significant risks of bodily injury or death. Along with safety hazards, an assessment of health hazards is necessary to determine risk reduction or mitigation.

The goal of the Health Hazard Assessment (HHA) is to incorporate biomedical knowledge and principles early in the design of a system to eliminate or control health hazards.

Early application will eliminate costly system retrofits and training restrictions resulting in enhanced soldier-system performance, readiness and cost savings. HHA is closely related to occupational health and preventive medicine but gets its distinctive character from its emphasis on soldier-system interactions of military unique systems and operations.

Health Hazard categories include acoustic energy, biological substances, chemical substances, oxygen deficiency, radiation energy, shock, temperature extremes and humidity, trauma, vibration, and other hazards. Health hazards include those areas that could cause death, injury, illness, disability, or a reduction in job performance.

### Organisational and Social

The seventh domain addresses the human factors issues associated with the socio-technical systems necessary for modern warfare. This domain has been recently added to investigate issues specific to Network Enabled Capability (NEC) also known as Network Centric Warfare (NCW). Elements such as dynamic command and control structures, data assimilation across mulitple platforms and its fusion into information easily understood by distributed operators are some of the issues investigated. A soldier survivability domain was also proposed but this was never fully integrated into the MANPRINT model.

### Domain Integration

Although each of the MANPRINT domains has been introduced separately, in practice they are often interrelated and tend to impact on one another. Changes in system design to correct a deficiency in one MANPRINT domain nearly always impact another domain.

## HUMAN FACTORS INTEGRATION

Areas of interest for human factors practitioners may include: training, staffing evaluation, communication, task analyses, functional requirements analyses and allocation, job descriptions and functions, procedures and procedure use, knowledge, skills, and abilities; organizational culture, human-machine interaction, workload on the human, fatigue, situational awareness, usability, user interface, learnability, attention, vigilance, human performance, human reliability, human-computer interaction, control and display design, stress, visualization of data, individual differences, aging, accessibility, safety, shift work, work in extreme environments including virtual environments, human error, and decision making.

### Real World Applications of Human Factors

#### *Multi-Modal Interfaces*

In many real world domains, ineffective communication occurs partially because of inappropriate and ineffective presentation of information. Many real world interfaces both allow user input and provide user output in a single modality (most often being either visual or auditory). This single modality presentation can often lead to data overload in that modality causing the user to become overwhelmed by information and cause him/her to overlook something. One way to address this issue is to use multi-modal interfaces.

*Reasons to use multimodal interfaces*:

- *Time sharing*: Helps avoid overloading one single modality
- *Redundancy*: Providing the same information in two different modalities helps assure that the user will see the information
- Allows for more diversity in users (blind can use tactile input; hearing impaired can use visual input and output)
- *Error prevention*: Having multiple modalities allows the user to choose the most appropriate modality for each task (for example, spatial tasks are best done in a visual modality and would be much harder in an olfactory modality)

*Examples of Well Known Multi-Modality Interfaces*:

- *Cell phone*: The average cell phone uses auditory, visual, and tactile output through use of a phone ringing, vibrating, and a visual display of caller ID.
- *ATM*: Both auditory and visual outputs

*Early Multi-Modal Interfaces by the Experts*:

- Bolts"Put That There" - 1980 - used speech and manual pointing
- Cohen and Oviatt's"Quickset" - multi user speech and gesture input

## Worker Safety and Health

One of the most prevalent types of work-related injuries are musculoskeletal disorders. Work-related musculoskeletal disorders (WRMDs) result in persistent pain, loss of functional capacity and work disability, but their initial diagnosis is difficult because they are mainly based on complaints of pain and other symptoms.

Every year 1.8 million U.S. workers experience WRMDs and nearly 600,000 of the injuries are serious enough to cause workers to miss work. Certain jobs or work conditions cause a higher rate worker complaints of undue strain, localized fatigue, discomfort, or pain that does not go away after overnight rest. These types of jobs are often those involving activities such as repetitive and forceful exertions; frequent, heavy, or overhead lifts; awkward work positions; or use of vibrating equipment.

The Occupational Safety and Health Admini-stration (OSHA) has found substantial evidence that ergonomics programs can cut workers' compensation costs, increase productivity and decrease employee turnover. Therefore, it is important to gather data to identify jobs or work conditions that are most problematic, using sources such as injury and illness logs, medical records, and job analyses.

Job analyses can be carried out using methods analysis, time studies, work sampling, or other established work measurement systems.

- Methods Analysis is the process of studying the tasks a worker completes using a step-by-step investi-gation. Each task in broken down into smaller steps until each motion the worker performs is described. Doing so enables you to see exactly where repetitive or straining tasks occur.
- Time studies determine the time required for a worker to complete each task. Time studies are often used to analyse cyclical jobs. They are considered" event based" studies because time measurements are triggered by the occurrence of predetermined events.
- Work Sampling is a method in which the job is sampled at random intervals to determine the proportion of total time spent on a particular task. It provides insight into how often workers are performing tasks which might cause strain on their bodies.
- Predetermined time systems are methods for analyzing the time spent by workers on a particular task. One of the most widely used predetermined time system is called Methods-Time-Measurement or MTM. Other common work measurement systems include MODAPTS and MOST.

## ERGONOMICS

Ergonomics is the science of designing the job, equipment, and workplace to fit the worker. Proper ergonomic design is necessary to prevent repetitive strain injuries, which can develop over time and can lead to long-term disability.

*The International Ergonomics Association defines ergonomics as follows*:

Ergonomics (or human factors) is the scientific discipline concerned with the understanding of interactions among humans and other elements of a system, and the profession that applies theory, principles, data and methods to design in order to optimize human well-being and overall system performance.

Ergonomics is employed to fulfill the two goals of health and productivity. It is relevant in the design of such things as safe furniture and easy-to-use interfaces to machines.

Ergonomics is concerned with the'fit' between people and their technological tools and environments. It takes account of the user's capabilities and limitations in seeking to ensure that tasks, equipment, information and the environment suit each user.

To assess the fit between a person and the used techno-logy, ergonomists consider the job (activity) being done and the demands on the user; the equipment used (its size, shape, and how appropriate it is for the task), and the information used (how it is presented, accessed, and changed). Ergonomics draws on many disciplines in its study of humans and their environments, including anthropometry, biomechanics, mechanical engineering, industrial engineering, industrial design, kinesiology, physiology and psychology.

Typically, an ergonomist will have a BA or BS in Psychology, Industrial/ Mechanical Engineering or Industrial Design or Health Sciences, and usually an MA, MS or PhD in a related discipline. Many universities offer Master of Science degrees in Ergonomics, while some offer Master of Ergonomics or Master of Human Factors degrees. In the 2000s, occupational therapists have been moving into the field of ergonomics and the field has been heralded as one of the top ten emerging practice areas.

## Domains

*The International Ergonomics Association (IEA) divides ergonomics broadly into three domains*:

- *Physical ergonomics*: Is concerned with human anatomical, and some of the anthropometric, physiological and biomechanical characteristics as they relate to physical activity. (Relevant topics include working postures, materials handling, repetitive movements, lifting, work related musculo-skeletal disorders, workplace layout, safety and health.)
- *Cognitive ergonomics*: Is concerned with mental processes, such as perception, memory, reasoning, and motor response, as they affect interactions among humans and other elements of a system. (Relevant topics include mental workload, decision-making, skilled performance, human-computer interaction, human reliability, work stress and training as these may relate to human-system and Human-Computer Interaction design.)
- *Organizational ergonomics*: Is concerned with the optimization of socio technical systems, including their organizational structures, policies, and processes.(Relevant topics include communication, crew resource management, work design, design of working times, teamwork, participatory design, community ergonomics, cooperative work, new work programs, virtual organizations, telework, and quality management.

## History and Etymology

The foundations of the science of ergonomics appear to have been laid within the context of the culture of Ancient Greece. A good deal of evidence indicates that Hellenic civilization in the 5th century BC used ergonomic principles in the design of their tools, jobs, and workplaces. One outstanding example of this can be found in the description Hippocrates gave of how a surgeon's workplace should be designed and how the tools he uses should be arranged. It is also true that archaeological records of the early Egyptians Dynasties made tools, household equipment, among others that illustrated ergonomic principles. It is therefore questionable whether the claim by Marmaras, et al., regarding the origin of ergonomics, can be justified.

The term ergonomics is derived from the Greek words ergon work and nomos natural laws and first entered the modern lexicon when Wojciech Jastrz?bowski used the word in his 1857 article Rys ergonomji czyli nauki o pracy, opartej na prawdach poczerpni?tych z Nauki Przyrody.

Later, in the 19th century, Frederick Winslow Taylor pioneered the"Scientific Management" method, which proposed a way to find the optimum method for carrying out a given task. Taylor found that he could, for example, triple the amount of coal that workers were shoveling by incrementally reducing the size and weight of coal shovels until the fastest shoveling rate was reached. Frank and Lillian Gilbreth expanded Taylor's methods in the early 1900s to develop"Time and Motion Studies". They aimed to improve efficiency by eliminating unnecessary steps and actions. By applying this approach, the Gilbreths reduced the number of motions in bricklaying from 18 to 4.5, allowing bricklayers to increase their productivity from 120 to 350 bricks per hour.

World War II marked the development of new and complex machines and weaponry, and these made new demands on operators' cognition. The decision-making, attention, situational awareness and hand-eye coordination of the machine's operator became key in the success or failure of a task. It was observed that fully functional aircraft, flown by the best-trained pilots, still crashed. In 1943, Alphonse Chapanis, a lieutenant in the U.S. Army, showed that this so-called"pilot error" could be greatly reduced when more logical and differentiable controls replaced confusing designs in airplane cockpits.

In the decades since the war, ergonomics has continued to flourish and diversify. The Space Age created new human factors issues such as weightlessness and extreme g-forces. How far could environments in space be tolerated, and what effects would they have on the mind and body? The dawn of the Information Age has resulted in the new ergonomics field of human-computer interaction (HCI). Likewise, the growing demand for and competition among consumer goods and electronics has resulted in more companies including human factors in product design.

However, the coining of the term Ergonomics is now widely attributed to Hywel Murrell, a psychologist in a meeting at the UK admirality in 1949. He used it to encompass the studies on which he had been engaged during and after the Second World War.

**Applications**

More than twenty technical subgroups within the Human Factors and Ergonomics Society (HFES) indicate the range of applications for ergonomics. Human factors engineering continues to be successfully applied in the fields of aerospace, aging, health care, IT, product design, transportation, training, nuclear and virtual environments, among others. Kim Vicente, a University of Toronto Professor of Ergonomics, argues that the nuclear disaster in Chernobyl is attributable to plant designers not paying enough attention to human factors."The operators were trained but the complexity of the reactor and the control panels nevertheless outstripped their ability to grasp what they were seeing [during the prelude to the disaster]."

Physical ergonomics is important in the medical field, particularly to those diagnosed with physiological ailments or disorders such as arthritis (both chronic and temporary) or carpal tunnel syndrome. Pressure that is insignificant or imperceptible to those unaffected by these disorders may be very painful, or render a device unusable, for those who are. Many ergonomically designed products are also used or recommended to treat or prevent such disorders, and to treat pressure-related chronic pain.

Human factors issues arise in simple systems and consumer products as well. Some examples include cellular telephones and other handheld devices that continue to shrink yet grow more complex (a phenomenon referred to as"creeping featurism"), millions of VCRs blinking"12:00" across the world because very few people can figure out how to programme them, or alarm clocks that allow sleepy users to inadvertently turn off the alarm when they mean to hit'snooze'. A user-centered design (UCD), also known as a systems approach or the usability engineering lifecycle aims to improve the user-system.

**Design of Ergonomics Experiments**

There is a specific series of steps that should be used in order to properly design an ergonomics experiment. First, one should select a problem that has practical impact. The problem should support or test a current theory. The user should select one or a few dependent variables which usually measures safety, health, and/or physiological performance. Independent variables should also be chosen at different levels. Normally, this involves paid participants, the existing environment, equipment, and/or software. When testing the users, one should give careful instructions describing the method or task and then get voluntary consent. The user should recognize all the possible combinations and interactions to notice the many differences that could occur. Multiple observations and trials should be conducted and compared to maximize the best results. Once completed, redesigning within and between subjects should be done to vary the data. It is often that permission is needed from the Institutional Review Board before an experiment can be done. A mathematical model should be used so that the data will be clear once the experiment is completed.

The experiment starts with a pilot test. Make sure in advance that the subjects understand the test, the equipment works, and that the test is able to be finished within the given time. When the experiment actually begins, the subjects should be paid for their work. All times and other measurements should be carefully measured and recorded. Once all the data is compiled, it should be analysed, reduced, and formatted in the right way. A report explaining the experiment should be written. It should often display statistics including an ANOVA table, plots, and means of central tendency. A final paper should be written and edited after numerous drafts to ensure an adequate report is the final product.

## Ergonomics in the Workplace

Outside of the discipline itself, the term'ergonomics' is generally used to refer to physical ergonomics as it relates to the workplace (as in for example ergonomic chairs and keyboards). Ergonomics in the workplace has to do largely with the safety of employees, both long and short-term. Ergonomics can help reduce costs by improving safety. This would decrease the money paid out in workers' compensation. For example, over five million workers sustain overextension injuries per year. Through ergonomics, workplaces can be designed so that workers do not have to overextend themselves and the manufacturing industry could save billions in workers' compensation.

Workplaces may either take the reactive or proactive approach when applying ergonomics practices. Reactive ergonomics is when something needs to be fixed, and corrective action is taken. Proactive ergonomics is the process of seeking areas that could be improved and fixing the issues before they become a large problem. Problems may be fixed through equipment design, task design, or environmental design. Equipment design changes the actual, physical devices used by people. Task design changes what people do with the equipment. Environmental design changes the environment in which people work, but not the physical equipment they use.

## Fields of Ergonomics

### *Engineering Psychology*

Engineering psychology is an interdisciplinary part of ergonomics and studies the relationships of people to machines, with the intent of improving such relationships. This may involve redesigning equipment, changing the way people use machines, or changing the location in which the work takes place. Often, the work of an engineering psychologist is described as making the relationship more"user-friendly."

Engineering psychology is an applied field of psychology concerned with psychological factors in the design and use of equipment. Human factors is broader than engineering psychology, which is focused specifically on designing systems that accommodate the information-processing capabilities of the brain.

### *Macroergonomics*

Macroergonomics is an approach to ergonomics that emphasizes a broad system view of design, examining organizational environments, culture, history, and work goals. It deals with the physical design of tools and the environment.

It is the study of the society/technology interface and their consequences for relationships, processes, and institutions. It also deals with the optimization of the designs of organiza-tional and work systems through the consideration of personnel, technological, and environmental variables and their interactions. The goal of macroergonomics is a completely efficient work system at both the macro- and micro-ergonomic level which results in improved productivity, and employee satisfaction, health, safety, and commitment. It analyses the whole system, finds how each element should be placed in the system, and considers all aspects for a fully efficient system. A misplaced element in the system can lead to total failure.

Macroergonomics, also known as organizational design and management factors, deals with the overall design of work systems. This domain did not begin to receive recognition as a sub-discipline of ergonomics until the beginning of the 1980s. The idea and current perspective of the discipline was the work of the U.S. Human Factors Society Select Committee on the Future of Human Factors, 1980-2000. This committee was formed to analyse trends in all aspects of life and to look at how they would impact ergonomics over the following 20 years.

*The developments they found include*:

- Breakthroughs in technology that would change the nature of work, such as the desktop computer,
- The need for organizations to adapt to the expecta-tions and needs of this more mature work force,
- Differences between the post-World War II gener-ation and the older generation regarding their expectations the nature of the new workplace,
- The inability of solely microergonomics to achieve reductions in lost-time accidents and injuries and increases in productivity,
- Increasing workplace liability litigation based on safety design deficiencies.

These predictions have become and continue to become reality. The macroergonomic intervention in the workplace has been particularly effective in establishing a work culture that promotes and sustains performance and safety improvements.

## Methods

- *Cognitive Walk-through Method*: This method is a usability inspection method in which the evaluators can apply user perspective to task scenarios to identify design problems. As applied to macroergonomics, evaluators are able to analyse the usability of work system designs to identify how well a work system is organized and how well the workflow is integrated.

- *Kansei Method*: This is a method that transforms consumer's responses to new products into design specifications. As applied to macroergonomics, this method can translate employee's responses to changes to a work system into design specifications.
- *High Integration of Technology, Organization, and People (HITOP)*: This is a manual procedure done step-by-step to apply technological change to the workplace. It allows managers to be more aware of the human and organizational aspects of their technology plans, allowing them to efficiently integrate technology in these contexts.
- *Top Modeler*: This model helps manufacturing companies identify the organizational changes needed when new technologies are being considered for their process.
- *Computer-integrated Manufacturing, Organization, and People System Design (CIMOP)*: This model allows for evaluating computer-integrated manufacturing, organization, and people system design based on knowledge of the system.
- *Anthropotechnology*: This method considers analysis and design modification of systems for the efficient transfer of technology from one culture to another.
- *Systems Analysis Tool (SAT)*: This is a method to conduct systematic trade-off evaluations of work-system intervention alternatives.
- *Macroergonomic Analysis of Structure (MAS)*: This method analyses the structure of work systems according to their compatibility with unique sociotechnical aspects.
- *Macroergonomic Analysis and Design (MEAD)*: This method assesses work-system processes by using a ten-step process.

## Seating Ergonomics

The best way to reduce pressure in the back is to be in a standing position. However, there are times when you need to sit. When sitting, the main part of the body weight is transferred to the seat. Some weight is also transferred to the floor, back rest, and armrests. Where the weight is transferred is the key to a good seat design. When the proper areas are not supported, sitting in a seat all day can put unwanted pressure on the back causing pain.

The lumbar (bottom five vertebrate in the spine) needs to be supported to decrease disc pressure. Providing both a seat back that inclines backwards and has a lumbar support is critical to prevent excessive low back pressures. The combination which minimizes pressure on the lower back is having a backrest inclination of 120 degrees and a lumbar support of 5 cm.

The 120 degrees inclination means the angle between the seat and the backrest should be 120 degrees. The lumbar support of 5 cm means the chair backrest supports the lumbar by sticking out 5 cm in the lower back area. One drawback to creating an open body angle by moving the backrest backwards is that it takes ones body away from the tasking position, which typically involves leaning inward towards a desk or table. One solution to this problem can be found in the kneeling chair.

A proper kneeling chair creates the open body angle by lowering the angle of the lower body, keeping the spine in alignment and the sitter properly positioned to task. The benefit of this position is that if one leans inward, the body angle remains 90 degrees or wider. One mis-perception regarding kneeling chairs is that the body's weight bears on the knees, and thus users with poor knees cannot use the chair. This misperception has led to a generation of kneeling chairs that attempt to correct this by providing a horizontal seating surface with an ancillary knee pad.

This design wholly defeats the purpose of the chair. In a proper kneeling chair, some of the weight bears on the shins, not the knees, but the primary function of the shin rests (knee rests) are to keep one from falling forward out of the chair. Most of the weight remains on the buttocks. Another way to keep the body from falling forward is with a saddle seat. This type of seat is generally seen in some sit stand stools, which seek to emulate the riding or saddle position of a horseback rider, the first"job" involving extended periods of sitting.

Another key to reducing lumbar disc pressure is the use of armrests. They help by putting the force of your body not entirely on the seat and back rest, but putting some of this pressure on the armrests. Armrest needs to be adjustable in height to assure shoulders are not overstressed.

**Organizations**

The International Ergonomics Association (IEA) is a federation of ergonomics and human factors societies from around the world. The mission of the IEA is to elaborate and advance ergonomics science and practice, and to improve the quality of life by expanding its scope of application and contribution to society. As of September 2008, the International Ergonomics Association has 46 federated societies and 2 affiliated societies.

The International Society of Automotive Engineers (SAE) is a professional organization for mobility engineering professionals in the aerospace, automotive, and commercial vehicle industries. The Society is a standards development organization for the engineering of powered vehicles of all kinds, including cars, trucks, boats, aircraft, and others. The Society of Automotive Engineers has established a number of standards used in the automotive industry and elsewhere. It encourages the design of vehicles in accordance with established Human Factors principles. It is one the most influential organizations with respect to Ergonomics work in Automotive Design. This society regularly holds conferences which address topics spanning all aspects of Human Factors/Ergonomics.

In the UK the professional body for ergonomists is the The Institute of Ergonomics and Human Factors and in the USA it is the Human Factors and

Ergonomics Society. In Europe professional certification is managed by the Centre for Registration of European Ergonomists (CREE). In the USA the Board of Certification in Professional Ergonomics performs this function.

## Interaction Design

Interaction design (IxD) is the study of devices with which a user can interact, in particular computer users. The practice typically centers around"embedding information technology into the ambient social complexities of the physical world." It can also apply to other types of non-electronic products and services, and even organizations. Interaction design defines the behaviour (the"interaction") of an artifact or system in response to its users. Malcolm McCullough has written,"As a consequence of pervasive computing, interaction design is poised to become one of the main liberal arts of the twenty-first century."

## Related Disciplines

### *Cognitive Psychology*

Certain basic principles of cognitive psychology provide grounding for interaction design. These include mental models, mapping, interface metaphors, and affordances. Many of these are laid out in Donald Norman's influential book The Psychology of Everyday Things.

### *Human Computer Interaction*

Academic research in human-computer interaction (HCI) includes methods for describing and testing the usability of interacting with an interface, such as cognitive dimensions and the cognitive walkthrough.

### *Design Research*

Interaction designers are typically informed through iterative cycles of user research. User research is used to identify the needs, motivations and behaviour of end users. They design with an emphasis on user goals and experience, and evaluate designs in terms of usability and affective influence.

### *Architecture*

As interaction designers increasingly deal with ubiquitous computing and urban computing, the architects' ability to make place and create context becomes a point of contact between the disciplines.

## User-centered Interaction Design

As technologies are often overly complex for their intended target audience, interaction design aims to minimize the learning curve and to increase accuracy and efficiency of a task without diminishing usefulness. The objective is to reduce frustration and increase user productivity and satisfaction. Interaction design attempts to improve the usability and experience of the product, by first researching and understanding certain users' needs and then designing to meet and exceed them. (Figuring out who needs to use it, and how those people would like to use it.)

Only by involving users who will use a product or system on a regular basis will designers be able to properly tailor and maximize usability. Involving real users, designers gain the ability to better understand user goals and experiences. (see also: User-centered design) There are also positive side effects which include enhanced system capability awareness and user ownership. It is important that the user be aware of system capabilities from an early stage so that expectations regarding functionality are both realistic and properly understood. Also, users who have been active participants in a product's development are more likely to feel a sense of ownership, thus increasing overall satisfaction.

**Relationship with Instructional Design**

Instructional design is a goal-oriented, user-centric approach to creating training and education software or written materials. Interaction design and instructional design both rely on cognitive psychology theories to focus on how users will interact with software. They both take an in-depth approach to analyzing the user's needs and goals. A needs analysis is often performed in both disciplines. Both, approach the design from the user's perspective. Both, involve gathering feedback from users, and making revisions until the product or service has been found to be effective. (Summative/ formative evaluations) In many ways, instructional design can be considered a precursor to interaction design.

**Relationship with User Interface Design**

Interaction Design is often associated with the design of system interfaces in a variety of media (see also: Interface design, Experience design) but concentrates on the aspects of the interface that define and present its behaviour over time, with a focus on developing the system to respond to the user's experience and not the other way around. The system interface can be thought of as the artifact (whether visual or other sensory) that represents an offering's designed interactions. Interactive voice response (Telephone User Interface) is an example of interaction design without graphical user interface as a media.

Interactivity, however, is not limited to technological systems. People have been interacting with each other as long as humans have been a species. Therefore, interaction design can be applied to the development of all solutions (or offerings), such as services and events. Those who design these offerings have, typically, performed interaction design inherently without naming it as such.

## Methodologies

Interaction designers often follow similar processes to create a solution (not the solution) to a known interface design problem. Designers build rapid prototypes and test them with the users to validate or rebut the idea. There are six major steps in interaction design. Based on user feedback, several iteration cycles of any set of steps may occur.

### *Design Research*

Using design research techniques (observations, interviews, questionnaires, and related activities), designers investigate users and their environment in order to learn more about them and thus be better able to design for them.

### *Research Analysis and Concept Generation*

Drawing on a combination of user research, technological possibilities, and business opportunities, designers create concepts for new software, products, services, or systems. This process may involve multiple rounds of brainstorming, discussion, and refinement. To help designers realise user requirements, they may use tools such as personas or user profiles that are reflective of their targeted user group.

From these personae, and the patterns of behaviour observed in the research, designers create scenarios (or user stories) or storyboards, which imagine a future work flow the users will go through using the product or service. After thorough analysis using various tools and models, designers create a high level summary spanning across all levels of user requirements. This includes a vision statement regarding the current and future goals of a project.

### *Alternative Design and Evaluation*

Once a clear view of the problem domain exists, designers develop alternative solutions with crude prototypes to help convey concepts and ideas. Proposed solutions are evaluated and, perhaps, merged. The end result should be a design that solves as many of the user requirements as possible.

Among the tools that may be used for this process are wireframing and flow diagrams. The features and functionality of a product or service are often outlined in a document known as a wireframe ("schematics" is an alternate term). Wireframes are a page-by-page or screen-by-screen detail of the system, which include notes ("annotations") describing how the system will operate. Flow Diagrams outline the logic and steps of the system or an individual feature.

The cognitive dimensions framework provides a specialized vocabulary to evaluate particular design solutions, and aid in the creation of new designs from existing ones through design manoeuvres.

### *Prototyping and Usability Testing*

Interaction designers use a variety of prototyping techniques to test aspects of design ideas. These can be roughly divided into three classes: those that test the role of an artifact, those that test its look and feel and those that test its implementation. Sometimes, these are called experience prototypes to emphasize their interactive nature. Prototypes can be physical or digital, high- or low-fidelity.

### *Implementation*

Interaction designers need to be involved during the development of the product or service to ensure that what was designed is implemented correctly. Often, changes need to be made during the building process, and interaction designers should be involved with any of the on-the-fly modifications to the design.

### *System Testing*

Once the system is built, often another round of testing, for both usability and errors ("bug catching") is performed. Ideally, the designer will be involved here as well, to make any modifications to the system that are required.

## ASPECTS OF INTERACTION DESIGN

### Social Interaction Design

Social interaction design (SxD) is emerging because many of our computing devices have become networked and have begun to integrate communication capabilities. Phones, digital assistants and the myriad connected devices from computers to games facilitate talk and social interaction. Social interaction design accounts for interactions among users as well as between users and their devices. The dynamics of inter-personal communication, speech and writing, the pragmatics of talk and interaction--these now become critical factors in the use of social technologies. And they are factors described less by an approach steeped in the rational choice approach taken by cognitive science than that by sociology, psychology, and anthropology.

### Affective Interaction Design

Throughout the process of interaction design, designers must be aware of key aspects in their designs that influence emotional responses in target users. The need for products to convey positive emotions and avoid negative ones is critical to product success. These aspects include positive, negative, motivational, learning, creative, social and persuasive influences to name a few. One method that can help convey such aspects is the use of expressive interfaces. In software, for example, the use of dynamic icons, animations and sound can help communicate a state of operation, creating a sense of interactivity and feedback. Interface aspects such as fonts, colour pallet, and graphical layouts can also influence an interface's perceived effectiveness. Studies have shown that affective aspects can affect a user's perception of usability.

Emotional and pleasure theories exist to explain peoples responses to the use of interactive products. These include Don Norman's emotional design model, Patrick Jordan's pleasure model, and McCarthy and Wright's Technology as Experience framework.

## INTERACTION DESIGN DOMAINS

Interaction designers work in many areas, including software interfaces, (business) information systems, internet, physical products, environments, services, and systems which may combine many of these. Each area requires its own skills and approaches, but there are aspects of interaction design common to all.

Interaction designers often work in interdisciplinary teams as their work requires expertise in many different domains, including graphic design, programming, psychology, user testing, product design, etc. Thus, they need to understand enough of these fields to work effectively with specialists.

The term interaction design was first proposed by Bill Moggridge and Bill Verplank in the late 1980s. To Verplank, it was an adaptation of the computer science term user interface design to the industrial design profession. To Moggridge, it was an improvement over soft-face, which he had coined in 1984 to refer to the application of industrial design to products containing software.

In 1989, Gillian Crampton-Smith established an interaction design MA at the Royal College of Art in London (originally entitled"computer-related design" and now known as"design interactions"). In 2001, she helped found the Interaction Design Institute Ivrea, a small institute in Northern Italy dedicated solely to interaction design; the institute moved to Milan in October 2005 and merged courses with Domus Academy. Today, some of the people originally involved with IDII have now set up a new institute in Copenhagen, called the Copenhagen Institute of Interaction Design or CIID. Today, interaction design is taught in many schools worldwide.

# 11

# Research Methods

Keeping tabs on the research produced in any given field is no small task. Such efforts range from discrete meta-analyses of specific concepts and topics to the ongoing maintenance of large bibliographic databases and informatics. Mass communication offers no exception to this variety of work as researchers in this field have regularly directed their efforts toward the research enterprise itself.

This work examines research in mass communication as far back as the 1930s and includes topics ranging from the content of specific journals to the use of specific methods, concept development, and broad trends in multiple journals spanning decades.

This chapter offers a unique element to the body of work examining the research in mass communication by providing a more detailed look at the use of research methods during the 1990s. This chapter also serves as a companion piece for two other published works. First, the material presented here is designed as a direct replication of Cooper, Potter, and Dupagne's 1994 "A Status Report on Methods Used in Mass Communication Research."

While a census is employed in this work rather than a sample as used by those authors, identical coding schemes are employed to provide a fairly direct comparison with the 1994 study. This allows examination of data spanning thirty-five years. second, this chapter serves as a comparison work for "Mass Communication Research Trends from 1980 to 1999" by Kamhawi and Weaver, providing support for some of the inferences made in their sample.

As in the previous work, an important focus of this chapter is on the use of quantitative versus qualitative methods. This chapter also directs additional attention to the use of mixed approaches in mass communication research. Some discussion of this phenomenon will be offered prior to describing the methods and results of this investigation.

## MIXED METHODS

The epistemological frictions of this field, as described by Cooper, Potter, and Dupagne, have hardly disappeared over the last decade. As they point out, the issue goes much deeper than "to count or not to count." The quantitative versus qualitative distinction is only the surface representation of a spectrum of fundamental orientations toward how the world may be known and how truth might be approached. It is when such philosophical contrasts become politicized that the matter can become divisive. Perhaps as a consequence, we tend to see some degree of split in our journals, in the orientation of our academic units, and in our graduate instruction-all of which tend to be regarded as either quantitative or qualitative in orientation. Although purely qualitative or purely quantitative units, journals, and such are uncommon, truly ecumenical circumstances are certainly not the rule.

There has been some attention paid to the combining of quantitative and qualitative approaches. Weaver observed an increase in this variety of work in the 1980s and predicted that mixed approaches would increase in popularity. An underlying phenomenon that may be on the rise, as Cooper, Potter, and Dupagne suggested, is that of broader training in our graduate programs.

In order to improve their competitive edge, doctoral students maybe equipping themselves with a wider range of research tools, either through personal initiative or as a consequence of programmatic requirements. This question must be left to researchers surveying the field's graduate programs. But the presence of mixed research in our journals might serve as evidence of such training. At the very least, identification and examination of this domain of research could provide useful exemplars for graduate training.

Historically, attention to the mixing of quantitative and qualitative approaches has resided most strongly in the area of measurement. There, most references turn to Campbell and Fiske's development of the multitrait-multimethod matrix method for evaluating the construct validity of a given measure. While such mixed approaches may be embraced by those rigorously developing formal measurement tools, they are less strongly represented in the texts often used to introduce mass communication graduate students to research methods. When the mixed approach is discussed it is often referred to as triangulation and defined as "the use of both qualitative and quantitative methods to fully understand the nature of a research problem."

The term "triangulation" is borrowed metaphorically from the navigational technique in which a position can be geometrically fixed through its observation from two or more points. Triangulation is not a developed concept in the field of communication and can easily be argued to be a poor metaphor for the actual use of mixed approaches in research. But the term does appear across a number of other fields in social and behavioral research, where it at least offers an approach for categorizing various forms of mixed work. To that extent it will be given some brief attention here.

Triangulation was perhaps first conceptually described as a technique in the social sciences by Feigl, and is traced through Webb et al. to the primary reference typically given to Denzen. Denzen elaborates six specific forms of triangulation: theory, data, methods, investigator, analysis, and multiple. In an effort to make triangulation a more viable option for researchers, Kimchi, Polivka, and Stevenson provide a set of operational definitions.

Each specific approach to triangulation can be elaborated extensively. However, the primary focus of this chapter (and that of Cooper, Potter, and Dupagne, and most methods texts) is the examination of quantitative versus qualitative approaches. As Erzberger and Prein point out, the notion of combining quantitative and qualitative observations is hardly new, and is also described by such terms as micro-macro integration. They describe the origins:

The starting point for this discussion was the idea that the different research methodologies-interpretative analysis of qualitative data on the one hand and statistical analysis of numerical data on the other- each have specific weaknesses but also specific strengths: the weaknesses should be overcome by combining qualitative and quantitative data sources and methods of analysis in the same research project.

They develop three arguments for the use of quantitative-qualitative triangulation. First, researchers may be motivated to achieve convergence, to confirm (or disconfirm) results across methods. second, complementarity might be sought. The motivation for this approach lies in a desire to use multiple approaches to allow the development of various pictures of the same phenomenon and provide a broader view. Finally, dissonance may be desired. In this case, different methods are employed in order to find divergent results and provide a provocative analysis.

Examples of studies explicitly using the term triangulation can be found across a range of the social sciences, including communication, education, nursing, community health, and evaluation. Here we ask to what degree this approach is used in mass communication research, whether by the term triangulation or not. Cooper, Potter, and Dupagne estimated that 7.2% of the work in the eight journals they examined between 1965 and 9 199 89 used both qualitative and quantitative methods. Kamhwai and Weaver estimate that 2.5% of articles in ten journals they examined between 1980 and 1999 used such mixed approaches. Neither offers a closer examination of how the two approaches were combined. This study will again report the occurrence of mixed research, and will also examine those studies to detail how this approach is represented in mass communication research.

## METHOD

In order to allow direct comparison, this study adopted with few exceptions the methods previously used by Cooper, Potter, and Dupagne. The previous work examined a longer time period and used a sampling strategy to reduce the amount of coding. Since the present study is constrained to a shorter period of time it was feasible to undertake a complete census. It should also be noted that the numbers provided by Cooper, Potter, and Dupagne are estimates. Direct comparisons between the studies must take that into consideration. Cooper, Potter, and Dupagne sampled approximately a third of the total population and had a sample size of 1,326, which would place their margin of error at about +/- 2.5%.

This study examines the same set of eight journals as did Cooper, Potter, and Dupagne: Communication Monographs, Communication Research, Critical Studies in Mass Communication, Human Communication Research, Journal of Broadcasting & Electronic Media, Journal of Communication .

Journalism & Mass Communication Quarterly, and Quarterly Journal of Speech. These journals were originally selected because they had circulations over 20,0 000 and had high standards demonstrated by peer acceptance rates under 20%. This is still the case for these journals. Kamhawi and Weaver also selected seven of these journals in the set of ten they examined.

As before, only articles presenting original research are examined. Coding categories are also taken directly from Cooper, Potter, and Dupagne, and include the research focus, use of theory, the data source, and the analysis procedure. Each of these is detailed in turn.

The research focus involves "the portion of mass media phenomenon that authors attempt to explain or interpret." Cooper, Potter, and Dupagne elaborated ten categories through consideration of the classic Lasswellian model of "who says what to whom in what channel to what effect." The same set of categories were used in this study for research focus: media industry; personalities in the media; production of messages; message content; audience analysis; distribution of messages; effects of media on individuals or groups; effects of media on institutions, society, or culture; regulation of media; and other.

The most significant departure made from Cooper, Potter, and Dupagne involved coding for the use of theory. They admit, as must be admitted here, that the coding scheme may lean toward the quantitative hypothetico-deductive approach and slight some qualitative work in which theory is developed, or grounded, rather than tested.

In order to capture a clearer picture of theory, additional categories were added to account for the other possible ways that theory might be used, especially with respect to the application of research questions and hypotheses as they might appear in qualitative work. Thus, articles were coded as displaying no use of theory, presenting research questions or hypotheses, specifying a hypothesis without supporting theory, offering a research question without supporting theory, offering a theory-based hypothesis or research question, and evoking theory without the specification of either a research question or a hypothesis.

No changes were made from Cooper, Potter, and Dupagne in the categories used for procedures and sources for data. Procedures included experiments, surveys, observation (e.g., participant observation, interviews), content analysis, and secondary analysis. Data sources included direct contact with people, direct contact with media messages, direct contact with archival data, analysis of existing qualitative data, analysis of existing qualitative data, and analysis of the research of others (e.g., meta analysis, reanalysis of published results).

There is one minor departure from previous coding on these variables. Cooper, Potter, and Dupagne allowed for more than one procedure to be coded per case. Rather than use this approach, a category for "multiple" was added to both variables, providing some additional detail.

Three coders were trained based on the methods reported in Cooper, Potter, and Dupagne. All were graduate students who had completed coursework in both theory and methods in a journalism graduate studies programme. Coders had little difficulty understanding the categories employed. A total of 2,649 articles were coded. A subsample (N = 130, 5%) of the content was randomly selected and independently receded. Intercoder agreement was calculated by Holsti's method and corrected for chance and number of categories by Scott's pi: method 92% (pi = 85%), procedure 91% (88%), source 92% (87%), focus 82% (76%), and use of theory 84% (41% for the five-category scheme introduced here, 67% if collapsed to match Cooper, Potter, and Dupagne).

## RESULTS

Tables and findings are presented in a manner generally matching Cooper, Potter, and Dupagne, and include their reported data to facilitate comparison. Here we see a clear quantitative versus qualitative distinction, at least as represented in the journals included in the analysis. The 57% quantitative dominance seen in this study's census of the content is a very close match to the estimate made by Cooper, Potter, and Dupagne. Cooper, Potter, and Dupagne report a trend across their time span in which emphasis shifts from qualitative to quantitative. While this trend appears reasonable, the amount of variance is fairly substantial and could mitigate that finding. The data presented here are fairly uniform across the decade; 1993 was the only year in which there was more qualitative than quantitative work published.

The more striking distinction between these results and Cooper, Potter, and Dupagne's lies in the prevalence of studies using both quantitative and qualitative approaches. It is conceivable that the broader discussion of mixed studies that appeared in a number of journals in the 1980s played itself out and that over the last decade such approaches have become less popular. It should also be noted, though, that the difference between the two studies on this category is small in magnitude (about 5%). The most conservative assessment of these findings is that quantitative-qualitative integration is not now, nor has it ever been, an especially common approach in the journals examined. Given an estimate of a +/-2.5% margin of error it may also be reasonable to conclude that mixed approaches were less prevalent in the 1990s than in the previous 25 years.

The results of the examination of research focus shows some interesting parallels to the previous work as well. Audience, content, and individual-level effects remain the most common foci of quantitative studies. For qualitative studies, industry remained a popular focus, and the popularity of content studies seems to have increased while studies of regulation have decreased. Overall, within this study there is divergence in focus between qualitative and quantitative studies, with a weak correlation (Spearman's rho, r) of.34 for the ranking of foci by both methods. This contrasts with the Cooper, Potter, and Dupagne data, in which r = -.37.

Content dominated as the most common focus within the mixed category in both studies, accounting for about a quarter of all mixed studies. This is reasonable as it might be argued that a content analysis offers the simplest domain in which to mix quantitative and qualitative methods. On one hand, a researcher might conduct a computer-aided analysis and enhance it with a discussion of a few excerpts.

On the other hand, a researcher might provide a few basic descriptive statistics to introduce an extensive discourse analysis. The consistency of the ranking of foci from Cooper, Potter, and Dupagne to this study is strongest for quantitative work (r =.88) and less so for the mixed (r =. 38) and qualitative (r =.14) categories. This may suggest that the topical interests of quantitative researchers vary less than those of their qualitative colleagues.

First, the percentage of atheoretical studies is likely to be smaller in the last decade than in the previous years, having dropped from Cooper, Potter, and Dupagne's estimate of 72% to this study's finding of 58% (summing the three atheoretical categories). This modest change is almost entirely in the realm of qualitative research, with the percentage of atheoretical work dropping from 97% to 59%. Cooper, Potter, and Dupagne do not elaborate this result by year, but we might presume a gradual change in this category.

This study does show a mild trend away from atheoretical work, with the high of 69% occurring in 1990 and the low of 51% in 1998, with only slight rebound in 2000 to 53%. The stronger trend is located in the qualitative work, but is also present in the mixed column, shifting from 90% atheoretical in Cooper, Potter, and Dupagne to 69% in this study.

Of the theoretical work done in the quantitative mode, the majority makes use of either a hypothesis or research question. Very likely this reflects the orientation of quantitative researchers toward a deductive approach and the use of inferential statistics.

The opposite is the case for the qualitative work, perhaps reflecting the stronger orientation toward induction. Closer examination, with categories collapsed to atheoretical, presentation of a hypothesis, and formal test of theory shows dependence between use of theory and methodology. Of the qualitative work, 58% is atheoretical with 32% presenting a hypothesis and only 11% formally testing. Of the quantitative work, again 58% is atheoretical but 8% presents a hypothesis while 38% formally test. Within the mixed category, 68% is atheoretical with 21% presenting a hypothesis and 10% formally testing.

Experiments, surveys, and content analysis-with their associated contact with people and media-remain the dominant approaches in quantitative work. It is more difficult to make comparisons with Cooper, Potter, and Dupagne in the qualitative column due to the low number of observations in the earlier study.

But in the 1990s we can see that qualitative studies rarely made use of experimental or survey approaches but do present more secondary analysis and reanalysis. Mixed research tended to involve content, with direct contact with people and media content as leading sources of data.

This study also allowed a category for multiple procedures and sources. Of the 62 studies using multiple procedures (e.g., combining a survey with content analysis), 29 (48%) were quantitative, 28 (44%) were mixed, and 5 (8%) were qualitative. Alternately, of the 60 mixed studies nearly half (45%) employed multiple procedures. A similar pattern presents itself for data sources. Of the 37 studies using multiple sources 22 (60%) were quantitative, 9 (24%) were mixed and 6 (16%) were qualitative.

Looking more closely at the multiple categories for procedure and source also reveals their characteristics. For sources of data, 20 of the 37 instances of multiple sources involve the combination of people and media content. For mixed procedures, about a quarter (23%) combine survey and content analysis. These may be agenda-setting studies (data on that detail were not collected). Another quarter combine observation and content analysis.

Finally, while a number of additional cross tabulations could be done with these data, readers are probably most interested in details on the journals examined. Two such analyses were run.

Dependence was observed between journal and use of theory as well as journal and method. The journal in which atheoretical articles appear least (4%) is Critical Studies in Mass Communication, which is strongly qualitative (91%). This observation may provide some credibility to the present study at least to the degree that observations on qualitative work do not appear to be biased against identification of the use of theory.

The journals in which atheoretical work appears most commonly are Journalism & Mass Communication Quarterly and Quarterly Journal of Speech, both with about 85% of their content being atheoretical.

If combined with its dominance in terms of the number of articles published (27% of chapters in this study), Journalism & Mass Communication Quarterly makes the greatest contribution (40%) to the body of atheoretical research in this group of eight journals. Interestingly, Journalism & Mass Communication Quarterly is also the leading venue for research using mixed methods, accounting for just over half of those studies.

## DISCUSSION

Very few studies were located in which methods were mixed. Each article listed combines quantitative and qualitative approaches and is indexed by the specific methods used. For example, the first chapter is an experiment and a survey combined, the second is an experiment and a content analysis, the third was survey only, the fourth begins a series of studies combining survey and observation, and so forth.

Not one of these chapters makes reference to triangulation or presents developed rationale for combining quantitative and qualitative approaches. And interestingly, an electronic search of Communication Abstracts for the term triangulation only returns five items, one of which is not relevant, and none of which appears in the eight journals examined here.

The overarching conclusion of this analysis seems to be that scholarship in these journals has reached a roughly 60/40 quantitative/qualitative split, rarely combines these approaches, and is almost devoid of triangulation as a formal approach to research.

To what degree might this argument be more broadly true of the field? It is certainly defensible that these journals represent our flagship outlets and are appropriately considered elite by virtue of their circulation and selectivity. But it is less clear what that actually means, especially in terms of influence over doctoral pedagogy. If these journals carry more credibility and exert more influence than other journals then the results of this study are more important than otherwise. A broader study of scholarship might paint a different picture and should be an invitation to further research.

To a limited degree a broader examination can be made by looking at the chapter described above by Kamhawi and Weaver, in which a sample of 889 articles in 10 journals were examined across the period 1980-1999. That study and the present one both report about the same proportion of articles using theory, 42% here and 39% in Kamhawi and Weaver. This is a useful concurrence given the differences between the studies in time span and journals examined. Kamhawi and Weaver found 70% of the articles in their sample using quantitative methods, while this study reports 57% (27% and 41% qualitative, 3% and 2% mixed, respectively). It is likely that these differences are largely due to the different journals examined, although some sampling and coding error must also be present.

Finally, there is good agreement between studies on the prevalence of experimental methods (15% and 13%), surveys (20% and 33%), content analysis (30% and 30%), and multiple approaches (2% and 3%). Due to differences in coding, these appear to be the only specific points of comparison for these two studies.

The original impetus for this chapter came from doctoral seminar discussions on the relative characteristics of quantitative versus qualitative research in this field, with some exploration of the characteristics of triangulation. Students in the seminar were required to write research proposals for their semester work, and were asked to integrate both quantitative and qualitative approaches to at least some degree.

While this N=1 observation is about as anecdotal as possible, most if not all seminar participants had considerable difficulty in conceptualizing studies with mixed methods. In fact, discussions over the course of the semester lead most participants to the conclusion that the additional difficulties of methods triangulation outweighed any potential benefits. This particular classroom observation seems to be reflected in the characteristics of articles published over the last decade in our leading journals.

In closing, readers are encouraged to consider the possibilities for their own research that might be embodied, especially in light of a broader trend in research. This broader trend involves the everincreasing encouragement for researchers to engage in interdisciplinary work that focuses on problems.

Major funding agencies are supporting such approaches and many universities are working to lower disciplinary boundaries. This is a world of research in which the kind of multiplicity parsed out cannot be avoided. In order for researchers in mass communication to join this world of research and take advantage of its opportunities it will be necessary to move away from descriptive studies that focus on quantitative puzzles and qualitative topics and embrace this multiplicity. Given mass communication's roots in so many different disciplines and approaches, this should be natural.

## MASS COMMUNICATION RESEARCH TRENDS

Scholars of mass communication-and indeed other fields-seem always to be interested in knowing research trends in their areas. Which methods are used most and least often? Which areas have been more or less studied? Which statistics are most and least in use? How does funding for research compare with that of other fields, and what kinds of studies are more or less likely to receive funding? Studies published in journals provide a good, but not entirely comprehensive, data source to answer these questions. Each year hundreds of articles on a wide range of topics are published in academic communication journals.

Viewing this literature from a distance, one can discern larger patterns and. trends in mass communication research. Knowing them can help researchers and students identify areas of strength and weakness, and of abundance and scarcity, in the research. Scholars may tackle topics that a meta-analysis shows have been ignored or they may refine a method to avoid problems identified in an analysis of dozens or even hundreds of individual studies. One problem with generalizing from published journal articles to the whole mass communication field is that books, monographs, book chapters, and convention papers are excluded. Despite this drawback, many researchers argue that journal articles are a barometer of research trends1 and reflect the evolution of communication research. For most mass communication scholars, journal articles are the main channel for reporting current research after convention and conference papers.

Several systematic reviews or meta-analyses of mass communication journal articles have already been carried out, especially in the 1970s and 1990s. This monitoring has been important in a field that changes rapidly, but many of these studies have been limited in scope. Some have analysed only one topic or one journal. The present thematic meta-analysis is wider in scope to provide a larger and more representative picture of recent research trends in mass communication. This study analyses ten major mass communication journals during the decades of the 1980s and 1990s.

These journals were chosen based on circulation, acceptance rate, and blind review process as the most widely read and highly esteemed in the mass communication field. The twenty-year time period covered by this present study was chosen to provide a long enough span to observe trends and also because the last decade has not yet been examined in detail. This time period also enables us to evaluate predictions made by previous meta-analyses about the future of mass communication research, if one keeps in mind that our findings are limited to the major journals of our field, publications whose focus most likely changes more slowly than conference papers, newer journals, and possibly books and book chapters.

## META-ANALYSES OF MASS COMMUNICATION RESEARCH

Previous meta-analyses of mass communication research have focused on the following topics. Qualitative versus Quantitative Methods, The emphasis on qualitative and quantitative research in mass communication journals has interested many researchers and scholars in general. Some studies have examined changes in methodology over time. Each has found an increase in the use of quantitative research.

Cooper, Potter, and Dupagne investigated the assumption that the amount of qualitative research has increased during the past decades. They studied eight journals during the 1965-1989 period. A systematic interval of three years was used to choose the sample from a population of twenty-five years. They did not find an expected increase in qualitative research. Instead, they found that qualitative research was actually more common in the late 1960s, but in the 1970s and 1980s quantitative research far exceeded it.

They argued that this finding did not mean that qualitative research was losing favour with researchers, but rather that the journals sampled might not have been ones that qualitative mass media researchers sought out, considering that many of the high circulation journals were still heavily quantitative in orientation during this time period.

Weaver, surveying trends in the field, urged more studies that combine qualitative and quantitative methods. Previous research has shown that very few such studies have been published.

In those studies that combined more than one method, the combinations tended to be quantitative. Weaver argued that there was an increase in research combining the two approaches in the 1980s. This trend was expected to continue. But subsequent studies have shown that qualitative research has not increased, at least not in high circulation communication journals. Their primary focus is still quantitative research, even though more researchers continue to attest to the larger role that qualitative research should be playing.

## Theoretical Frameworks

Several reviews of mass communication research have focused on whether there was an explicit theoretical framework evident in the articles. Riffe and Freitag found that only a fourth of the articles employing content analysis included an explicit theoretical framework, and fewer than half of them had clearly stated hypotheses or research questions that guided the analysis. Overall, research in mass communication has been found lacking in theoretical development by this and other reviews.

## Medium

Print media have been the focus of many research studies. Weaver and Gray found that 56% of the articles between 1955 and 1974 in Journalism Quarterly dealt with print media. Electronic media or a combination of electronic and print media constituted 26%.

They attributed this dominance to numerous historical articles on newspapers, magazines, and books. Other studies have also demonstrated the dominance of research on print media in mass communication journals. But these results were derived from only one journal-Journalism Quarterly. Since then the journal has widened its scope, and in 1995 it changed its name to Journalism & Mass Communication Quarterly.

One might ask today whether studies of print media still dominate. Television is the medium with the highest exposure among most groups in society. It is only logical that it will receive attention in proportion to its reach in society. There are newly discovered areas in television research that have drawn increased interest. In the past, visual aspects of television have not received a great deal of attention.

Television has mostly been studied in terms of its verbal messages (for theoretical and methodological reasons), but now there is an increased interest in studying visual images and how they interact with the verbal content of television to affect the audience. The Internet does not seem to have dethroned television yet as a focus for research, although there are increasing numbers of communication studies about the Internet.

### Funding

Mass communication research has traditionally received less frequent funding than any of the other social sciences, according to studies by Weaver and Gray, and Zhi and Swiencicki. Weaver and Gray, studying the period from 1954 to 1978, found only one-fourth of the mass communication studies reported in Journalism Quarterly and Public Opinion Quarterly acknowledged funding, while the average funding rate for journals from the three disciplines of psychology, sociology, and political science was 55%. Zhu and Swiencicki studied the 1983-1993 period for these two journals plus Journal of Communication, Journal of Broadcasting & Electronic Media, Critical Studies in Mass Communication, and Communication Research.

They found only 22% of the sampled articles reported funding compared to 56% in the other disciplines. In their analysis of two major journals from 1954 to 1978, Weaver and Gray found that research funding was evenly balanced among university, government, and private sources. This present study checks on this balance during the 1980s and 1990s.

## METHOD

The objective of this present study is to investigate trends in published mass communication research during the decades of the 1980s and 1990s in ten major journals. We were particularly interested in the use of qualitative and quantitative methods, the presence of theoretical frameworks, the medium (or media) being studied, and acknowledgment of funding (its presence or lack of, and sources of).

### Sample

As mentioned earlier, many meta-analyses have focused on single journals, but generalizing from one journal to most journals in the field is questionable. Studying more than one journal allows for wider generalization. We have analysed mass communication research published in the twenty years between 1980 and 1999 in ten major mass communication journals in the United States. We have excluded book reviews, essays, and commentaries as well as articles not dealing with mass communication. "Research-in-brief" articles also were not included.

Major mass communication journals were defined as those that have a circulation of more than 1,500, employ a blind review process, and have a typical acceptance rate under 20%. Based on these criteria, the selection was made from The Iowa Guide.

Four of these journals-Journalism & Mass Communication Quarterly, Journal of Communication, Journal of Broadcasting & Electronic Media, and Critical Studies in Mass Communication-are the official publications on mass communication research of four major professional societies. We realise that the results of this study are influenced by the sample used. From the outset, for example, excluding "research in brief" meant that a certain line of research published in the selected journals was not included in our sample. We excluded these reports because they rarely included information on many of our key variables.

The choice of "major" or "big" journals also restricts the kind of research we analysed, but we thought that studying the more general and larger circulation journals (as opposed to the more narrowly focused and smaller circulation publications) would be the most representative of mass communication research since these journals likely reach more scholars in the field than the newer journals. The fact remains that our findings can only be generalized to these journals and that different results would be likely from a wider selection of journals and publications than we analysed.

For each journal, one issue was selected randomly to represent each year. Thus there are a total of 196 issues analysed in this study. A table of random numbers was used to make the issue selection for each journal. A range was set (from 1 to 4 if the journal was quarterly, or 1 to 6 if it was bi-monthly). A random starting point was chosen, and then the researchers moved down the table taking the first number that fell within the range.

Twenty numbers were selected for each journal, each representing a year. A total of 889 research articles related to mass communication published in the ten journals between January 1980 and December 1999 were included in this analysis.

## Coding Instrument

Variables coded for each article included the general method of research (qualitative, quantitative, or a mix of both), the data gathering procedure (survey, content analysis, etc.), the theory behind the study (if any), the source of funding, and the time period from which data were gathered. If the method by which the results were determined involved numerical or counting procedures and statistics were used to report data, the chapter was classified as quantitative.

Quantitative research included mostly content analyses, surveys, and experiments. Qualitative research involves being closely involved with the subjects to increase depth of understanding. It does not convert what is observed into numerical form in order to perform mathematical procedures. It often includes focus groups, direct observation, in-depth interviews, and case studies, as well as legal, policy, and historical research.

If more than one data gathering procedure was used, the method was coded as a mixture of quantitative if all the methods were quantitative, a mixture of qualitative if all the methods were qualitative, or a combination of both qualitative and quantitative when both kinds of methods were used. For example, a survey in addition to in-depth interviews would be coded as a combination of qualitative and quantitative methods.

We also coded the communication medium studied. An article was classified as print if it dealt exclusively with print media (newspapers, magazines, trade journals). It was considered broadcast if it dealt with television and/or radio. When print and broadcast were both studied, the article was coded as a combination. Studies of the Internet were coded separately. Some studies that did not mention any particular medium were coded as "media in general." Finally, an "others" option included other mass media studies too infrequent to have their own categories. These included videotext, cinema, wire services, public relations, and video games, as well as non-media studies (such as studies of mass communication students or faculty).

Theory was among the most difficult variables to code. We specifically looked for any theory mentioned. When no theory was specifically mentioned, we re-examined whether any theory was strongly implied but fell short of being mentioned. When more than one theory was mentioned, the dominant one was coded. When more than one seemed dominant, the first one mentioned was coded.

Funding source options included university, government, and private. More than one funding source could be checked for a single article; the category "combination" was included to be used for this situation. The funding status and funding source were coded based on the acknowledgment made by the author(s) in the text, footnotes, or the endnotes.

Study length was coded as an interval variable. It was later receded for ease of analysis. The categories created were (1) less than three months, (2) from more than three months to one year and (3) more than one year.

## Data Collection

One mass communication doctoral student did the coding. An intercoder reliability test of a sample of 26 articles using Krippendorf's alpha showed 78% agreement. The lowest agreement was over data gathering method (65%) and the highest agreement was over the theory mentioned (100%).

## Statistics

Considering the exploratory nature of this study, the statistical significance level was set at.05 to minimize Type II errors (overlooking real relationships). The statistic most employed was the difference of proportions test, mainly to examine whether the changes over the decades were significant or not. These tests are usually two-tailed.

## Findings

*Methods.* It has been widely asserted and assumed that qualitative methods have re-emerged in mass communication research. This assumption is evident in U.S. mass communication programs where the number of courses in qualitative methodologies appears to be growing. Contrary to expectations, however, qualitative research was not given as much attention as quantitative research in the 1980s in the 8 journals studied by Cooper, Potter, and Dupagne. They speculated that these journals might have been biased against publishing qualitative research, and that such research might have been published in other journals that were more qualitatively oriented. But their analysis included most of the leading journals with the largest circulations in the field. A reanalysis of the 1980s using our 10 journals (7 of which overlapped with those analysed by Cooper, Potter, and Dupagne), and an analysis of the 1990s, confirms their findings.

The use of qualitative methods did not increase significantly during the twenty-year period we analysed. There was a slight increase of 4% from the early 1980s to the late1990s. Even in the 1990s, non-qualitative studies clearly dominated in the 10 mass communication journals we analysed. Incorporating 1970s data from Cooper, Potter, and Dupagne, the gap between qualitative and quantitative research seems to have increased from the 1970s to the 1980s and then leveled off in the 1990s. The use of both methods jointly in single studies has been rare, especially in the 1980s and 1990s.

Experiments ranked third, nearly doubling in frequency from the early 1980s to the late 1990s. One reason that these three methods are used the most may be related to funding, considering that studies employing quantitative methods are more likely to have received funding than those not using such methods.

Increased use of experiments is consistent with the rise of the cognitive approach that uses experiments as the main method of data gathering and also with an increase in funding of experimental research.

## Use of Theory

The use of theory was not common, even for articles using quantitative methods. Of the 889 studies only 39% referred to a theory (30.5% specifically mentioned and 8.7% implied). Most of these theories were cited in quantitative studies, especially surveys.

The theories most frequently mentioned were ones relating to uses and effects of media, and also that only three theories (Information Processing, Uses and Gratifications, and Media Construction of Social Reality) were cited in 10% or more of the studies.

## Medium

The traditional broadcast and print media were most likely to be studied in leading mass communication research journals during the last two decades. Studies on broadcast exceeded studies on print in both decades. The overall difference of 13.5% between the two areas is statistically significant. Although we are now in the age of the Internet and the World Wide Web, this was not yet reflected in mass communication research published in major journals in the 1990s. There was a slight increase from the 1980s to almost 7% in the late 1990s, but overall studies about the Internet constituted only 2% of all the articles we analysed. Almost all of these studies appeared in the1990s, when the Internet began to be considered a mass medium.

Broadcast research exceeded print research in all the five-year intervals studied. When broadcast research increased, print research decreased, and vice versa. Looking only at the first and last time periods, it is clear that broadcast research decreased about 10% while print research remained at the same level. The decrease in broadcast research seemed to be due mainly to an increase in research on the Internet and other media, and non-media studies.

**Funding**

For the two decades combined, only 254 or slightly more than one-fourth (28.6%) of the published studies we analysed acknowledged receipt of financial support from an intramural or extramural source.

Weaver and Gray, studying funding between 1954 and 1978, found a similar pattern: only 26% of their studies mentioned a funding source. This funding rate is also roughly comparable to the one found by Zhu and Swiencicki who studied mass communication research funding from 1983 to 1993. Overall, 22% of their studies were funded. A clear trend can be detected from our data.

There has been a gradual decrease over the years in frequency of funding. While 36.2% of all studies were funded in 1980-1984, this decreased significantly to 23.8% in 1995-1999. Funding in the early 1980s for published studies was nearly evenly split between university, government, and private sources with no one source dominating, similar to Weaver and Gray's findings for the 1950s, 60s and 70s. They regarded this diversity in funding sources as healthy. But toward the late 1980s and early 1990s, we found government funding decreased proportionally with a small rebound in the late 1990s.

Private funding increased slightly in the late 1980s, but decreased notably in the 1990s, especially in the last half of the decade. University funding increased steadily during the 1980s and 1990s, becoming by far the dominant funding source in the 1990s. The dominance in university funding can be regarded as a positive development because of the freedom of inquiry usually supported by academic institutions, but as Weaver noted, the relatively low level of funding provided by universities as compared with government and private sources also restricts the kind of research that can be done.

We found no correlation between funding and the time period covered by a study. In other words, there was no significant difference in proportion of funded studies by time span of the study (less than three months, from three months to one year, or more than one year). But there was definitely a greater tendency for quantitative studies to receive funding.

**Discussion**

This study sought to analyse and update trends in mass communication research published in ten leading journals during the past two decades, with special attention to whether the debate over approaches has resulted in changes in methods used, which media are most and least studied, how theory-guided the research is, which theories are most often relied upon, and whether funding levels and sources have changed.

One notable finding is the lack of any increase in qualitative research articles in the journals sampled and the continued emphasis on the funding of quantitative studies.

The reasons why qualitative research is not more prominent in major journals could be further investigated. Is this due to the perceived orientation of these journals or to the actual orientation of these journals? In other words, is there a "bias" among the major journal editors in favour of quantitative research or do qualitative researchers not submit to these journals because of a perceived bias, page length restrictions, or other reasons? These questions could be further examined in surveys of journal editors and qualitative researchers.

One of the limits of our findings is that using the article as the unit of analysis does not account for the space devoted to such articles. Qualitative research generally requires more pages to report than does quantitative. Thus we would expect journals that carry fewer articles to publish relatively more qualitative research per issue.

In the six journals with lower article frequency (they carried 12% of total articles analysed), both methods of research are represented equally, while in the four journals with higher article frequency (they accounted for 88% of the sampled articles) qualitative methods are significantly less likely to be used, confirming our expectation.

Because our sample of articles came mainly from the four journals that averaged more than three articles per issue, these articles are most likely to be shorter and thus to employ quantitative methods. These findings confirm the dominance of the quantitative social science research approach in major mass communication journals in the last two decades of the Twentieth Century. However, these generalizations can be applied only to the ten journals studied here.

Our findings may create the impression that relatively little qualitative research is conducted in the mass communication field, but it seems likely that more qualitative research is published in other more specialized (and lower circulation) journals, book chapters, monographs, and books. Our sample of journals did not include many of the journals that qualitative researchers typically read and publish in, although it did include some, such as Critical Studies in Mass Communication and Journalism & Mass Communication Monographs.

Another major finding of this analysis is the dominance of mass communication studies focused on traditional broadcast and print media, especially television, and newspapers. Will these media continue to dominate research as we enter further into the "Internet age"?

So far there has been only a slight decrease in traditional media research and a slight increase in mass communication research about the Internet. Some of the reasons may be the difficulty of conducting Internet studies, the slow acceptance of the Internet as a mass medium, the failure of the Internet to replace traditional media, and its fairly limited reach. Yet more research on new media is expected in the coming years, at least more than was evident in our sample of articles.

One indication of this is a recent analysis by Kim and Weaver of the index of Communication Abstracts from 1995 through 1999. This abstracting service includes studies broadly related to communication from more than 200 journals, as well as reports and books.

Kim and Weaver found that Internet-related publications increased rapidly from only ten in 1995 to 188 in 1999, an increase from 0.7% to 9.5%. In addition, some new online journals have emerged, such as Convergence and the Web Journal of Mass Communication Research, and much research about the Internet is published in such journals as Journal of Computer Mediated Communication and New Media & Society.

Theoretical development is probably the main consideration in evaluating the disciplinary status of the field. As our field grows in scope and complexity, the pressure for theoretical integration increases. It seems that scholars in the field should be developing and testing theories to explain the process and effects of mass communication. However, that was not widely evident in our sample.

Overall only 39% of the studies referred to any theory, and most of these references were to previously existing theories. DeFleur's analysis of the state of theory building seems to apply to our results. Most of the articles we analysed seemed to be one-shot studies without a theoretical trail. This information is not news to mass communication researchers. A 1991 survey of major scholars in the field of communication revealed that only 37% of them thought theoretical development of the field was either good or very good.

Funding is of central importance to any field of research. However, the data we have about funding for mass communication research is limited, as few studies have empirically investigated this issue, which almost all communication scholars must face. While mass communication has been growing in terms of more and new media channels, a larger labour force, and more colleges offering mass communication education, there has been no corresponding increase in the proportion of funded research. This study finds that overall funding for mass communication remains low; there has been a steady decline in proportions of funded research from the early 1980s to the late 1990s, at least that research published in major journals analysed in this study.

In addition, a balance between university, government, and private funding sources was no longer evident in the 1990s, when the university became the main source of funding. This has one advantage: unlike government and private sectors, the university typically does not have an agenda favoring one sort of research more than another. Thus, theoretical as well as applied research can be pursued, but university funding tends to be lower in actual dollars than that from private and government sources. The decline of government support for mass communication studies may be due to government funding agencies not recognizing mass communication as an academic discipline.

Mass communication scholars have a long way to go before being fully recognized by funding sources within the government. The decline in private funding is harder to explain. The increase in university funding may imply that within the university, mass communication is becoming more accepted as a legitimate field. More systematic investigation as to the cause of the changes in funding patterns would be useful.

Contrary to Berelson's 1959 declaration that the field of mass communication research was "withering away,"51 the field has actually grown and blossomed in the five decades that have followed. This is apparent from the proliferation of communication schools, doctoral programs, associations and divisions in the associations, graduate student enrollment, journals, and books.

In spite of such growth, the findings of this review of mass communication research published in ten leading journals suggest considerable stability in methods, media, and funding patterns during the 1980s and 1990s, as compared with the previous two or three decades. There were some changes in methods and in the theories most and least studied, but the general picture was one of more stability than change, at least in these major journals.

It must be remembered, however, that this observation does not include the dozens of conference papers, books, book chapters, and articles in newer, less widely circulated journals. There seems to be much change already going on in the mass communication field, but not yet in the major journals of the field.

Depending on one's view of the value of continuity and change, this can be interpreted as positive or negative. It does seem likely, however, given the dramatic changes in communication media and scholarship during the past decade, that research in the major journals in mass communication will also change in the coming decade.

This study examined one issue from each of the twenty years of investigation for each of the ten journals selected. Thus while this research of mass communication research trends is one of the most ambitious so far in terms of population studied and variables examined, we are aware that the sample may be skewed in favour of quantitative research. A larger sample that includes different journals and books (and even conference research papers) would likely yield different results. We leave that formidable task to others to explore.

## EXPLICATING WEB PORTALS FOR COMMUNICATION RESEARCH

One of the unique features of the World Wide Web as a mass medium lies in the fact that message sources are indistinct from message receivers. The Web is literally a web woven collectively by all citizens of the Internet, resulting in massive amounts of information being disseminated by both professional gatekeepers and laypersons.

For casual users interested in efficiently obtaining news and information on the net, this proves burdensome because they now have the arduous additional task of sifting through information of unknown pedigree and determining its veridicality instead of simply attending to news of established credibility.

This might be the reason why portals, which help to make sense of information avalanches by establishing gatekeeping guidelines and streamlining information flow, are among the most popular sites on the Web, and why some scholars and practitioners believe that the portal is the key organizing unit for gaining a better understanding of the new medium.

Literature suggests that although the term "portal" is widely used, a majority of existing perspectives consider the term a "buzzword" that requires little definition or explanation. This might be one reason why the term has been under-explicated and suffers from theoretical abstraction. Indeed, little progress has been made beyond early postulations of "portals like Yahoo" or portals as sites that "consist almost exclusively of absolute links to a large number of other sites." Although such definitions serve as a rudimentary starting point, they contribute very little toward a conceptual framework that is necessary for conducting a programme of research on the topic of portals.

Even as portals are increasing in their presence as well as importance, the absence of suitable ontological definitions precludes us from not only developing a "portal typology" to facilitate better conceptual understanding but also makes empirical investigation difficult. Indeed, consistent with Strauss's opinion, portals suffer from "confusing and often contradictory definitions," which perhaps explains why, even though the "portal" has supplemented the "Web site" in Internet terminology, media researchers have devoted little attention to the topic of portals.

The primary goal of this chapter is to delineate the applicability of portals as a promising venue of research in communication technology. Specifically, it proposes a classification system for portals by performing an explication based on metaphors that are useful for describing the different kinds of portals on the Web. In accordance with the metaphorbased approach, it identifies distinguishing features of portals and outlines pertinent theoretical propositions. Finally, it examines operational considerations for studying portals and advances useful propositions aimed at building a research agenda around the concept of "portals." We first discuss the importance of metaphors in communication research before explicating the concept of portals.

## METAPHORS AND COMMUNICATION

Metaphors in communication have received extensive attention, from the time Aristotle proposed that they can be seen primarily as analogies, commonly referred to as the comparison theory of metaphor. Metaphors are universally employed to illustrate something novel by orienting to something more commonly understood. Indeed, as several scholars have argued, metaphors are not just pretty linguistic artifices but critical devices when faced with the task of reducing an abstract concept to something that is easily comprehensible. As Centner and Jeziorski state, "...a faculty for analogical reasoning is an innate part of human cognition...." Recent proliferation of research on metaphors has shown that metaphors are central to communication processes, and that they can be especially useful for elucidating abstract theoretical terms or concepts.

Metaphors have also enjoyed a rich history in the formulation of several mass communication theories. Indeed, Wilbur Schramm's early postulations regarding the effects of mass media were based on metaphorical allusion when he suggested that the process and effects of mass communication was similar to that of calcareous water dripping slowly from stalagmite on a cave floor.

Schramm offered this metaphorical analogy to suggest that the effects of mass communication were both gradual and incremental, and hence needed study over time. Not surprisingly, several prominent theoretical frameworks and propositions in the field have employed metaphorical devices. These include "magic bullet," "two-step flow," "diffusion," "cultivation," "agenda setting," "spiral of silence," and "sleeper effect," among others.

Metaphors are akin to heuristics because they help to ease cognitive overload by allowing users to develop their own mental shortcuts. Fundamentally, metaphors are "linguistic comparisons of the form 'A is B.'" That is, although perceptions of "A" and "B" may vary based on individual differences, they are essentially two distinct terms or conceptual realms that can be linked together by deployment of metaphors.

Consistent with Boyd's belief that metaphors are essential in the comprehension of new scientific propositions, a metaphor-based approach is particularly useful when explicating technological "buzz-words" (such as "portal") that suffer from conceptual and empirical obscurity. Boyd sees the role of "theory-constitutive" metaphors as affording "epistemic access" to "important and interesting aspects of reality." Applying this rationale to Web portals, a metaphor-based explication appears to be particularly useful because portals are both relatively novel in media research and conceptually fuzzy. By classifying portals in terms of intelligible and everyday metaphors, and also by drawing out the defining features of each metaphor, such an explication has the potential to offer "epistemic access" of portals to Web users in terms of those variables that are relevant to communication research.

As an alternative to the popular technique outlined by Chaffee, the metaphor-based approach to explication has certain distinct advantages: (1) it leads to conceptual clarity by examining connections in terms of familiar, intelligible analogies; (2) it assists in identification of distinctive features of each metaphor; and (3) it better facilitates the all-important leap from the conceptual realm to the empirical domain by exemplifying-and therefore concretizing-the concept. For these reasons, we perform a metaphor-based explication of portals.

Although there are several theoretical frameworks underlying metaphor research, our approach draws on the perspective of equating a "topic" to a "vehicle."

According to metaphor scholars, the purpose of employing the "topic" and "vehicle" approach is to uncover an efficient way of allowing a concept to represent those properties and underlying characteristics that are most applicable to the concept. That is, the deployment of a metaphor allows useful bits of information to be conveyed from the topic to the vehicle.

To clarify, consider the following statement: "The United States is a melting pot." Here, "United States" is the topic and "melting pot" is the vehicle. The central idea is that most people would find the meaning of the base term ("United States") to be instigated by the ease and efficiency with which they can comprehend the meaning of the vehicle ("melting pot"). That is, individuals' assessment of the United States would be based on construing it as a melting pot enmeshing various cultures, races, and identities.

Ultimately, the effectiveness of a strong metaphor lies in its potential to represent familiar features and hence answer "how things are." Indeed, as Black pointed out, the appropriateness of representational features is what may be eventually useful to elucidate the psychological and informational facets of successful metaphors. Given what we are attempting to accomplish in this chapter, we offer five metaphorical conceptions (or vehicles) of the topic of "portals" for stimulating theoretically driven social-science research on this unique venue of online mass communication. These are the vehicles of gateways, billboards, networks, niches, and brands. These metaphors are derived by a process of meaning analysis.

The particular metaphors were selected because they are most evocative and applicable to most portals, and hence most conducive to empirical examination using the variable-centered approach recommended by Nass and Mason. Thus, we identify five distinctive variables that best represent the metaphors of gateways, billboards, networks, niches, and brands.

These variables refer to the "5Cs" of control, content, community, customization, and commerce. They accentuate each of the five metaphors by meeting the exhaustiveness and distinctiveness criteria as well as by representing prominent variables in online communication.

Portals Are Gateways. At a rudimentary level, a portal can be conceptualized as a Web site that serves as a primary starting point for users connecting to the Internet. Some of the current major portals, according to this definition, include iGoogle, Yahoo!, and Netvibes. Ruefli, Whinston, and Wiggins opine that AOL and CompuServe can also be considered portals in that they symbolize entry points for their customers to get on the Web.

Cohen equates a portal to a "point of presence" or gateway access to the Internet. According to IBM, an Internet portal is "a single integrated, ubiquitous, and useful [point of] access to information, applications, and people." Connolly states that "a portal is a gateway to the Web that allows the plethora of information available on Internet and Intranet Web sites to be organized and customized through a single entry point."

These definitions suggest that the consensus perception is one where a portal is treated as a "door" to access information on the Web or to access the Web itself.

The "portals are gateways" metaphor also points to the importance of control as a principal defining feature. Control can be examined at two levels. For instance, the "gateway" can certainly exert some semblance of control because it not only dictates what features will be offered to users but also how users will access those features. At another level, users can also exercise control over the nature of their entry into the Web by choosing specific gateways whose gatekeeping practices are in line with their interests (e.g., AOL). For users, exercising such control will likely lead to greater empowerment.

Portals Are Billboards. A portal can also play a powerful role in building consumer awareness and confidence in other portals or Web sites. This is especially true of megaportals (mammoth or extra-large portals such as Yahoo! and WebMD). When users enter such a megaportal, their eyeballs are immediately captured, and the brands they see there can make an impression and conceivably stimulate clicking behaviour. This would be especially true if the megaportal enjoys perceptions of high credibility with its users, which may then influence their perceptions of the advertised portal or Web site.

Of course, portal designers and owners are aware of this marketing function that they potentially serve, and established portals enjoy high advertising demand. For the advertising site, it is difficult to build traffic on an isolated Web site. As a result, many online sellers establish alliances with portals such as Yahoo! and MSN so that they can maximize the "billboard" potential of these portals and hence increase the likelihood of their own content enjoying high visibility.

Thus, the portal is a veritable gallery that serves as a billboard advertising a diversity of content, both informational and commercial. From a user's perspective, both the availability of content as well as the awareness of different types of content is increased because one is exposed to a variety of content from multiple vendors and information sources.

**Portals Are Networks**

Online networks are analogous to Rheingold's conceptualization of virtual communities as "social aggregations that emerge from the Net when enough people carry on those public discussions long enough, with sufficient human feeling, to form webs of personal relationships in cyberspace."

The fundamental ways in which online networks differ from "traditional" offline networks pertain to how the former are not constrained by barriers of time and space, but formed on the basis of commonality of interests. Thus, the information-delivery capability of the Internet hasn't so much built a new business as it has created new Net-based community networks.

These networks need not be comprised entirely of known others, but from shared experiences with unknown others. For example, Paul McCartney's concert at the Cavern Club in Liverpool forty years later was not broadcast on television but on the Internet, creating a shared experience for Beatles fans who know that they are part of a specific network of similar others. Therefore, a significant feature of successful portals is that they should be able to leverage commonality of interests, or "affinity," to form a network of likeminded users who come together to serve a specific purpose or share similar interests. Such users may perceive a strong sense of membership.

Membership refers to the feeling that individuals have devoted part of themselves to becoming a member, and therefore believes they have a certain entitlement to belong. As research in community psychology has shown, factors such as membership and a sense of belonging can effectively nurture a sense of community. For example, HaReshima. com is a portal that brings together a network of Jewish users to discuss such varied issues as Jewish study, Kosher resources, Jewish culture, Israel, and so on.

Portals Are Niches. Portals also have the potential to target certain specialized consumers. Researchers have suggested that targeted information may be perceived as effective because unique advertising features have been customized to the attributes of a targeted consumer segment, and the target population will make mental connections between the presented information and themselves. Correspondingly, niche marketing concentrates on select, specialized segments that are most likely to be receptive to the products/ services being advertised.

That is, by focusing on a specific target or niche segment, portals can offer enhanced customer-centric services. Depending on the degree of specialization being offered, the term "portal" assumes two meanings. In addition to traditional, general interest, horizontal portals like Yahoo!, we are witnessing a rapid proliferation of vertical or niche portals. Horizontal portals cover a wide array of topics and features, and also act as repositories for an extensive range of information. In contrast, vertical portals, or vortals, are considered to represent category leaders in a given topical group or cater to a specific segment of users.

Essentially, horizontal portals (e.g., Yahoo!, Lycos, MSN) may be considered as all-purpose portals because they cater to a wide demographic segment. On the other hand, vortals cater to a specialized demographic segment, and hence are referred to as specific-purpose portals. For example, MissionAllergy.com is a vortal because it offers a wide range of services and information pertaining to allergies.

Thus, the distinction between horizontal portals and vertical portals is largely contingent on the degree of "nicheness," which relates to the specificity with which customized value can be created and delivered to each user. The element of customization is an important distinguishing feature of niche portals, because vertical portals offer more tailoring and customization features than horizontal portals. For example, MyYahoo.com is a niche portal (compared to the more generic Yahoo!) because it offers a wide range of selections customized to the individual user.

**Portals Are Brands**

Branding is an important issue when considering successful portal design. Brand loyalty in the online domain is quite different from that in the analog world. Factors that affect brand loyalty in the online environment are speed, ease of use, and the ability to deliver what a user is looking for. In fact, some findings suggest that users weigh these factors more heavily, compared to other factors such as pricing advantage. That is, brand loyalty is derived from users' experiences when using the portal or site.

In fact, the portal experience becomes one of the most important means for building and reinforcing brand identity and preferences. How well the portal performs its intended function (namely, providing a gateway to the Web as in AOL, creating a vibrant community as in BET.com, or providing up-to-date information as in CNN.com) is likely to dictate the association of a particular portal with a particular identity. In effect, a portal becomes a brand name for a given category or genre of Web-based communication. Sometimes, this branding derives from corporate identity established with older media (e.g., CNN and MSNBC), but other times, new brands emerge within the Web medium (e.g. salon.com, drudgereport.com).

Thus, we may propose that the portal is the brand. The "portals are brands" classification is especially pertinent when examined from the commercial or transactional perspective. That is, a portal acts not only as a gateway but also as a one-stop shopping complex.

Users are likely to find-and fulfill-all or a specific expected domain of their transactional needs by visiting that site. For example, the process of purchasing a used car would include product research (e.g., make, model), product discovery (finding an appropriate used car), quality check, pricing, and extended warranty. Thus, a portal like cars.com is a one-stop full-service operation, where a potential buyer can execute every step involved in purchasing the car.

## DEFINING FEATURES OF THE "PORTAL AS METAPHOR" CLASSIFICATION

Yet another way of facilitating our theoretical understanding of portals is by examining their salient features. Searle suggests that the primary function of metaphors is to "call to mind" the mechanisms which can link a metaphorical phrase to a speaker's interpretation of the particular metaphor.48 In the human-Web site interaction context, merely identifying a portal in terms of metaphorical dimensions, while ontologically useful, would still not make explicit the underlying properties of the site suggested by the metaphor.

For that to happen, the metaphor has to be drawn out in terms that can be empirically observed. Our explication thus far of metaphors enables us to distill distinct attributes that typify portals and hence specify outcomes, i.e., we can identify certain distinctive features based on what portals can do. Although there probably are other attributes that necessitate consideration, we propose that the features of customization, content, control, community, and commerce-the 5Cs-are particularly noteworthy in developing theoretical propositions and related operationalizations. Each of these important features is discussed below.

### Customization

The use of terms such as "proactive," "user-centered," and "user-controlled" to describe portals is an implicit recognition of their customization potential. Portals can not only empower users by giving them the ability to customise content, but they can also anticipate a user's wants and deliver relevant content.

The ability to isolate individual users and target content specifically toward them is recognized as an important attribute of portals. It is therefore not surprising that the consensus opinion seems to be that "better customization makes for a better portal."

Furthermore, the elements of control, content, community, and commerce are influenced by customization. That is, presenting users the opportunity to customise information gives them greater control over their portal experience. Moreover, the customization feature can provide individualized content, can effectively build a spirit of community, and can facilitate transaction. In order to avoid being overwhelmed by "portal glut," strategies such as customization and personalization may be adopted by portals to cultivate feelings of loyalty and desire to revisit the portal site.

**Content**

Portals cover a wide array of topics and features, and also act as repositories for an extensive range of information. Although sometimes referred to as horizontal portals, they typically feature a search engine, a directory of Web sites, headline news, weather information, stock quotes, telephone and e-mail directories, possibly map information, chat groups, message boards or forums, and sometimes e-mail service and personal Web sites. All these different content features are available as "channels" or "windows," and users can customise the portal such that they can select and arrange only those channels that interest them.

A portal can also be likened to a catalog in that it is a compendium of stored information that is up-to-date and available in multimedia formats. In a similar vein, a portal is analogous to a collection, or "an accumulation of information resources intended for a user community or a set of communities." The underlying characteristic here is that such a collection should be user-centered and user-controlled. By selecting what information they choose to receive from portals, users perform the gate-keeping function themselves. Because users can effectively act as gate-keepers, it gives them a greater choice of content.

An implicit acknowledgement here is that offering users the ability to customise their content preferences will determine their ability to navigate through a maze of information, and help them select information that will be most useful to them. This conceptualization assumes that portals are user-centered and can empower users to construct personal information systems that are receptive to individual needs by their ability to respond in an interactive manner. Thus, by providing not only a gateway to content, but also a venue where content can be created, portals offer easy access to an immense amount of information.

**Control**

Because of their functionality, portals have the potential to offer a high degree of user empowerment compared to ordinary Web sites. Some important elements that users desire control over are exploitation, exposure, functionality, and content. Exploitation refers to how user information is used, and by whom. Users loathe the idea of their personal information being disseminated without their permission. They also demand control over how the information is used. That is, will the information be used to offer better site experiences, or will it be used to send invasive, undifferentiated messages?

Exposure, functionality, and content all relate to the degree of control mat a portal offers. These refer to how and when the user has access to customized offers or content. Exposure and functionality include being able to view recommendations based on prior behaviour, or based on the behaviors of other users with matching profiles. The degree of control is also predicated on the portal's ability to offer customized content (such as My BBC, My Lycos, My Yahoo), a feature that many users appreciate. In addition, interface functionality allows the portal to inform a user when certain events occur (e.g., a special airfare to a particular destination), and the ability to be selective about the type of content that is displayed (e.g., to receive news about their favourite sports team).

**Community**

A successful portal is one capable of leveraging "community knowledge," that is, relevant knowledge that a site acquires about users with similar tastes and values, enabling them to cater to user needs. Thus, some portals not only cater to a target network of users but they also have the capability to build an awareness of community. Portals nurture a true sense of community by allowing users access to comments and activities of likeminded others. By generating an impression of community, portals help to strengthen the sense that each member of the network has a role and stake in the portal.

Furthermore, Web 2.0 technologies have made it possible for portals to carry highly specific RSS feeds relevant to a narrowly defined community. Users can now share ideas and impressions with one another by way of blog comments and other feedback mechanisms built into portals. Several newer portals such as Netvibes let users feature their sharing (e.g., Flickr) and social networking (e.g., Facebook) sites on the main page, thus converting one's portal into a reflection of one's own community.

**Commerce**

Given the vast transactional potential of the Internet, portals can also be conceptualized in terms of commerce. In general, commercial portals are password-protected, with the underlying assumption being that a single log-in can facilitate easy navigation and accomplish a variety of transactional activities. These portals also employ encryption technologies (e.g., SSL) to ensure secure transactions. Typically, commercial portals should be able to provide customers personalized product offerings from a range of available content.

For instance, an individual interested in purchasing a computer can log into Dell Online, customise a computer based on his/her preferences, and complete the transaction. Amazon.com is a proactive interface in that it tries to influence transactions by offering individuals customized recommendations. The commerce element is also inherent in B2B portals because they cater to specific businesses by offering industry-specific information and facilitating transaction (e.g., Plastics.net).

## Synopsis of the 5Cs Framework

In summary, our postulation of the 5Cs framework resides in charting those features of metaphors that lend themselves best to empirical investigation using the variable-centered approach. Thus, when equating the topic of "portal" to the metaphor of "gateway," the attribute or feature that is most relevant is that of control. In a similar vein, when proposing how a portal is analogous to a network, billboard, niche, and brand, the features that best exemplify each of these metaphorical mappings are those of community, content, customization, and commerce, respectively.

This does not mean that there is not-or could not be-an overlap between or among these features based on the different vehicles; rather, we suggest that each of these portal metaphors accentuates one essential element more so than any other element. That is, the feature of control would be foremost in the conceptualization of a portal as a gateway but not as much to any of the other vehicles of network, billboard, niche, and brand. If the conceptualization established a feature that could potentially be equally spread across two vehicles, then it would dispossess the metaphorical allusion of its distinctiveness and hence deprive the conceptualization of theoretical clarity.

Based on the explication, we can illustrate how each portal metaphor signifies a role served by a specific (dominant) feature. Our discussion of outcome-based specifications suggests that, although each of the 5 Cs is distinctive on its own, it also is related to one (or more) features along psychological and/or ontological dimensions. The interconnectedness between-and among-the 5Cs indicates the variable nature of portals. That is, each of the 5Cs can be present in specific types of portals, with some Cs being reflected more prominently in certain types of portals, compared to others.

## Propositions for Empirical Research

Our conceptual exposition of Web portals is only as valid as the empirical support for theoretical propositions generated from it. A useful starting point is to consider the focal concept and ask whether it can be thought of as a variable. A portal can be conceived as a variable to the same extent that a Web site can be regarded as a variable. That is to say, when we talk about applying operationalizations to Web sites, we do so by manipulating specific elements that are assumed to be defining characteristics of Web sites. Based on our explication, then, we forward the following propositions that would benefit from empirical investigation.

P1: Each classification of a portal according to a specific superordinate category is contingent on the portal manifesting the defining feature of that particular superordinate category.

Fundamentally, a portal is a subordinate category of one of five superordinate categories (gateways, billboards, networks, niches, and brands). A superordinate category subsumes subordinate categories by making explicit certain properties or features that should be displayed by the subordinate category for membership into the superordinate group. For a portal to be seen as being included as part of a certain superordinate class, it will have to unambiguously display a distinct feature that defines that particular class. P1, then, specifies the necessary conditions for a portal to fulfill the class inclusion property of metaphors. Thus, for a portal to be included under the (superordinate) class of gateways, it should reflect the "control" element. Similarly, for a portal to be included under the class of billboards, networks, niches, and brands, it should manifest the elements of content, community, customization, and commerce, respectively.

P2: For effective portal comprehension, each of the five categorizations of portals should reflect the defining feature most closely associated with the specific superordinate classification, more so than any other feature(s).

This proposition underlines the importance of what Schon referred to as "frame conflict" and "frame restructuring" in metaphor research. That is, frame conflict arises when several different meanings of a frame are created and each meaning, while convincing and persuasive in its own right, also singularly differs from other meanings or mappings. One strategy for resolving this conflict is by identifying new features that may serve to connect the frame with its corresponding metaphor.

A frame is likely to be perceived as belonging to a unique category if it affords the distillation of a particular feature, while subsuming other features. In the context of portals, the isomorphism between a particular conceptualization and a valid operationalization is likely to be realized most effectively if users are able to pinpoint the particular (variable-based) feature that is most closely associated with that specific conceptualization.

Like P1, this proposition can also be tested empirically. Applied to our explication, then, exposure to a "niche" portal should evoke (from users) perceptions of customization to a significantly greater extent than perceptions of control, content, community, and commerce. Similarly, perceptions of control, content, community, and commerce should predominate when users are exposed to portals that are conceptualized as "gateways," "billboards," "networks," and "brands," respectively.

It should be noted that users may perceive more than one dominant feature upon exposure to a specific portal (e.g., they may rate a "niche" portal as possessing both the features of customization and commerce).

Under such circumstances, a possible "frame conflict" could lead to ambiguity regarding portal nomenclature (e.g., whether the conceptualization of the "niche" portal needs to be re-thought, depending on the primary objective of the portal). In reality, though, portal designers and producers may wish to offer combinations of elements to users (e.g., a niche shopping portal that accentuates both the features of customization and commerce to an equal degree). Such a decision may divest the portal of its uniqueness (e.g., inability to categorize the portal as either a "niche" or "brand," especially if both customization and commerce are perceived to be present equally), but ultimately, the cost-benefit tradeoff can be tested empirically.

P3: The defining feature of a given categorization of a portal should influence subsequent information processing in terms of attitudes, cognition, and behaviors. One of the aims of employing metaphors to represent a term or phrase that is not readily comprehensible is to provide a meaning analysis. Empirically, the extraction of meaning can be accomplished by measures of attitude, cognition, and behaviour (or behavioral intention).

Based on our explication, user responses to portals should eventually be contingent on the strength of the specific feature that the portal offers (or is supposed to offer). So, user perceptions of a portal in terms of attitudes, cognitions, and behaviors will be influenced by discerning the defining feature of that particular portal.

For users exposed to a "niche" portal, their attitudes toward the portal would be informed by their ability to perceive the degree of customization that is offered by the portal. Additionally, their memory for information featured on the portal site as well as their navigational behaviors (such as hyperlinks clicked on) would also be dictated by their perception of customization on the portal site.

In a similar vein, user attitudes, cognitions, and behaviors upon exposure to portals labeled as "gateways," "billboards," "networks," and "brands" should be motivated by perceptions of control, content, community, and commerce, respectively.

Although we submit these propositions based on our explication and in the hope of advancing an empirical programme of research on portals, emerging scholarship on portals has begun to examine some of these predictions. In one of the first experimental studies of portals, Kalyanaraman and Sundar operationalized a "niche" portal based on the degree of customization. Consistent with P1, they found that participants exposed to different versions of customized portals (low, medium, high) were able to recognize the degree of customized information that the portal offered, with the highly customized version evoking perceptions of the portal as a "niche" site.

In addition, participants rated customization as being the most salient feature of the portal. In accordance with P2, even though participants reported that the portal had elements of community, this feature was not rated to be a defining element of the portal compared to the customization feature. Finally, as predicted by P3, participants' attitudes and navigational behaviors were dictated by the customization feature.

That is, higher levels of customization resulted in significantly more positive attitudes toward the niche portal. Also, participants' navigational activity (such as number of links clicked on, use of search function, time spent on each site) was a direct function of customization. A similar pattern of findings was observed in another recent study. Beier examined user perceptions of online news portals by varying levels of customization and found results consistent with Kalyanaraman and Sundar.

As for P3, Beier also showed that the customization feature can influence cognition-participants' score on memory for news stories was significantly higher when the news stories were customized than when they were not. Although these findings are restricted to one of the five types of portals that have been explicated in this chapter (niche portals), they provide preliminary empirical validation to the propositions and suggest a promising programme of research for mass communication scholars interested in uses and effects of Web portals.

Although the term "portal" enjoys ubiquitous presence in current new media terminology, it has attracted surprisingly little empirical attention from communication scholars. The lack of a cohesive conceptual framework has meant that the role and meaning of "portal" has been in a state of flux. Such concerns motivated us to develop a framework for understanding portals and subjecting them to empirical research.

The methodological importance of this chapter lies in its metaphor-based approach to concept explication. This approach is particularly constructive for explicating those concepts that have not been subjected to extensive academic research but have gained the status of well-accepted buzzwords. In that sense, the explication outlined in this chapter adds to Chaffee's popular method of explication by showing how to perform a meaning analysis with metaphorical conceptions rather than theoretical-operational conceptualizations that are subject to reification. In this chapter, we have restricted our focus to "vital" metaphors-consistent with Black's contention that identification of metaphors should be conceptually interesting. Thus, while there may certainly be many other instances of the "portal as metaphor" criterion, we have sought to confine our attention to those metaphors that we believe provide not just a framework for empirical research but which also help advance theoretical understanding of both the base concept (portal) as well as the variables that emphasize the concept.

Based on our explication, then, we recommend that portals be conceptualized by drawing on the defining features of each metaphor. Rather than using popular catch-all terms such as "user-centered" or "proactive" that tend to be empirically ineffectual, we suggest that a portal be conceptualized in terms of a Web interface that takes into account the elements of customization, control, content, community, and commerce. By referring to portals in terms of one or more of these elements (by employing adjectival modifiers, as needed), we not only lessen the probability of misunderstanding or misinterpreting "hazy" terminology, but also offer a variable-centered approach to facilitate empirical investigation.

The variable-centered approach affords empirical isolation of such specific variables as types of content (news versus product sales) and types of features (e.g., customization) aimed at specific outcomes such as sense of community, with consequences not only for theory development but also for business practices. For instance, Priceline.com was the undisputed market leader in its niche area (airline tickets). However, its subsequent foray into other domains (e.g., grocery shopping) eroded the site's market value even in its niche domain.

Applying the metaphors we identified earlier, the Priceline business strategy signifies a "metaphorical shift" from "niche portals" to "brand portals." This leads to some important questions, namely, the perceived trade-off between customization and commerce as well as the relative psychological importance of each of the 5Cs, providing fertile ground for empirical research.

In conclusion, and in the spirit of the metaphorical approach that stimulated this chapter, we hope to have cut the Gordian knot on portals. To that extent, this chapter is a starting point for communication research on portals and will hopefully stimulate empirical research on the emergent concept. A systematic programme of research in this direction will provide a nuanced understanding of portals in particular and the online medium in general.

## COMMUNICATION RESEARCH: THE "RHETORICAL ENVIRONMENT"

No informed person questions... the indispensability of objective data-gathering and of the exhaustive statistical analysis of those data for all they are worth. The only question... raised here concerns the need to ask, "What are they worth for what?".

A few sentences later, Lynd wondered whether, in many instances, the answer to this question is "to give more lectures and to supervise the writing of more dissertations". (Should anyone, by the way, read between the lines and guess that this chapter will make the claim that the only good communication research is that which seeks to offer practical guidance in solving a real-life problem, let me be unequivocal: such a guess is way off the mark.)

Lynd's doubts about the usefulness of social scientific research in the late 1930s are essentially the same as many of those voiced by critics in the 1970s, 1980s, and 1990s. For example, the social psychologist Kenneth Gergen, in a wide-ranging critique of the social sciences as he viewed them in the early 1980s, lamented that the number of research publications in the sociobehavioral sciences has multiplied exponentially over the past three decades. Yet one is hard pressed to locate substantial gains in knowledge. After noting the daily occurrence of major crises, both in society at large and in people's personal lives, he posed this double-barreled question:

Is it just a matter of "more hard work" before the [social] sciences will begin to discern the constancies, the enduring principles beneath the vicissitudes of common experience? Will more time, more funding, more research, and greater theoretical effort finally allow the behavioral scientist to answer the rudiments of human conduct, and to return manifold to society its investments to date? [His laconic answer:] There is room for suspicion.

We should take careful note of the phrase, "to return manifold to society its investments." In my view, Gergen is reminding us that there may come a time when society will question whether it should continue to provide financial and other resources to support social scientific research that appears to contribute very little to enriching the quality of human life on this planet. The distinguished psychologist Seymour Sarason, in his recent autobiography, provides a thoughtful assessment of the state of the psychological sciences. Admitting that many of his colleagues will register vigorous dissent, he deliberately walks out to the end of a limb when he declares that any field like psychology should be judged by the degree to which it understands, anticipates, and takes action in regard to changes in society.

And, more recently, in their comprehensive critique of contemporary America, The Good Society, Bellah and his associates take it as a matter of self-evident truth that "All social science is implicitly normative as well as descriptive". I refrain from piling up more quotations from credible observers. The central issue that these and a host of other critics are addressing, epitomized in Lynd's "knowledge for what," I shall hereafter, for the-sake of convenience, designate by the shorthand term, the social relevance issue. Two cautionary notes: I am not urging that everyone is obligated to agree with the specific opinions of anyone I have cited. It is enough that we remind ourselves that such opinions have been voiced by responsible social scientists. My point is that the social relevance issue exists, and every researcher needs to give it careful thought.

Social relevance must be sharply differentiated from direct application of research results to specific problems in society. By social relevance I mean only the degree to which informed observers could say of a given example of research that it gives fair promise of casting light, now or in the future, on matters related to the quality of human life.

A theory may be highly abstract, or a set of empirical findings may make no specific reference to any real-life problem. However, such a study could still be said to have social relevance if an informed observer could perceive that it deals with concepts that constitute stepping stones toward an understanding of at least one important area of human existence. So far I've been talking about social science in general. Since, wisely or unwisely, communication researchers commonly describe themselves as social scientists, I shall be devoting the remainder of this chapter to that area of social science we call (again, wisely or unwisely) the "discipline" of human communication studies.

More specifically, I shall be introducing and explicating the key concept, rhetorical environment, as the centre piece of a strategy-one strategy-that should make it difficult for "outsiders" to overlook the contributions of communication researchers, whether to socially relevant concerns or to significant conceptual advances. The Summer 1993 issue of the Journal of Communication, a sequel to the famous "Ferment in the Field" issue of ten years ago, is devoted entirely to the theme, "The Future of the Field."

Its pages reflect the continuing struggles of communication specialists to define exactly what it is that we do; and to convince ourselves that, whatever we are doing, it is right and proper that--at least after some repair work-we should continue doing it. There are critics who argue that we are squandering our energies on interminable controversies about the identity of our field; we should instead devote ourselves to the formidable task of producing research of uncontestably high quality. If we succeed in doing this, the argument goes, recognition of our worth will be automatic.

Colleagues in the social sciences and the humanities (and practitioners in the "real world"?) will be pounding on our doors to gain access to our warehouse of intellectual treasures. While I concede that these arguments are not without merit, a perusal of the Journal is sufficient to confirm me in the conviction that continuing the dialogue of self-criticism within our field is not only an encouraging sign of intellectual vigour, but is downright essential. Professor Beniger offers an arresting metaphor, but one that is, in my judgment, only a half-truth, when he declares:

Bibliometric studies over the past 15 years depict the field of communication as an intellectual ghetto, one that rarely cites outside itself and is even more rarely cited by other disciplines. I would agree that the great majority of scholars affiliated with the academic field of communication are cited only infrequently by authors in other fields. However, I would disagree with Beniger when he says our field is one that "rarely cites outside itself." Indeed, in my judgment, one of the indicators of our disciplinary weakness is that a very large proportion of the published research of communication scholars is top heavy with citations from "non-communication" sources. For years we have heard complaints that communication theorists have borrowed most of their seminal concepts and many of their theoretical models from "outsiders".

*Nevertheless, Beniger is certainly right when he says*:

Although no one discipline could possibly embrace the entire range of academic interest in information and communication, certainly any organized field that calls itself communication might be expected to play a central role. Alas, just the opposite has been true.

Assuming this state of affairs to be the case--and it is hard to deny--we now face the really gut-level question: Why? Two possible answers have been suggested: First, too much of our research, it is said, is simply second-rate work. Too much of it is trivial, or derivative, or unimaginative, or biased, or downright incompetent. It is also charged that too many of our studies are conducted in a vacuum, ignoring possible relationships with other studies or other "variables." Indeed, I myself have long criticized a goodly portion of communication research on these grounds. This, as you might guess, has been particularly true in my own specialty, organizational communication. (For example, it has suffered from its historic bias, corrected only very recently, in favour of investigating almost exclusively problems originated by management.)

But this whole argument fails to take into account that the other social sciences have been found guilty of the same crimes as those charged against the communication discipline. And yet the other social sciences enjoy, by common consent, a much higher place in the academic pecking order than do we.

The second suggested answer to the "why" question is that we have done a poor job of communication: we have failed to let the rest of the academic, not to mention the non-academic, world know of our work, even when that work is of the highest quality and when that work is clearly relevant to an understanding of high-profile social problems.

For example, your dean, Professor Wartella, delivered an address last year in Wichita that has sometimes been referred to as a "call to arms." Professor Wartella's central argument was that "communication research and scholarship can make a difference in children's media, but... they usually do not". She urged communication researchers to "put aside our paradigm debates and focus instead on the public nature of our enterprise".

She pointed to three specific examples of important public policy issues: the Children's Television Act of 1990, the development of Whittle Communications's "Channel One," and the 1992 congressional debate over the funding of public broadcasting. Then she laid it on the line:

These are but a few of the current public issues which cry out for reasoned discussions and informed communication scholarship. Yet too often communication research is either not mentioned in the discussion, is irrelevant, or uninformative, or all three.

If only I had the courage to be a plagiarist, I would be claiming authorship of those words. That the field of communication study, then, falls short of the potential it ought to enjoy, both in academe and in the larger society, seems to be an indisputable conclusion. We are on thin ice, for example, when many large foundations do not even list "communication" among the specialties available for financial support. We are on thin ice when the administrations of major universities propose abolishing departments of communication-and on several campuses in recent years, such efforts have been successful. (Do administrations consider wiping out departments of English, or psychology, or history?) We are on thin ice when, in a major university with a prestigious department of speech communication on campus, the department of political science is awarded-competitively-a grant to support a study explicitly devoted to an analysis of the rhetoric of presidential campaign speeches.

The president of the Speech Communication Association, the president of the Central States Speech Communication Association, and a candidate for the presidency of the International Communication Association, all have issued written statements in 1993 sounding the alarm bell. In the words of one of them, "Our discipline is currently under siege on campuses across the U. S. I am not so presumptuous as to offer myself as the savior of the discipline.

*But I will hazard a few recommendations*:

- I know this is obvious, but we simply must find ways to reduce the proportion of publish-or-perish potboilers that appear in journals under our control. Simultaneously, perhaps enhancing our efforts by creating more awards for outstanding scholarship, we must find ways to stimulate the production of superior studies. This will mean, in many cases, encouraging researchers to explore innovative, non-traditional methods. (I shall come back to this later, with special reference to the concept of rhetorical environment.)
- No doubt about it, we must indeed find ways to spread the word, in both academic and non-academic circles, when we feel confident that a given study will almost certainly meet with the acclaim of sophisticated critics, both "insiders" and "outsiders."
- We must engage in a concerted effort of "consciousness raising" among all our researchers about the social significance issue. I do not mean that every study we produce must be saturated with social significance. What I do mean is that, everytime-I repeat, every time-we select a problem for investigation, we force ourselves to confront the question: What are the probabilities that this study will emerge with findings that, directly or indirectly, now or in the foreseeable future, will contribute to our understanding of at least one important problem facing human beings in their everyday lives?
- Then, should our study yield such findings, we must not be content to let those findings lie interred forever in the pages of an academic journal. We must initiate efforts to publicize the study, either among other academic disciplines, or in the mass media-preferably both. For decades, the traditional attitude among social scientists could be described in such terms as these: "I am the theoretician; I am the scientist. When I have completed a study, my obligation ends there. It is up to others (creatures of lesser talents, no doubt) to do what they will with the findings." This attitude is still widespread. But, in my judgment, it is one of the most vicious and irresponsible tenets ever put forth in supposedly intelligent circles. I would hope that, at least among communication researchers, it can be stamped out.

(For an encouraging counterexample, we can take note of the Association of Atomic Scientists, a group of natural scientists who have striven, vigorously and unceasingly, to inform the general public about the consequences of splitting the atom.)

- Finally I am about to make a suggestion that, I am sure, will strike many of you--perhaps even all of you-as inexcusably romantic. I am going to talk about passion. That's right-passion. Suppose a researcher happens to find a subject, especially if it derives from an urgent social malaise, that arouses strong feelings. The feelings, shall we say, are unusually powerful: the researcher's inner voice cries, "This is outrageous. Something has to be done, and I must be involved in whatever that something is." This is an example of passion. Be assured: I do not for a moment propose that every researcher must be fired up with an all-consuming passion about any research problem. But, occasions do arise when a researcher is really turned on by a problem--whether it be a disastrous social condition, or a cruel life style of an oppressed group, or a source of widespread interpersonal distress. When this happens, the researcher may decide to devote most, or even all, of his or her research labors to investigating topics (within his or her area of expertise, of course) that show promise of contributing to an understanding of the problem.

Does this mean the abandonment of true research for impassioned advocacy? Not at all. To be sure, there is always this danger. The researcher may indeed, as a citizen, assume the role of advocate, but the roles of public advocate and nonpartisan scholar must at all times be separated. Let me tell you now about the case of Professor Charles Perrow.

Perrow, of Yale University, has long been recognized as one of the most distinguished organizational sociologists in the English-speaking world. He is the author of numerous studies dealing with a wide range of organizational phenomena-including the classic Complex Organizations-A Critical Essay.

Hence, the Speech Communication Association was indeed fortunate to have Perrow as a speaker at its 1988 convention in New Orleans. In a wrap-up session of a preconvention conference, he was asked by an audience member to tell us about his research plans for the near future. I can still vividly recall the substance of his response, for he spoke passionately of his conviction that the worldwide epidemic of AIDS will become, in the next century, one of the most catastrophic scourges ever visited upon humankind. He told us he was so depressed and so alarmed that he would devote all his future organizational studies to the investigation of topics related to combatting the AIDS epidemic.

This meant, he confessed, the abandonment of his current programme of research. Now that is real passion. And I have not the slightest doubt that

Charles Perrow's scientific research of the future will be just as brilliant as it always has been-possibly the most brilliant of his entire career. I must now tell you that/feel almost as passionate as Perrow, when I contemplate the deplorable state of many rhetorical environments in late twentieth-century America.

But before explaining why I feel that way, I must, of course, tell you what I mean by "rhetorical environment." I use the term in the following sense: For a specified group, organization, community, or public; and at a specified time, it is frequently possible to identify a cluster of attributes that characterize most of the persuasive or argumentative discourse--that is, the rhetoric--that takes place. This identifiable cluster of attributes is what I call the rhetorical environment. It includes linguistic styles, argumentative tactics, preferences for certain topics over others, and the like.

Researchers who are interested in depicting what they believe is a specified rhetorical environment will find themselves asking a set of criterial questions. Following are examples of such questions-the list is illustrative, not exhaustive. (It will be noted that I deliberately make prominent use of examples from organizational communication.)

- What topics are most commonly at the centre of rhetorical discourse? For example, in discussing candidates for high political office, the media in recent years have engaged in feeding frenzies based on alleged sins or goofs in the candidates' private lives. In many corporations, "empowerment," "meeting global competition," "total quality," and "rightsizing" are among the current buzzwords.
- What topics, ideas, or lines of reasoning are taboo? For example, it is frequently charged that radio and television talk shows almost never feature speakers who question the basic pillars of the American system of capitalist democracy; the so-called controversies tend to focus on proposals for tinkering with the status quo. And we are all familiar with that bumper-sticker commandment: "America-love it or leave it!" In the corporate world, there are many topics for potential discussion that are off-limits to all but the very highest echelons of management. For example, even in some of the most "progressive" and "humanistic" companies, employees who are heard saying anything good about labour unions can quickly become members of an endangered species.
- What are the attitudes toward, and what are the typical ways of conducting, controversy? Is it the practice, for example, to avoid open debate about major issues, to sweep troublesome problems under the rug? If serious issues are given exposure at all, is such exposure presented in such a manner as to facilitate thoughtful analysis? We are all familiar with the two-minute, the one-minute, the thirty-second, or even the ten-second sound bite as examples of

what all too often passes for serious argumentation on television. And, of course, in the organizational world, only a handful of companies or government agencies go so far as to permit-not to mention encourage-open debate on the pro's and con's of corporate policies or actions. Moreover, the suppression of dissent in many unions has been a serious blot upon the labour movement.

- To what degree is most of the rhetoric honest, fair-minded, rational?--or is most of it deceptive, manipulative, demagogic? Are opponents respected in their rights to speak out, or are they subjected to insults or intimidation? When we apply this question to the organizational world, we find ourselves investigating the attitudes of management--whether in a government agency, in a corporation, or in a labour union--toward those organizational members who openly express dissent (the extreme case being the whistle-blower). Some years ago an organizational critic hypothesized a four-stage model representing the most typical ways in which organizations deal with dissenters.

Although not yet put to rigorous empirical test, the model is supported by much anecdotal evidence. Briefly stated, O'Day posits two phases in the handling of dissenters; and each phase contains two "rituals." Phase One he calls "indirect intimidation." Here the dissenter is subjected first to the ritual of "nullification," in which his or her statements are regarded simply as errors.

But if the dissenter persists, then the ritual of "isolation" is brought into play. This consists of cutting the culprit off from communication with other organizational members, and from various kinds of resources. If the dissenter's voice has still not been silenced, Phase Two, "Direct Intimidation" follows. The first ritual here is "defamation," featuring charges of subversion, evil purposes, psychopathology, or gross incompetence. Finally, if defamation fails to squelch the culprit, the last ritual-expulsion--is enacted; in other words, the dissenter is fired.

More questions--many more questions--remain to be asked by any researcher desiring to create a valid description of a selected rhetorical environment. But I hope enough has been said to convey a reasonably clear idea of the sort of entities I have in mind when I speak of rhetorical environments. Incidentally, those who are familiar with the exciting work of Irving Janis and his associates in developing the concept they call groupthink, will quickly recognize the groupthink experience as an example of one particular rhetorical environment. Earlier in the chapter I confessed to feeling real passion upon contemplating what I described as "the deplorable state of many rhetorical environments in late twentiethcentury America." The logical corollary is obvious: Were I in the early years of my academic career, I know I would be passionate about devoting most of my research labors to studies that promise a high probability of improving our understanding of rhetorical environments-especially, of course, in organizations.

Why such strong feelings about this particular topic? One reason is attributable to the simple fact that, day in and day out, I am an observer--or "consumer," if you will--of a constant barrage of debased rhetoric emanating from the print and electronic media, especially television. One day a year or so ago it struck me that we are all immersed in a polluted "environment of the word," and that the most polluted area of all lies in the domain of rhetorical discourse.

It is rhetorical discourse that makes possible public policy debate, that makes possible campaigns for public office, and that makes possible virtually all organizational decision making.

Bellah and his associates, authors of The Good Society articulated my feelings with remarkable precision when they wrote of "the debasement of public discourse," declaring that "debate has degenerated into... media mass with little sustained intellectual content". I shall have a bit more to say about this later. But, at this point I think it appropriate to focus upon my area of special study, organizational communication, to identify the most influential source of my distress about rhetorical environments.

Over a period of many years (more than I like to contemplate!) I have observed hundreds of employees, including managers, in dozens of organizations. I have observed, first-hand and close-up, how human beings spend big chunks of their everyday workplace lives. A lengthy convalescence this year gave me an opportunity to look back upon all those years of observation, to see if I could distill from them a single Grand Conclusion. Whether or not it is a Grand Conclusion, what I came up with was this: Millions of people in twentieth-century America are experiencing innumerable miseries on the job; and, in my judgment, many of these miseries could be alleviated were it possible to modify the rhetorical environments of innumerable organizations.

Let me be more specific by recounting for you a vivid first-hand experience with two sharply contrasting rhetorical environments within the same corporation. What I shall call Division A of Company X was a large manufacturer of heavy industrial equipment, with a workforce of more than 20,000 employees.

After only a few hours in Division A I came to realise that the place was a human jungle. No one seemed to trust anyone else, and the prevailing mode of decision making featured personal insults, withholding of valuable information, and the prompt shooting down of everyone else's ideas. One index of the rhetorical environment was that many managers found it prudent to maintain "JIC" files ("Just in Case"-sometimes rendered by the less elegant "CMA"-"Cover My Ass"), to be used in self-defence. The ultimate disease symptom was the "bugging" of several lower-level managers' offices by top executives. Division B, with about 6,000 employees, presented a starting contrast. In spite of the need for security clearance in many areas of the plant, management invited honest participation in many (admittedly, not all) decisions. Dissent, albeit within limits, was actually encouraged.

And the office walls displayed satiric cartoons lampooning managers. Most amazing of all, management even, from time to time, publicized (on bulletin boards) confessions of selected mistakes it had made. I regret to report that I have never encountered another organization with the kind of rhetorical environment that prevailed in Division B of Company X.

In recent years a small but highly respected group of organizational specialists have produced a body of writings dealing with various aspects of what I would call rhetorical environments in contemporary organizations. A good example is a book published back in 1977, Freedom Inside the Organization. It is significant to note that the author, David Ewing, was at one time an executive editor of the Harvard Business Review.

Basing much of his information on first-hand observations in many different organizations, Ewing reported in vivid detail the ubiquity of restrictions on employees' freedom of speech. He concluded that "the evidence leaves no doubt whatever that tyranny at work is an important fact of life. [And] in much of the workplace despotism flourishes". It is worth noting, by the way, that Ewing is no advocate of complete "democracy" as a practical mode of governance in the average organization:

There must be discipline. There must be control. There must be scope for quick and arbitrary judgments by decision makers.

Whether or not we agree with Ewing's philosophy of governance, we must concur with him--and many other organizational experts--that making employees afraid to speak up can be a formula for organizational disaster. Ah, some will object, "Ewing was writing in 1977.

This is 1993. Surely the intervening sixteen years have witnessed radical changes in management methods and organizational structures." To be sure, especially during the 1980s there occurred what can only be called revolutions in the theories and practices of organizational management. In recent years it has become almost obligatory for managements to demonstrate that they have "empowered" their employees.

The trouble is that there exists a great mass of evidence to suggest that these Glorious Revolutions have not greatly changed things in thousands of organizations. Indeed, as recently as 1988 Levering himself, coauthor of The 100 Best Companies, wrote a book called A Great Place to Work. But we need to pay close attention to the subtitle; it reads: What Makes Some Employers So Good (And Most So Bad).

How about employees fearing to speak up? Well, in 1991 a book came out under the title Driving Fear Out of the Workplace. It reported a survey in which 70 per cent of 260 interviewees (employees working in a variety of companies) testified that they were indeed afraid to "speak up" in the workplace.

As recently as a couple of weeks ago, the Chicago Tribune provided an account of what it is like to work in many of the companies that sort mail for the U. S. Postal Service (the Postal Service is in the middle of a major policy shift, contracting out its mail sorting to private employers).

Both union officials and nonpartisan technology experts charge, according to the Tribune, that the Postal Service's new programme has resulted in creating "low-wage jobs in 20th Century sweatshops." And employees of a large California facility--which is recording a 50 per cent turnover rate in a state with high unemployment--complain of a "strict, military-style approach" toward employees.

A rich storehouse of horror stories about deplorable rhetorical environments--featuring lies, broken promises, deceptive messages, and so on--is to be found in the recent best-seller by two investigative reporters for the Philadelphia Inquirer: America--What Went Wrong?. But time does not permit the further accumulation of evidence demonstrating that the conditions Ewing observed in the 1970s can be found throughout much of the organizational world in the 1990s.

It shall suffice to quote the words of Barbara Garson, author of The Electronic Sweatshop. Speaking of the exponential growth in recent years of devices for facilitating constant (and frequently unobtrusive) surveillance of workers every moment they are on the job, Garson arrived at the following conclusion:

Among stockbrokers and middle managers, [electronic] monitoring entailed subtle loss of autonomy and signaled a decline in prestige. For clerical workers whose keystrokes are counted by the minute or airline clerks whose "stats" axe posted daily, electronic monitoring has been linked to pain, stress and serious disease.

Each of the white-collar labour-controlling devices we've so far encountered has been essentially an extension of nineteenth-century management practices. It should be obvious that an atmosphere of close surveillance is unlikely to foster a healthy rhetorical environment.

As some of you may have noted, much of what I have been talking about is commonly categorized under such headings as "organizational culture" or "communication climate."

What advantage accrues, it may be asked, in adding the concept "rhetorical environment" to these already-available designations? I concede at once that rhetorical environment can plausibly be treated as a component of either "culture" or "climate." But, as one of almost innumerable components, the strictly rhetorical aspects of culture or climate are usually given only cursory treatment--if they are mentioned at all.

Should anyone ask, "So what?" let me make explicit a basic premise that has probably been only implicit up to this point: In my judgment, the rhetorical are the most crucial of all the innumerable communication acts that take place every hour of every day in every organization. It is primarily through the exercise of rhetoric that decisions are made and actions are implemented. Hence, I am urging that the rhetorical environment be singled out for special attention, and that it be known by its own special label.

This position, I must make clear, by no means implies that rhetorical phenomena be studied in isolation from other components of cultures and climates, or that the researcher can ignore such forces as the political and economic environments in which all organizations are immersed. I shall go no further in recounting the organizational-communication origins of my passionate concern with rhetorical environments.

I propose now to conclude by suggesting a few of the many ways in which interested researchers might incorporate the concept in their work. What I am going to propose will also serve, incidentally, to add some specifics to the recommendations I made, earlier in the chapter, for enhancing the prestige and acceptance of communication research in general.

But first, some caveats. Caveat number one. Rhetorical environments are both cause and effect. Innumerable communication acts, when aggregated over a period of time, can coalesce around a cluster of attributes, thus making it possible for an observer to claim identification of a rhetorical environment.

Once created (albeit while undergoing changes m its contents) the rhetorical environment exercises, in its mm, immense-but not deterministic--influence upon the ways in which members of a given language community typically engage in rhetorical discourse. This means that researchers can focus either upon phenomena considered to be antecedents or upon those considered to be consequents of a specified rhetorical environment.

Caveat number two. As I view the concept, a rhetorical environment can never be regarded as a neatly packaged entity, amenable to precise measurement. For one thing, researchers must decide which data sources-including both observers and documentswill be used to identify a particular cluster of attributes as constituting a specific rhetorical environment.

A moment's reflection will confirm that different observers of the same social scene may (and usually will) provide different opinions on such matters as (a) whether any rhetorical environment can be identified at all; and, if so, (b) what its attributes are.

Moreover, many rhetorical environments that appear to be obvious to the researcher or other "outsiders" are totally invisible to the participants themselves.

This is likely to be the case whenever we are dealing with "unobtrusive controls" (whether in the internal governance of an organization or in society at large). Some scholars may wish to make use here of such concepts as "hegemony" and "ideology" (in any of its various meanings). On unobtrusive control in the organizational setting, researchers should consult the definitive analysis of Tompkins & Cheney.

Caveat number three. Researchers must not fall into the trap of assuming that, for any selected social entity, only one rhetorical environment will emerge--one can recall the case of Divisions A and B of Company X. Two or more distinctly different rhetorical environments will often exist, side by side, in the same group or organizational unit.

Thus, it is now acknowledged that, in many of the fabled high-tech companies in the equally fabled Silicon Valley of California, at least two cultures--hence, rhetorical environments--co-exist.

The laid-back, non-hierarchical, free-wheeling culture of the professionals--the scientists and technologists--frequently fails to percolate down to the lower-level production and maintenance workers. At these lower levels, in fact, harsh and regimented working conditions are widespread, with greatly restricted opportunities in the workplace for informal interpersonal communication or even for relaxation.

With these caveats out of the way, let me briefly sketch just a few of the ways in which researchers, if they are so inclined, might make use of the concept of rhetorical environment.

- Investigators should keep in mind that rhetorical environments can be examined in a wide diversity of settings. Although I have (understandably) drawn examples from organizations and, to a lesser extent, from public discourse, the concept can be applied to the study of families, small groups, communities, and other social entities, as well as from the more obvious cases of political campaigns, television treatment of public issues, radio and TV talk shows, and the like-not to mention organizations.
- No researcher is obligated to make a given rhetorical environment, taken as a Gestalt, the centre piece of a particular study. Indeed, I would prefer that scholars with various interests and areas of expertise would apply their talents most of the time to selected aspects of a rhetorical environment rather than attempt to encompass the whole thing at one fell swoop.

  Let me cite a single, admittedly modest, example. A team of two researchers from a business school chose to examine just one componentadmittedly a highly influential component--of what is actually the rhetorical environment (no, the authors never used the term) within a single company, the Dana Corporation. This company gives high prominence to a basic document called "The Philosophy and Policies of Dana." A significant feature is that, unlike many official corporate documents, its authorship is identified as the "Policy Committee"--a four-member group. This fact made it possible for the researchers to seek out the real-life "rhetors" and interview them. The objective was to discover what the writers perceived as the rhetorical options available to them, and what their reasoning was in making their choices among these options. In other words, here was a magnificent opportunity to track down an official document and to find out how it was actually composed. (Most of us, I am sure, would dearly love to trace many policy statements, rules, regulations, and instructions to their original authors, asking them just how they came up with such monstrosities.)

Here, then, is an example of research featuring a close examination of a quantitatively small, but qualitatively influential, component of the rhetorical environment in a real-life company. I commend the Rogers & Swales paper to future researchers seeking ideas for selecting topics relevant to rhetorical environments.

- In addition to its other features, described above, the Rogers & Swales study illustrates the application of my next suggestion: that we should encourage research projects in which two or more academic specialties are combined for purposes of analyzing the same events, or data bases, from different perspectives. Professor Priscilla Rogers, although employed in a business school, brought to the study her expertise as a rhetorical scholar; and Professor John Swales, employed in the same business school, was able to contribute his knowledge of linguistic analysis. The result was almost certainly a more insightful study than either investigator would have produced, working alone.

  What I am urging, however, goes beyond the two-member team represented by Rogers and Swales. I have in mind what may be called integrated multi-disciplinary research teams. Such teams are not simply convenient, haphazard combinations of scholars drawn from several different disciplines or theoretical orientations. Rather, they are closely-knit, carefully constructed organic entities. They would bring to bear a synthesis of different--even sharply divergent--strategies upon a concerted, or integrated, study of a commonly shared event or data base.

  To indicate what I mean, one can try imagining teams made up of three or more experts representing some or all of the following specialties (the order of items is random):

  An anthropologist a communication experimentalist a rhetorical critic a social psychologist a sociologist a Critical Theorist an organizational theorist a political scientist an interpersonal-communication specialist a discourse analyst an ethicist [Hold onto your hats!] a theologian.

  It is my conviction that rhetorical environments are of such a nature that they are best investigated by such integrated multi-disciplinary teams-if such teams can be created!

- A corollary of the third suggestion is that communication researchers should screw up their courage (not hard to do if they are protected by tenure) and fearlessly try out non-traditional research methods. But by non-traditional I do not mean flaky. Indeed, a number of non-traditional methodologies have been successfully applied by a small number of respected scholars. For example, there is the Socratic-dialogue-argumentative-confrontational depth interview (vs. the bloodless, neutral survey interview) employed by Bellah and associates in their Habits of the Heart. It is a technique they say they copied from the political scientist Robert Lane, author of the classic Political Ideology: Why the American Common Man Believes What He Does.

This type of interview may easily be the most appropriate for researchers attempting (a) to ferret out the dominant premises (some of which are seldom articulated) in a given rhetorical environment; (b) to learn the reasons individuals offer for their commitment to these premises; and to find out how or why individual partisans defend their adherence to positions widely regarded as "extremist." For example, it would be enlightening to conduct Socratic interviews with respondents who are strong defenders of the following pronouncement by the Rev. Pat Robertson (who campaigned in 1988 for the Republican presidental nomination):

[The Iowa ERA amendment is part of] a feminist agenda... that is not about equal rights for women. It is about a socialist, anti-family political movement that encourages women to leave their husbands, kill their children, practice witchcraft, destroy capitalism, and become lesbians. [Verbatim quotation as found in several newspapers and magazines]

- All rhetorical environments have histories, some brief, some extending over many years. Hence, the craft of the historian can be highly useful in many studies of rhetorical environments. When and how did a given environment apparently get started? With what persons and what events was it dominantly associated? These are a few of the questions that historically-oriented researchers might address in efforts to identify the antecedents of a given rhetorical environment.

Let me cite an excellent example of historical method applied to the analysis of a real-life rhetorical environment. I refer to Manchester's famous depiction of the "general atmosphere of hate" that prevailed in Dallas when President Kennedy made his ill-fated visit in November of 1963. What Manchester did was to trace the antecedents of this "atmosphere of hate" (that is, rhetorical environment) in the history and culture of Dallas.

It is worth noting that this historical approach is congruent with the position advocated some years ago by a political scientist who has specialized in the study of organizations. L. B. Mohr, in his book Explaining Organizational Behaviour (1982) challenged the value of constantly multiplying conventional studies that accomplish no more than add dozens of variables to an already huge and bewildering accumulation, from which very few really robust generalizations have emerged. He urged researchers to devote closer attention to the study of dependent--rather than independent--variables.

One obviously important way of doing this is the retrospective investigation of antecedents.

- One obvious implication of the foregoing suggestion is that we should explore ways of undertaking long-term studies, in which observations are made and data gathered over periods of several years. Would such an endeavor require generous funding? It most certainly would. Probably something on the order of magnitude of the $20 million grant that Walter Annenberg announced, just a few months ago, to the University of Pennsylvania, for the establishment and support of a new "Public Policy Centre." (Incidentally, the brochure describing the Centre lists, among possible research questions, a number of topics closely related to the rhetorical environment concept.)

Therefore that we must keep constantly in mind the issue of social relevance. And that, in the concept of rhetorical environment, we have a splendid opportunity to undertake research that will be fruitful in developing socially relevant findings (while at the same time, of course, providing a context for generating respectable theories). I entertain the hope that there will be others who will share my passionate determination to do something about the deplorable state of public discourse in contemporary America. Indeed, in my soberest moments, I fear that the current rhetorical environment threatens the very survival of democracy itself. Can we, in our dual roles as nonpartisan researchers and as citizen advocates, really make a difference--a difference in the desperately urgent task of combatting an abysmal rhetorical environment that trivializes (when it does not completely smother) discussion of important public issues?

Can we dream an impossible dream? How about several universities combining forces to create something like a "Consortium for the Study of Public Discourse"? Think about the possibilities. Such an entity could become one of the preferred sources of information for both academic and mass-media representatives seeking the latest research-buttressed information. It could be a powerful instrument for attracting funding to support communication research--especially expensive long-term research. It could also disseminate, from time to time, critical--but nonpartisan--appraisals of selected aspects of the general rhetorical environment. And communication scholars could finally put to rest the question, "Knowledge for What?"

## THE STATUS OF INTERNET-BASED RESEARCH

Although the Internet may be portrayed as a communication technology unique to the 1990s, this depiction is somewhat misleading. The Internet's origins are in fact traceable to the 1960s development of the military-funded communication network, ARPANET, with the Internet officially making its debut as a civilian tool for communication in 1983.

However, widespread public awareness of the Internet's existence did not occur within the United States until the early 1990s when it was privatized and online services such as America Online (AOL) were developed to serve the general public. Hence, there is a tendency to think of it as a turn-of-the-twenty-first-century phenomenon.

Prior to the 1990s, early public access to the Internet was limited mostly to government agencies, universities, and computer-related organizations, such as hardware and software developers. Initially, users experienced the Internet in the form of text-based communication applications such as e-mail and navigation systems such as Telnet.

In 1992, the World Wide Web (WWW) became publicly available in the United States and began to diffuse widely in 1993 with the release of the iconbased web browser Mosaic, which made web navigation more "user friendly" and visually appealing. Subsequently, use of the Web helped to popularize the Internet in general. As use of the Internet has shifted from a small community of researchers and government employees to a worldwide community, researchers recognize the Internet as an important area in need of study. The widespread diffusion and adoption of the Internet in the United States and abroad provides scholars with numerous research opportunities.

Because the Internet functions as a channel for communication, this is especially true for the field of communication. However, as with any innovation, it can be difficult at first to know how to approach the investigation of an innovation's contribution to and effects on the society into which it is introduced. With regard to the Internet, communication researchers, as well as others, must grapple with numerous decisions, such as determining how applicable existing theories and methods of inquiry are to this newest communication technology.

While the arguments for why and how to study the Internet vary, a common theme to arise within our discipline concerns the unique opportunity that today's communication scholars have to witness and record, first hand, the introduction of a major communication technology. Scholarly journals are one forum where communication researchers record the results of their research for the benefit of current and future generations of scholars.

Published articles inform other researchers of the types of approaches being used to study a wide variety of topics, including the Internet. A number of disciplines are conducting Internet research as is evident when searching electronic databases. For example, a simple keyword search conducted in December 1999 in the Social Sciences Abstracts database on the term "Internet" yielded a return of 969 articles published across a diversity of disciplines, most notably in the areas of business, demographics, law, and policy studies.

Each discipline, including communication, typically contains a core set of journals considered to be "leaders" among all others in terms of their coverage of subject matter, length of publication, and quality of published articles. The question asked in this study concerns how leading journals in the field represent Internet-based research conducted by communication scholars, because an important goal of scholarly journals is to document a field's evolution over time.

This study examines the content, frequency, and pattern of published Internet-based research articles-studies that focus on some aspect of the Internet-in leading communication journals for the purpose of assessing how these journals are keeping pace with the Internet's influence on the communication process. It also considers how these journals represent our response to these changes to other disciplines in the social sciences.

## THE IMPORTANCE OF COMMUNICATION SCHOLARS RESEARCHING THE INTERNET

Within the discipline, a handful of articles has addressed the importance of communication scholars studying the Internet. The reasons for study as well as the ways in which the Internet should be studied are varied. For example, in 1996, the Journal of Communication devoted the majority of its winter issue to "The Net." Within this issue, in a dialogue between Newhagen & Rafaeli, Rafeali pointed out that the development of the Internet, in part, is rooted in academe and, as such, "this alone behooves our involvement" in its study.

Beyond this statement Rafeali suggested that researchers focus on what he called the "five defining qualities of communication" on the Internet which, although somewhat abstract, included "multimedia, hypertextuality, packet switching, synchronicity, and interactivity." Newhagen argued that communication researchers must take a more active role in understanding the Internet by first understanding computer architecture, an area often left to engineers.

A bridge must be constructed between the worlds of communication and engineering so that communication researchers no longer find themselves in the position "where the engineers roll out a new technology, and we hold up numbers from 1 to 10, rating it."

Concerning the benefits of studying virtual reality, Biocca stated, "Communication researchers rarely have had the chance to observe the introduction, diffusion, and sociocultural presence of what may become the next dominant communication medium." However, he cautioned against viewing new communication technologies as a revolutionary by stating that many "new" technologies build upon, and borrow from, existing ones.

As such, researchers are likely to start out using existing theories and methods to study a new technology. He suggested focusing on questions such as the shape the medium is taking, and how the medium shapes and is shaped by the user-areas well suited to communication research. In a 1993 article, writing more broadly about humancomputer interface design, Biocca, as Newhagen was to do later in 1996, called for communication scholars to be more proactive in researching computer-mediated communication (CMC) by taking part in the design and development of new communication technologies.

Although, both of Biocca's articles were written just prior to the Internet's widespread public diffusion, his ideas, as if in anticipation of its introduction, are very applicable to the Internet and have been echoed in the later writing of Newhagen and Rafaeli.

Other communication scholars assuming the importance of studying the Internet have suggested additional approaches to its study. December argued for the need to define specific units of analysis for Internet research that would act as guideposts for researchers, helping to facilitate cross study comparisons.

These four units were defined as media space, media class, media object, and media instance. He also proposed a definition of Internet-based computer-mediated communication as that which involves information exchange that takes place on the global, cooperative collection of networks using the TCP / IP protocol suite and the client-server model for data communication.

Messages may undergo a range of time and distribution manipulations and encode a variety of media types. The resulting information content exchanged can involve a wide range of symbols people use for communication.

As such, he argued that the Internet is not a single medium but is instead made up of several media. Additionally, he cautioned that researchers studying on-line services such as Prodigy or America OnLine (AOL) should be aware that they were not actually conducting Internet-based research because these access providers offer proprietary services not available on the Internet. While this caveat is technically correct, it is perhaps overly restrictive. In addition to offering proprietary services to its users, on-line vendors such as AOL also function as Internet Service Providers (ISPs), allowing for communications to be exchanged via the global network.

In contrast to December, Morris and Ogan viewed the Internet as a single flexible mass medium capable of the synchronous and asynchronous transmission of text, audio, and video communication. They argued that the Internet provides the opportunity for communication researchers to rethink rather than abandon traditional views on mass media and to adopt a more flexible perspective on communication models. Additionally, they suggested that researchers study the Internet using a variety of existing frameworks, such as network analysis, and theories, such as social presence. In summary, these scholars essentially argue that communication in relation to other disciplines should be a leader, if not the leader, in researching the Internet because it is a communication phenomenon.

Communication scholars need to be proactive and creative in their research designs in order to reach this goal. To do this, they must possess a thorough understanding of how the technology works by taking an active role in the design and evaluation of future Internet applications.

## RATIONALE

Knowledge of the extent to which Internet-related topics have been addressed and what methods of inquiry have been applied can assist communication researchers in placing their work within a broader range of studies. This information also identifies over- and under-emphasized topics and methods. Lastly, knowledge of the degree to which the Internet is represented within a discipline can provide researchers with a sense of the area's development and relative importance to the field as a whole.

It is not uncommon for communication researchers to analyse articles within an individual journal or a range of journals in order to assess the status of the discipline as a whole with respect to a particular issue. Examples of these studies include analyzing the frequency with which qualitative research is published, investigating the content and quality of published content analyses, and assessing the status of published mass communication articles by women across eight journals. Continuing this type of inquiry, this study examines the publication history of Internet research among five leading journals in the field.

## JOURNAL SELECTION CRITERIA

While acknowledging the presence of newer electronic Internet and new technology-specific publications such as Internet Research and Journal of Computer-Mediated Communication, this study purposely focuses on mainstream, established communication journals. The reasons for this emphasis are threefold. First, and most obvious, the Internet is a channel for communication and as such it falls within the realm for study by communication researchers and, in turn, publication in our leading, established communication journals.

Second, established journals-those in existence for a period of decades-have the distinct advantage of having built both a reputation and a following over time. These journals are widely read within the discipline, contributing to scholars' perceptions of and currency with changes in the field. A third reason, closely related to the second, is that established journals can be viewed as historical records that document the field's evolution. Ideally, these journals reflect trends in the development of a discipline and the segments of society with which it deals as accurately as possible for the benefit of current and future scholars. Selection of the five journals examined in this study employed two criteria: previous research identifying leading journals in the field and the reputation of Social Sciences Abstracts as a valid resource for communication research. In a content analysis of women's published research in mass communication, Dupagne, Potter, and Cooper identified eight leading communication journals, defined according to high circulation counts and low acceptance rates.

The journals identified in their study included: Communication Monographs, Communication Research, Critical Studies in Mass Communication, Human Communication Research, Journal of Broadcasting and Electronic Media, Journal of Communication, Journalism Quarterly, and Quarterly Journal of Speech. These journals functioned as a starting point for this study; however, application of the second criterion, communication research indexed in Social Sciences Abstracts, resulted in the omission of four titles from the original list.

The decision to further limit the journals examined was based on a twofold rationale. First, electronic databases are increasingly used by scholars to conduct literature searches because of their ease of use and convenience in comparison to print indexes. Within the vast realm of electronic indexes available for searching, Social Sciences Abstracts is a widely used leading index published by the highly reputable indexing service, H. W. Wilson Company. Second, subject-specific indexes, such as Social Sciences Abstracts, are typically more useful to and more likely to be used by scholars than general indexes, such as Expanded Academic Index, because they cover indexed journals in more detail, are more likely to index all articles in a journal rather than a chosen few, and they provide longer, more detailed abstracts.

By restricting the focus to leading communication journals indexed in Social Sciences Abstracts, this study attempts to take into consideration a broader view concerning how scholars in other disciplines might perceive the role of our discipline in the area of Internet research based on the presence of communication journal articles contained in the index. With the application of this second criterion, the final list of journals examined in this study include: Communication Research, Human Communication Research, Journal of Broadcasting & Electronic Media, Journal of Communication, and Journalism & Mass Communication Quarterly.

## MEASURES

This study uses December's definition of Internet-based communication but with a slightly more liberal view on what constituted Internet-based communication. An article was considered Internetbased if it focused on computer-mediated communication technologies requiring access to an ISP, including services such as AOL or Prodigy, or closely simulated an Internet-based communication environment (e.g., intranets, e-mail exchange between AOL members). This definition broadly included the Internet in general, intranets, World Wide Web (WWW), e-mail, mailing lists, bulletin boards, newsgroups, chat, virtual reality games such as multi-user domains (MUDs), and video/audio/ text computer conferencing. From the interfaces specified above, it can be seen that in most instances Internet access was necessary for communication to occur.

As with any area of research, certain information is useful in providing scholars with an overall sense of an area's progress or current status. For the purpose of this study, the concept of current status is operationalized into nine measures-author name, authorship, author rank, affiliation, topic, interface, method, total number of Internet-based articles per issue, and total number of research articles per issue.

Identification of an area's primary researchers provides scholars with a sense of which perspectives may be dominant in an area of study. While quantity of publication by an author does not necessarily equate with quality of research, it can provide scholars, especially those new to an area, with a starting point in the literature. The same can be said for the order of authorship on an article.

Distinguishing between primary and secondary authors can indicate, but not necessarily guarantee, which researchers are initiating studies, taking primary responsibility for the studies, and acting as primary contacts or "experts" in an area.

Knowledge of which universities or organizations are conducting research in a particular area is beneficial for those interested in matters such as networking, educational, and employment opportunities. The rank (e.g., faculty, staff, student) of an author provides information on the diversity or homogeneity of the contributors to an area of research.

## RESEARCH QUESTIONS

This study attempts to answer two basic questions. First, what is the frequency and pattern, if any, of published Internet-based research articles in five of the leading communication journals? Second, what do the contents of these articles reveal about the status of Internet research within and outside of the communication discipline?

## METHOD

### Unit of Analysis

The unit of analysis for this study was the scholarly communication research article that focused on Internet-based communication. This included "research in brief" articles but excluded editorials, rejoinders, and book reviews. Coders primarily read titles and abstracts to determine if an article fit this study's definition of Internetbased research. In instances where article titles and abstracts did not provide sufficient information, coders skimmed the articles for details.

**Population Data**

All research articles were examined in four major communication journals between the years 1994-1999. Because frequency of publication over time was one question asked by this study, population data were used instead of sample data in an effort to obtain a more accurate depiction of publishing trends across time by these journals.

The four journals selected for the main study included Communication Research, Human Communication Research, Journal of Broadcasting & Electronic Media, and Journal of Communication.

A fifth journal, Journalism fa Mass Communication Quarterly, was selected for a pilot study to test the codebook. To identify leading communication journals publishing Internet-related articles, a basic keyword search was conducted using the term "Internet" in the Social Sciences Abstracts electronic database; four journals were consistently referenced in the search results and thus selected for closer examination. One limitation of this selection process concerns the exclusion of some communication journal titles from the Social Sciences Abstracts index.

However, this limitation was considered acceptable given the broader focus of the study discussed earlier. Despite this limitation, the five journals selected for this study are examples of the mainstream publication outlets available through most of the field's major associations: the Association for Education in Journalism and Mass Communication, Broadcast Education Association, and International Communication Association.

The starting year for the study, 1994, was selected because, based on the Social Sciences Abstracts search results, in general, Internet publications did not begin to increase until that point in time. The first recorded Internet article in the database occurred in 1992; one article was referenced in 1993. However, in each year thereafter, the number of articles increased steadily. This pattern is consistent with the growing popularity of the Internet with the general public in the United States.

The communication journals selected for study during this time frame contained a total of 961 research articles (323 from the pilot study and 638 from the main study). Each article was examined to determine if it met the definition of Internet-based research. Those articles that qualified were then coded.

**Operational Definitions**

To answer the questions proposed in this study, nine measures were recorded for each Internet-based research article: author name, authorship, author rank, affiliation, topic, interface, method, total number of Internet-based articles per issue, and total number of research articles per issue. For each article the last name and initials of all authors were recorded. Authorship was coded as primary (first author) or secondary (all additional authors). The rank of each author was coded as faculty, student, staff (university affiliated, nonfaculty/non-student employees), government employee, business employee, or other. Author affiliation was recorded as the name of the university or organization with which the author was identified at the time of publication.

Rather than attempt to anticipate the range in subject matter, article topic was recorded as open text by each coder and then later grouped into six broad categories: access, adoption/diffusion, policy, research/theory, social interaction, and other. Interface, the application used to communicate via a computer, was divided into eight categories: World Wide Web, e-mail, mailing lists/newsgroups/bulletin boards, chat rooms, virtual reality game sites (e.g., MUDs, MOOs), video/audio/text-based conferencing, Internet in general (no specific interface identified), and other (coders recorded the specific interface).

Method of inquiry was coded as policy study, critique/essay (non-policy studies), interview/case study, content analysis (qualitative and quantitative), experiment, survey, other (coders recorded the specific method) and combination for multiple methods used within a single study (each method was recorded and then weighted). Lastly, for each journal issue, coders recorded the total number of Internet-based articles and overall total number of research articles.

### Coding Procedures

The author and another communication researcher acted as coders. The codebook was created by the author and reviewed for clarity by the second coder. A pilot test to check for intercoder reliability was conducted on all issues of Journalism & Mass Communication Quarterly, 1994-1999, resulting in a 100% overlap of 323 articles. Discrepancies in coding were discussed, and slight modifications for the purpose of clarification were made to the codebook before proceeding to the four journals selected for the main study. Reliabilities for the number of Internet-based research articles and total number of articles for the pilot test were at the acceptable levels allowing for the inclusion of these articles in the study, under separate reporting.

Intercoder reliability for the main study was calculated using a 20% overlap. Issues for the reliability check were selected using a stratified random sample. The total overlap between the coders contained 128 articles.

### Intercoder Reliability

For the main study, the level of agreement concerning which articles qualified as Internet-based research was 98.4%. Percentages of agreement and

Scott's pi corrections for chance (where applicable) were as follows for the measures: author name, 97.9%; authorship, 97.9%,.96; author rank, 97.9%,.97; affiliation, 97.9%; topic, 94.3%; interface, 96.9%,.96; method, 97.7%,.97; and total number of research articles per issue, 96.9%. For the pilot study, percentage of agreement for Internet-based research articles was 84.6% and 99.7% for total number of articles per issue.

## RESULTS

Frequency analyses are reported for each measure. With the exception of overall trends in publishing, all other measures report data collected from the four journals in the main study. This is because intercoder reliability for the pilot study was only reached on the two measures: Internet-based articles per issue and total articles per issue.

### Trends in Publishing

Of the 961 research articles analysed, 37 (3.9%) were Internet-based. Among the four journals in the main study, 4.1% (26 of 638 articles) were Internet-based. Trends in the publication of Internet-based articles across the five journals revealed no distinct pattern of increase, decrease, or stabilization during the six-year time period. This finding was also the case within each of the five journals.

Overall, the Journal of Communication (32%) published Internet research articles the most frequently followed by Journalism & Mass Communication Quarterly (30%), Journal of Broadcasting & Electronic Media (24%), Human Communication Research (8%), and Communication Research (6%). The percentage of published Internet-based research articles varied widely by year; however, a trend line reflecting a moving average suggests that the number of articles has increased over time.

### Topic, Interface, and Method

Social interaction (31%) was the topic most often researched. This was followed by research/theory (23%); other (15%), which included the topics of competition among local news web sites, digital art on the WWW, TV audience feedback via email, and portrayals of the Internet in magazines; access (12%) and adoption/diffusion (12%); and policy issues (7%). The interface studied most often was the Internet in general (42%) followed by mailing lists/ newsgroups/bulletin boards (19%), WWW (15%), email (12%), and chat rooms (4%), video/audio/text conferencing (4%), and other (4%) which included an Internet-based interactive health programme.

The two most frequently used methods of inquiry were content analysis (27%) and critique/essay (27%). These were followed by experiment (11%) and survey (11%), and, lastly, policy study (8%), interview/case study (8%), and combination (8%), which included groupings such as network analysis and content analysis, and surveys and content analysis.

## DISCUSSION

The results of this study present a somewhat vague picture as to where this newest area of study is positioned within the selected journals. In part, this is due to the low number of Internet articles available for examination and thus discussion.

The results also indicate that scholars searching the Social Sciences Abstracts would find a scarcity of Internet-related research in our leading journals. It may be that the infrequent and uneven publication of Internet research in the journals examined is simply a typical reflection of any field's initial attempts to come to terms with a new area of study.

This finding suggests that Internet research is an area within the field that is clearly open for study. Within the four journals analysed, only two authors stood out in total number of publications potentially providing greater opportunity for other scholars to become better known through their research in comparison to more established areas in communication. Not surprisingly, faculty are the dominant group publishing Internet research articles, but, again, because of the newness of the area student authors may have more opportunities to publish than in more established areas. While certain universities are represented more than others, it remains to be seen which programs will eventually come to the fore regarding Internet-based communication research.

In the areas of topic, interface, and methods, similar opportunities for growth exist. However, as speculated by Biocca and Morris and Ogan, thus far, communication researchers primarily are using traditional methods to study the Internet (e.g., content analysis, essays/ critiques) with a few studies employing network analysis, as suggested by Morris and Ogan.

Additionally, research has tended to focus largely on the Internet in general, leaving specific interfaces such as mailing lists and e-mail in need of attention. Topics also seem to follow widely used categories (e.g., adoption/ diffusion, social interaction) in communication research. This trend may be useful for making comparisons across different types of media; however, it also risks overlooking effects that may be unique to the Internet.

The low number of Internet-based research articles (3.9%) and the sporadic publication of the articles within the five communication journals examined may be attributed to several factors. To begin with, the Internet, despite nearly a three-decade history, is still a relatively new area of study. Although the World Wide Web, which helped make the Internet popular, became publicly available in 1992, it was not until 1995 that awareness of the Internet by the media and the general public began to increase. With this increased awareness among the populace, researchers are realizing the importance of researching the Internet, but this can be a slow process.

In 1995, Dennis Davis, the editor of Journal of Broadcasting & Electronic Media, wrote in his annual summary, "One of my editorial priorities is to increase the number of articles dealing with new technologies. To do this, the number of submissions will need to be increased. This past year 10 submissions (4.9%) dealt with new industries or new technologies. Three times as many manuscripts dealt with existing industries (30 papers, 14.8%). I would like to see a more even balance between submissions dealing with old and new industries."

To its credit, the Journal of Communication published a symposium on "The Net" in its 1996 winter issue. Factoring in the timeframe necessary for the review, decision, and printing process, the calls to action contained within this issue may partially explain the noticeable increase in the publication of articles during 1998. The drop off in 1999 may be a reflection of this cycle as well, or possibly a reflection of changes in editors' interests. Still, it seems clear that some of these journals are demonstrating a desire to publish Internet-based research articles; however, as Davis indicates, perhaps few studies are being submitted.

Alternatively, it may be that a number of studies are being submitted; however, because of the relative newness of Internet-based research some of these studies may lack the theoretical grounding often desired in published works by our leading journals. A review of the literature reveals that communication researchers are attempting to unveil the parallels and distinctions between new and traditional technology theories and methodologies, but the research waters are still murky in this area. Additionally, the emergence of new technology journals such as Internet Research and New Media and Society, may serve as alternative outlets for these studies, thus siphoning off submissions to the mainstream, established communication journals. As well, given the crossdisciplinary nature of the Internet (e.g., computing, communication, human factors), depending on the topic, communication researchers may be submitting their works to journals in other fields. If this is the case, then the communication journals examined might more actively solicit Internet research submissions in an attempt to better represent the amount and type of research being conducted in this area.

While this author does not advocate the lowering of acceptance standards for research articles, communication journals could potentially foster increased publication of Internet research, following the lead of the Journal of Communication, by dedicating issues to symposia on the topic. These symposia could be viewed as debuts of Internet research that, while possibly less theoretically rigorous, would be considered valuable contributors to the development of future, more theoretically based studies.

The main point to be emphasized is that the communication research community is widely dispersed across numerous universities and organizations worldwide. Scholarly journals function, in part, as a communication link between researchers. Communication scholars interested in studying the Internet benefit most by knowing who else is researching in the area and what results have been found. Leading journals play an important role in conveying this information, but only if that information is being published. If it is the case, which remains to be seen, that Internet research is not being published because of a lack of strong theoretical foundations, then an important question needs to be addressed. Namely, how are scholars to build theory if they do not have access, which these journals can provide, to studies on which to build a foundation? The answer may lie in the emergence of topic-specific journals such as New Media and Society.

In 1996, Morris and Ogan, commenting on the Internet's growth (25 million at the time), asked, "Why, then, have communication researchers, historically concerned with exploring the effects of mass media, nearly ignored the Internet?" This is a question still in need of an answer, or possibly reformulation. We might also ask why our leading journals appear to be slow on the uptake. Notably, Wartella and Reeves, in a 1985 study that examined historical trends in publishing about children and the media, observed "that the relationship between research activity and media popularity is not simultaneous." Their findings illustrated that research related to a communication technology (e.g., film, radio, television) often lags behind the diffusion rate of the technology, a pattern confirmed in this study.

Nevertheless, Internet research appears to be an area of study with which communication researchers must become more comfortable and skilled at conducting. Unlike television, radio, or print media, the computer requires certain knowledge and skills to operate-and ultimately to study. As Biocca and Newhagen and Rafaeli argue, communication scholars are being called upon to take a more active role in the understanding and design of new communication technologies. These challenges, as well as knowledge and skills requirements, may act as barriers for some researchers who are less technically oriented. This particular barrier may be offset over time as communication programs develop tracks of study in new technologies on both the graduate and undergraduate levels that emphasize familiarity with and understanding of computer communication technologies.

Additionally, the Internet can simultaneously function as an interpersonal and mass channel for communication. This hybrid nature tends to blur the traditional lines used to distinguish different types of communication from one another. Is the Internet really a form of mass communication? Questions such as this one make it difficult for communication scholars to identify perspectives from which to study the Internet.

Finally, because Internet research is more or less in its infancy and as such lacks a strong history of research on which to build, communication researchers must be especially thoughtful about and creative in their approach to its study. They must also make the effort to network, outside of journal publications, with other Internet researchers to share research strategies and results. Certainly, not every communication researcher is interested in studying the Internet nor, given the numerous areas available for study within the field, should it be the focus of every communication scholar or the sole topic of our leading publications. However, in general, to overlook the Internet as an area for study is to be remiss as a discipline.

Before concluding, two limitations must be addressed regarding the narrow focus of the research. First, the conclusions drawn from this study are primarily limited to the five journals examined. It should be noted, though, that these journals have historically attempted to keep pace with changes in the discipline so that cautious speculations of a more general nature about the discipline's response to the Internet might be made. However, additional research examining a broader range of communication journals is necessary to confirm these speculations. Second, the definition used to identify Internet-based research excluded articles examining computer-mediated communication more generally. Future studies may wish to examine this broader category of research as well.

This study makes two primary contributions to the field. First, it informs communication scholars of the content and amount of published Internet research in leading journals that represent our research efforts both within and outside of the discipline. Second, it generates discussion concerning why the numbers are relatively low in light of earlier calls to action regarding the importance of studying the Internet. Both communication journals and communication scholars play important roles in determining where Internet research will be positioned within the discipline, as well as where the discipline will be placed relative to other fields investigating the technology. Despite the small number of Internetbased articles published by five of our leading journals during the sixyear time period examined, communication scholars studying the Internet should be encouraged in that, overall, the number of articles published appears to be increasing.

However, to more accurately reflect the Internet's importance as a research topic within the discipline, it is hoped that the findings in this study will encourage communication scholars to submit more of their Internet-based research to our leading journals while current and future editors of these journals will be encouraged to include more of these articles in their publications. As a discipline we possess the potential be a leader in Internet research, and our core journals can, and should, reflect this potential not only to scholars within the field but also to the larger academic community.

# Index

## M



## N



## O



## P



## Q



## R



## S



## T



## U



## V



## W